C-1150   CAREER EXAMINATION SERIES

*This is your
PASSBOOK for...*

Building Plan Examiner

*Test Preparation Study Guide
Questions & Answers*

NATIONAL LEARNING CORPORATION®

COPYRIGHT NOTICE

This book is SOLELY intended for, is sold ONLY to, and its use is RESTRICTED to individual, bona fide applicants or candidates who qualify by virtue of having seriously filed applications for appropriate license, certificate, professional and/or promotional advancement, higher school matriculation, scholarship, or other legitimate requirements of education and/or governmental authorities.

This book is NOT intended for use, class instruction, tutoring, training, duplication, copying, reprinting, excerption, or adaptation, etc., by:

1) Other publishers
2) Proprietors and/or Instructors of "Coaching" and/or Preparatory Courses
3) Personnel and/or Training Divisions of commercial, industrial, and governmental organizations
4) Schools, colleges, or universities and/or their departments and staffs, including teachers and other personnel
5) Testing Agencies or Bureaus
6) Study groups which seek by the purchase of a single volume to copy and/or duplicate and/or adapt this material for use by the group as a whole without having purchased individual volumes for each of the members of the group
7) Et al.

Such persons would be in violation of appropriate Federal and State statutes.

PROVISION OF LICENSING AGREEMENTS – Recognized educational, commercial, industrial, and governmental institutions and organizations, and others legitimately engaged in educational pursuits, including training, testing, and measurement activities, may address request for a licensing agreement to the copyright owners, who will determine whether, and under what conditions, including fees and charges, the materials in this book may be used them. In other words, a licensing facility exists for the legitimate use of the material in this book on other than an individual basis. However, it is asseverated and affirmed here that the material in this book CANNOT be used without the receipt of the express permission of such a licensing agreement from the Publishers. Inquiries re licensing should be addressed to the company, attention rights and permissions department.

All rights reserved, including the right of reproduction in whole or in part, in any form or by any means, electronic or mechanical, including photocopying, recording, or by any information storage and retrieval system, without permission in writing from the Publisher.

Copyright © 2024 by
National Learning Corporation

212 Michael Drive, Syosset, NY 11791
(516) 921-8888 • www.passbooks.com
E-mail: info@passbooks.com

PUBLISHED IN THE UNITED STATES OF AMERICA

PASSBOOK® SERIES

THE *PASSBOOK® SERIES* has been created to prepare applicants and candidates for the ultimate academic battlefield – the examination room.

At some time in our lives, each and every one of us may be required to take an examination – for validation, matriculation, admission, qualification, registration, certification, or licensure.

Based on the assumption that every applicant or candidate has met the basic formal educational standards, has taken the required number of courses, and read the necessary texts, the *PASSBOOK® SERIES* furnishes the one special preparation which may assure passing with confidence, instead of failing with insecurity. Examination questions – together with answers – are furnished as the basic vehicle for study so that the mysteries of the examination and its compounding difficulties may be eliminated or diminished by a sure method.

This book is meant to help you pass your examination provided that you qualify and are serious in your objective.

The entire field is reviewed through the huge store of content information which is succinctly presented through a provocative and challenging approach – the question-and-answer method.

A climate of success is established by furnishing the correct answers at the end of each test.

You soon learn to recognize types of questions, forms of questions, and patterns of questioning. You may even begin to anticipate expected outcomes.

You perceive that many questions are repeated or adapted so that you can gain acute insights, which may enable you to score many sure points.

You learn how to confront new questions, or types of questions, and to attack them confidently and work out the correct answers.

You note objectives and emphases, and recognize pitfalls and dangers, so that you may make positive educational adjustments.

Moreover, you are kept fully informed in relation to new concepts, methods, practices, and directions in the field.

You discover that you are actually taking the examination all the time: you are preparing for the examination by "taking" an examination, not by reading extraneous and/or supererogatory textbooks.

In short, this PASSBOOK®, used directedly, should be an important factor in helping you to pass your test.

BUILDING PLAN EXAMINER

DUTIES:
Examines building plans to ensure compliance with pertinent codes, laws and ordinances. Under supervision, an employee in this class is responsible for the analysis and review, prior to the issuance of a building permit, of building plans and specifications for structural soundness and types of materials used. The employee is responsible for maintaining a current file on all new and significant changes in materials and types of construction methods used in the building construction field. Work requires discussing defects in plans or specifications before a permit may be issued. Performs related work as required.

SCOPE OF THE EXAMINATION:
The written test will cover knowledge, skills and/or abilities in such areas as:
1. **Inspection procedures and principles** - These questions test for knowledge of the appropriate practices and methods to use when inspecting various types of building facilities and projects, including proper adherence to plans and codes, dealing with residents, owners and contractors, and inspection record keeping.
2. **Building construction and rehabilitation** - These questions test for knowledge of the various methods and materials used when constructing or renovating various types of buildings and their components.
3. **Understanding and interpreting building plans and requirements** - These questions test for the ability to read, analyze and perform computations based on technical drawings and written technical material related to building facilities and projects. All the information needed to answer the questions will be presented in the written material and/or drawings.
4. **Building, housing and zoning laws and codes** - These questions test for knowledge of, and the ability to apply, provisions of the Building and Residential Codes of New York State (and the portions of other codes applicable to these two codes), and the general concepts of zoning, including related laws and regulations.
5. **Understanding and interpreting written material** - These questions test how well you comprehend written material. You will be provided with brief reading selections and will be asked questions about the selections. All the information required to answer the questions will be presented in the selections; you will not be required to have any special knowledge relating to the subject areas of the selections.

HOW TO TAKE A TEST

I. YOU MUST PASS AN EXAMINATION

A. *WHAT EVERY CANDIDATE SHOULD KNOW*

Examination applicants often ask us for help in preparing for the written test. What can I study in advance? What kinds of questions will be asked? How will the test be given? How will the papers be graded?

As an applicant for a civil service examination, you may be wondering about some of these things. Our purpose here is to suggest effective methods of advance study and to describe civil service examinations.

Your chances for success on this examination can be increased if you know how to prepare. Those "pre-examination jitters" can be reduced if you know what to expect. You can even experience an adventure in good citizenship if you know why civil service exams are given.

B. *WHY ARE CIVIL SERVICE EXAMINATIONS GIVEN?*

Civil service examinations are important to you in two ways. As a citizen, you want public jobs filled by employees who know how to do their work. As a job seeker, you want a fair chance to compete for that job on an equal footing with other candidates. The best-known means of accomplishing this two-fold goal is the competitive examination.

Exams are widely publicized throughout the nation. They may be administered for jobs in federal, state, city, municipal, town or village governments or agencies.

Any citizen may apply, with some limitations, such as the age or residence of applicants. Your experience and education may be reviewed to see whether you meet the requirements for the particular examination. When these requirements exist, they are reasonable and applied consistently to all applicants. Thus, a competitive examination may cause you some uneasiness now, but it is your privilege and safeguard.

C. *HOW ARE CIVIL SERVICE EXAMS DEVELOPED?*

Examinations are carefully written by trained technicians who are specialists in the field known as "psychological measurement," in consultation with recognized authorities in the field of work that the test will cover. These experts recommend the subject matter areas or skills to be tested; only those knowledges or skills important to your success on the job are included. The most reliable books and source materials available are used as references. Together, the experts and technicians judge the difficulty level of the questions.

Test technicians know how to phrase questions so that the problem is clearly stated. Their ethics do not permit "trick" or "catch" questions. Questions may have been tried out on sample groups, or subjected to statistical analysis, to determine their usefulness.

Written tests are often used in combination with performance tests, ratings of training and experience, and oral interviews. All of these measures combine to form the best-known means of finding the right person for the right job.

II. HOW TO PASS THE WRITTEN TEST

A. NATURE OF THE EXAMINATION

To prepare intelligently for civil service examinations, you should know how they differ from school examinations you have taken. In school you were assigned certain definite pages to read or subjects to cover. The examination questions were quite detailed and usually emphasized memory. Civil service exams, on the other hand, try to discover your present ability to perform the duties of a position, plus your potentiality to learn these duties. In other words, a civil service exam attempts to predict how successful you will be. Questions cover such a broad area that they cannot be as minute and detailed as school exam questions.

In the public service similar kinds of work, or positions, are grouped together in one "class." This process is known as *position-classification*. All the positions in a class are paid according to the salary range for that class. One class title covers all of these positions, and they are all tested by the same examination.

B. FOUR BASIC STEPS

1) Study the announcement

How, then, can you know what subjects to study? Our best answer is: "Learn as much as possible about the class of positions for which you've applied." The exam will test the knowledge, skills and abilities needed to do the work.

Your most valuable source of information about the position you want is the official exam announcement. This announcement lists the training and experience qualifications. Check these standards and apply only if you come reasonably close to meeting them.

The brief description of the position in the examination announcement offers some clues to the subjects which will be tested. Think about the job itself. Review the duties in your mind. Can you perform them, or are there some in which you are rusty? Fill in the blank spots in your preparation.

Many jurisdictions preview the written test in the exam announcement by including a section called "Knowledge and Abilities Required," "Scope of the Examination," or some similar heading. Here you will find out specifically what fields will be tested.

2) Review your own background

Once you learn in general what the position is all about, and what you need to know to do the work, ask yourself which subjects you already know fairly well and which need improvement. You may wonder whether to concentrate on improving your strong areas or on building some background in your fields of weakness. When the announcement has specified "some knowledge" or "considerable knowledge," or has used adjectives like "beginning principles of..." or "advanced ... methods," you can get a clue as to the number and difficulty of questions to be asked in any given field. More questions, and hence broader coverage, would be included for those subjects which are more important in the work. Now weigh your strengths and weaknesses against the job requirements and prepare accordingly.

3) Determine the level of the position

Another way to tell how intensively you should prepare is to understand the level of the job for which you are applying. Is it the entering level? In other words, is this the position in which beginners in a field of work are hired? Or is it an intermediate or advanced level? Sometimes this is indicated by such words as "Junior" or "Senior" in the class title. Other jurisdictions use Roman numerals to designate the level – Clerk I, Clerk II, for example. The word "Supervisor" sometimes appears in the title. If the level is not indicated by the title, check the description of duties. Will you be working under very close supervision, or will you have responsibility for independent decisions in this work?

4) Choose appropriate study materials

Now that you know the subjects to be examined and the relative amount of each subject to be covered, you can choose suitable study materials. For beginning level jobs, or even advanced ones, if you have a pronounced weakness in some aspect of your training, read a modern, standard textbook in that field. Be sure it is up to date and has general coverage. Such books are normally available at your library, and the librarian will be glad to help you locate one. For entry-level positions, questions of appropriate difficulty are chosen – neither highly advanced questions, nor those too simple. Such questions require careful thought but not advanced training.

If the position for which you are applying is technical or advanced, you will read more advanced, specialized material. If you are already familiar with the basic principles of your field, elementary textbooks would waste your time. Concentrate on advanced textbooks and technical periodicals. Think through the concepts and review difficult problems in your field.

These are all general sources. You can get more ideas on your own initiative, following these leads. For example, training manuals and publications of the government agency which employs workers in your field can be useful, particularly for technical and professional positions. A letter or visit to the government department involved may result in more specific study suggestions, and certainly will provide you with a more definite idea of the exact nature of the position you are seeking.

III. KINDS OF TESTS

Tests are used for purposes other than measuring knowledge and ability to perform specified duties. For some positions, it is equally important to test ability to make adjustments to new situations or to profit from training. In others, basic mental abilities not dependent on information are essential. Questions which test these things may not appear as pertinent to the duties of the position as those which test for knowledge and information. Yet they are often highly important parts of a fair examination. For very general questions, it is almost impossible to help you direct your study efforts. What we can do is to point out some of the more common of these general abilities needed in public service positions and describe some typical questions.

1) General information

Broad, general information has been found useful for predicting job success in some kinds of work. This is tested in a variety of ways, from vocabulary lists to questions about current events. Basic background in some field of work, such as sociology or economics, may be sampled in a group of questions. Often these are principles which have become familiar to most persons through exposure rather than through formal training. It is difficult to advise you how to study for these questions; being alert to the world around you is our best suggestion.

2) Verbal ability

An example of an ability needed in many positions is verbal or language ability. Verbal ability is, in brief, the ability to use and understand words. Vocabulary and grammar tests are typical measures of this ability. Reading comprehension or paragraph interpretation questions are common in many kinds of civil service tests. You are given a paragraph of written material and asked to find its central meaning.

3) Numerical ability

Number skills can be tested by the familiar arithmetic problem, by checking paired lists of numbers to see which are alike and which are different, or by interpreting charts and graphs. In the latter test, a graph may be printed in the test booklet which you are asked to use as the basis for answering questions.

4) Observation

A popular test for law-enforcement positions is the observation test. A picture is shown to you for several minutes, then taken away. Questions about the picture test your ability to observe both details and larger elements.

5) Following directions

In many positions in the public service, the employee must be able to carry out written instructions dependably and accurately. You may be given a chart with several columns, each column listing a variety of information. The questions require you to carry out directions involving the information given in the chart.

6) Skills and aptitudes

Performance tests effectively measure some manual skills and aptitudes. When the skill is one in which you are trained, such as typing or shorthand, you can practice. These tests are often very much like those given in business school or high school courses. For many of the other skills and aptitudes, however, no short-time preparation can be made. Skills and abilities natural to you or that you have developed throughout your lifetime are being tested.

Many of the general questions just described provide all the data needed to answer the questions and ask you to use your reasoning ability to find the answers. Your best preparation for these tests, as well as for tests of facts and ideas, is to be at your physical and mental best. You, no doubt, have your own methods of getting into an exam-taking mood and keeping "in shape." The next section lists some ideas on this subject.

IV. KINDS OF QUESTIONS

Only rarely is the "essay" question, which you answer in narrative form, used in civil service tests. Civil service tests are usually of the short-answer type. Full instructions for answering these questions will be given to you at the examination. But in case this is your first experience with short-answer questions and separate answer sheets, here is what you need to know:

1) Multiple-choice Questions

Most popular of the short-answer questions is the "multiple choice" or "best answer" question. It can be used, for example, to test for factual knowledge, ability to solve problems or judgment in meeting situations found at work.

A multiple-choice question is normally one of three types—
- It can begin with an incomplete statement followed by several possible endings. You are to find the one ending which *best* completes the statement, although some of the others may not be entirely wrong.
- It can also be a complete statement in the form of a question which is answered by choosing one of the statements listed.

- It can be in the form of a problem – again you select the best answer.

Here is an example of a multiple-choice question with a discussion which should give you some clues as to the method for choosing the right answer:

When an employee has a complaint about his assignment, the action which will *best* help him overcome his difficulty is to
    A. discuss his difficulty with his coworkers
    B. take the problem to the head of the organization
    C. take the problem to the person who gave him the assignment
    D. say nothing to anyone about his complaint

In answering this question, you should study each of the choices to find which is best. Consider choice "A" – Certainly an employee may discuss his complaint with fellow employees, but no change or improvement can result, and the complaint remains unresolved. Choice "B" is a poor choice since the head of the organization probably does not know what assignment you have been given, and taking your problem to him is known as "going over the head" of the supervisor. The supervisor, or person who made the assignment, is the person who can clarify it or correct any injustice. Choice "C" is, therefore, correct. To say nothing, as in choice "D," is unwise. Supervisors have and interest in knowing the problems employees are facing, and the employee is seeking a solution to his problem.

2) True/False Questions

The "true/false" or "right/wrong" form of question is sometimes used. Here a complete statement is given. Your job is to decide whether the statement is right or wrong.

SAMPLE: A roaming cell-phone call to a nearby city costs less than a non-roaming call to a distant city.

This statement is wrong, or false, since roaming calls are more expensive.

This is not a complete list of all possible question forms, although most of the others are variations of these common types. You will always get complete directions for answering questions. Be sure you understand *how* to mark your answers – ask questions until you do.

V. RECORDING YOUR ANSWERS

Computer terminals are used more and more today for many different kinds of exams.

For an examination with very few applicants, you may be told to record your answers in the test booklet itself. Separate answer sheets are much more common. If this separate answer sheet is to be scored by machine – and this is often the case – it is highly important that you mark your answers correctly in order to get credit.

An electronic scoring machine is often used in civil service offices because of the speed with which papers can be scored. Machine-scored answer sheets must be marked with a pencil, which will be given to you. This pencil has a high graphite content which responds to the electronic scoring machine. As a matter of fact, stray dots may register as answers, so do not let your pencil rest on the answer sheet while you are pondering the correct answer. Also, if your pencil lead breaks or is otherwise defective, ask for another.

Since the answer sheet will be dropped in a slot in the scoring machine, be careful not to bend the corners or get the paper crumpled.

The answer sheet normally has five vertical columns of numbers, with 30 numbers to a column. These numbers correspond to the question numbers in your test booklet. After each number, going across the page are four or five pairs of dotted lines. These short dotted lines have small letters or numbers above them. The first two pairs may also have a "T" or "F" above the letters. This indicates that the first two pairs only are to be used if the questions are of the true-false type. If the questions are multiple choice, disregard the "T" and "F" and pay attention only to the small letters or numbers.

Answer your questions in the manner of the sample that follows:

32. The largest city in the United States is
   A. Washington, D.C.
   B. New York City
   C. Chicago
   D. Detroit
   E. San Francisco

1) Choose the answer you think is best. (New York City is the largest, so "B" is correct.)
2) Find the row of dotted lines numbered the same as the question you are answering. (Find row number 32)
3) Find the pair of dotted lines corresponding to the answer. (Find the pair of lines under the mark "B.")
4) Make a solid black mark between the dotted lines.

VI. BEFORE THE TEST

Common sense will help you find procedures to follow to get ready for an examination. Too many of us, however, overlook these sensible measures. Indeed, nervousness and fatigue have been found to be the most serious reasons why applicants fail to do their best on civil service tests. Here is a list of reminders:

- Begin your preparation early – Don't wait until the last minute to go scurrying around for books and materials or to find out what the position is all about.
- Prepare continuously – An hour a night for a week is better than an all-night cram session. This has been definitely established. What is more, a night a week for a month will return better dividends than crowding your study into a shorter period of time.
- Locate the place of the exam – You have been sent a notice telling you when and where to report for the examination. If the location is in a different town or otherwise unfamiliar to you, it would be well to inquire the best route and learn something about the building.
- Relax the night before the test – Allow your mind to rest. Do not study at all that night. Plan some mild recreation or diversion; then go to bed early and get a good night's sleep.
- Get up early enough to make a leisurely trip to the place for the test – This way unforeseen events, traffic snarls, unfamiliar buildings, etc. will not upset you.
- Dress comfortably – A written test is not a fashion show. You will be known by number and not by name, so wear something comfortable.

- Leave excess paraphernalia at home – Shopping bags and odd bundles will get in your way. You need bring only the items mentioned in the official notice you received; usually everything you need is provided. Do not bring reference books to the exam. They will only confuse those last minutes and be taken away from you when in the test room.
- Arrive somewhat ahead of time – If because of transportation schedules you must get there very early, bring a newspaper or magazine to take your mind off yourself while waiting.
- Locate the examination room – When you have found the proper room, you will be directed to the seat or part of the room where you will sit. Sometimes you are given a sheet of instructions to read while you are waiting. Do not fill out any forms until you are told to do so; just read them and be prepared.
- Relax and prepare to listen to the instructions
- If you have any physical problem that may keep you from doing your best, be sure to tell the test administrator. If you are sick or in poor health, you really cannot do your best on the exam. You can come back and take the test some other time.

VII. AT THE TEST

The day of the test is here and you have the test booklet in your hand. The temptation to get going is very strong. Caution! There is more to success than knowing the right answers. You must know how to identify your papers and understand variations in the type of short-answer question used in this particular examination. Follow these suggestions for maximum results from your efforts:

1) Cooperate with the monitor

The test administrator has a duty to create a situation in which you can be as much at ease as possible. He will give instructions, tell you when to begin, check to see that you are marking your answer sheet correctly, and so on. He is not there to guard you, although he will see that your competitors do not take unfair advantage. He wants to help you do your best.

2) Listen to all instructions

Don't jump the gun! Wait until you understand all directions. In most civil service tests you get more time than you need to answer the questions. So don't be in a hurry. Read each word of instructions until you clearly understand the meaning. Study the examples, listen to all announcements and follow directions. Ask questions if you do not understand what to do.

3) Identify your papers

Civil service exams are usually identified by number only. You will be assigned a number; you must not put your name on your test papers. Be sure to copy your number correctly. Since more than one exam may be given, copy your exact examination title.

4) Plan your time

Unless you are told that a test is a "speed" or "rate of work" test, speed itself is usually not important. Time enough to answer all the questions will be provided, but this does not mean that you have all day. An overall time limit has been set. Divide the total time (in minutes) by the number of questions to determine the approximate time you have for each question.

5) Do not linger over difficult questions

If you come across a difficult question, mark it with a paper clip (useful to have along) and come back to it when you have been through the booklet. One caution if you do this – be sure to skip a number on your answer sheet as well. Check often to be sure that you have not lost your place and that you are marking in the row numbered the same as the question you are answering.

6) Read the questions

Be sure you know what the question asks! Many capable people are unsuccessful because they failed to *read* the questions correctly.

7) Answer all questions

Unless you have been instructed that a penalty will be deducted for incorrect answers, it is better to guess than to omit a question.

8) Speed tests

It is often better NOT to guess on speed tests. It has been found that on timed tests people are tempted to spend the last few seconds before time is called in marking answers at random – without even reading them – in the hope of picking up a few extra points. To discourage this practice, the instructions may warn you that your score will be "corrected" for guessing. That is, a penalty will be applied. The incorrect answers will be deducted from the correct ones, or some other penalty formula will be used.

9) Review your answers

If you finish before time is called, go back to the questions you guessed or omitted to give them further thought. Review other answers if you have time.

10) Return your test materials

If you are ready to leave before others have finished or time is called, take ALL your materials to the monitor and leave quietly. Never take any test material with you. The monitor can discover whose papers are not complete, and taking a test booklet may be grounds for disqualification.

VIII. EXAMINATION TECHNIQUES

1) Read the general instructions carefully. These are usually printed on the first page of the exam booklet. As a rule, these instructions refer to the timing of the examination; the fact that you should not start work until the signal and must stop work at a signal, etc. If there are any *special* instructions, such as a choice of questions to be answered, make sure that you note this instruction carefully.

2) When you are ready to start work on the examination, that is as soon as the signal has been given, read the instructions to each question booklet, underline any key words or phrases, such as *least, best, outline, describe* and the like. In this way you will tend to answer as requested rather than discover on reviewing your paper that you *listed without describing*, that you selected the *worst* choice rather than the *best* choice, etc.

3) If the examination is of the objective or multiple-choice type – that is, each question will also give a series of possible answers: A, B, C or D, and you are called upon to select the best answer and write the letter next to that answer on your answer paper – it is advisable to start answering each question in turn. There may be anywhere from 50 to 100 such questions in the three or four hours allotted and you can see how much time would be taken if you read through all the questions before beginning to answer any. Furthermore, if you come across a question or group of questions which you know would be difficult to answer, it would undoubtedly affect your handling of all the other questions.

4) If the examination is of the essay type and contains but a few questions, it is a moot point as to whether you should read all the questions before starting to answer any one. Of course, if you are given a choice – say five out of seven and the like – then it is essential to read all the questions so you can eliminate the two that are most difficult. If, however, you are asked to answer all the questions, there may be danger in trying to answer the easiest one first because you may find that you will spend too much time on it. The best technique is to answer the first question, then proceed to the second, etc.

5) Time your answers. Before the exam begins, write down the time it started, then add the time allowed for the examination and write down the time it must be completed, then divide the time available somewhat as follows:
    - If 3-1/2 hours are allowed, that would be 210 minutes. If you have 80 objective-type questions, that would be an average of 2-1/2 minutes per question. Allow yourself no more than 2 minutes per question, or a total of 160 minutes, which will permit about 50 minutes to review.
    - If for the time allotment of 210 minutes there are 7 essay questions to answer, that would average about 30 minutes a question. Give yourself only 25 minutes per question so that you have about 35 minutes to review.

6) The most important instruction is to *read each question* and make sure you know what is wanted. The second most important instruction is to *time yourself properly* so that you answer every question. The third most important instruction is to *answer every question*. Guess if you have to but include something for each question. Remember that you will receive no credit for a blank and will probably receive some credit if you write something in answer to an essay question. If you guess a letter – say "B" for a multiple-choice question – you may have guessed right. If you leave a blank as an answer to a multiple-choice question, the examiners may respect your feelings but it will not add a point to your score. Some exams may penalize you for wrong answers, so in such cases *only*, you may not want to guess unless you have some basis for your answer.

7) Suggestions
    a. Objective-type questions
        1. Examine the question booklet for proper sequence of pages and questions
        2. Read all instructions carefully
        3. Skip any question which seems too difficult; return to it after all other questions have been answered
        4. Apportion your time properly; do not spend too much time on any single question or group of questions

5. Note and underline key words – *all, most, fewest, least, best, worst, same, opposite,* etc.
6. Pay particular attention to negatives
7. Note unusual option, e.g., unduly long, short, complex, different or similar in content to the body of the question
8. Observe the use of "hedging" words – *probably, may, most likely,* etc.
9. Make sure that your answer is put next to the same number as the question
10. Do not second-guess unless you have good reason to believe the second answer is definitely more correct
11. Cross out original answer if you decide another answer is more accurate; do not erase until you are ready to hand your paper in
12. Answer all questions; guess unless instructed otherwise
13. Leave time for review

   b. Essay questions
   1. Read each question carefully
   2. Determine exactly what is wanted. Underline key words or phrases.
   3. Decide on outline or paragraph answer
   4. Include many different points and elements unless asked to develop any one or two points or elements
   5. Show impartiality by giving pros and cons unless directed to select one side only
   6. Make and write down any assumptions you find necessary to answer the questions
   7. Watch your English, grammar, punctuation and choice of words
   8. Time your answers; don't crowd material

8) Answering the essay question

Most essay questions can be answered by framing the specific response around several key words or ideas. Here are a few such key words or ideas:

M's: manpower, materials, methods, money, management
P's: purpose, program, policy, plan, procedure, practice, problems, pitfalls, personnel, public relations

   a. Six basic steps in handling problems:
   1. Preliminary plan and background development
   2. Collect information, data and facts
   3. Analyze and interpret information, data and facts
   4. Analyze and develop solutions as well as make recommendations
   5. Prepare report and sell recommendations
   6. Install recommendations and follow up effectiveness

   b. Pitfalls to avoid
   1. *Taking things for granted* – A statement of the situation does not necessarily imply that each of the elements is necessarily true; for example, a complaint may be invalid and biased so that all that can be taken for granted is that a complaint has been registered

2. *Considering only one side of a situation* – Wherever possible, indicate several alternatives and then point out the reasons you selected the best one
3. *Failing to indicate follow up* – Whenever your answer indicates action on your part, make certain that you will take proper follow-up action to see how successful your recommendations, procedures or actions turn out to be
4. *Taking too long in answering any single question* – Remember to time your answers properly

IX. AFTER THE TEST

Scoring procedures differ in detail among civil service jurisdictions although the general principles are the same. Whether the papers are hand-scored or graded by machine we have described, they are nearly always graded by number. That is, the person who marks the paper knows only the number – never the name – of the applicant. Not until all the papers have been graded will they be matched with names. If other tests, such as training and experience or oral interview ratings have been given, scores will be combined. Different parts of the examination usually have different weights. For example, the written test might count 60 percent of the final grade, and a rating of training and experience 40 percent. In many jurisdictions, veterans will have a certain number of points added to their grades.

After the final grade has been determined, the names are placed in grade order and an eligible list is established. There are various methods for resolving ties between those who get the same final grade – probably the most common is to place first the name of the person whose application was received first. Job offers are made from the eligible list in the order the names appear on it. You will be notified of your grade and your rank as soon as all these computations have been made. This will be done as rapidly as possible.

People who are found to meet the requirements in the announcement are called "eligibles." Their names are put on a list of eligible candidates. An eligible's chances of getting a job depend on how high he stands on this list and how fast agencies are filling jobs from the list.

When a job is to be filled from a list of eligibles, the agency asks for the names of people on the list of eligibles for that job. When the civil service commission receives this request, it sends to the agency the names of the three people highest on this list. Or, if the job to be filled has specialized requirements, the office sends the agency the names of the top three persons who meet these requirements from the general list.

The appointing officer makes a choice from among the three people whose names were sent to him. If the selected person accepts the appointment, the names of the others are put back on the list to be considered for future openings.

That is the rule in hiring from all kinds of eligible lists, whether they are for typist, carpenter, chemist, or something else. For every vacancy, the appointing officer has his choice of any one of the top three eligibles on the list. This explains why the person whose name is on top of the list sometimes does not get an appointment when some of the persons lower on the list do. If the appointing officer chooses the second or third eligible, the No. 1 eligible does not get a job at once, but stays on the list until he is appointed or the list is terminated.

X. HOW TO PASS THE INTERVIEW TEST

The examination for which you applied requires an oral interview test. You have already taken the written test and you are now being called for the interview test – the final part of the formal examination.

You may think that it is not possible to prepare for an interview test and that there are no procedures to follow during an interview. Our purpose is to point out some things you can do in advance that will help you and some good rules to follow and pitfalls to avoid while you are being interviewed.

What is an interview supposed to test?

The written examination is designed to test the technical knowledge and competence of the candidate; the oral is designed to evaluate intangible qualities, not readily measured otherwise, and to establish a list showing the relative fitness of each candidate – as measured against his competitors – for the position sought. Scoring is not on the basis of "right" and "wrong," but on a sliding scale of values ranging from "not passable" to "outstanding." As a matter of fact, it is possible to achieve a relatively low score without a single "incorrect" answer because of evident weakness in the qualities being measured.

Occasionally, an examination may consist entirely of an oral test – either an individual or a group oral. In such cases, information is sought concerning the technical knowledges and abilities of the candidate, since there has been no written examination for this purpose. More commonly, however, an oral test is used to supplement a written examination.

Who conducts interviews?

The composition of oral boards varies among different jurisdictions. In nearly all, a representative of the personnel department serves as chairman. One of the members of the board may be a representative of the department in which the candidate would work. In some cases, "outside experts" are used, and, frequently, a businessman or some other representative of the general public is asked to serve. Labor and management or other special groups may be represented. The aim is to secure the services of experts in the appropriate field.

However the board is composed, it is a good idea (and not at all improper or unethical) to ascertain in advance of the interview who the members are and what groups they represent. When you are introduced to them, you will have some idea of their backgrounds and interests, and at least you will not stutter and stammer over their names.

What should be done before the interview?

While knowledge about the board members is useful and takes some of the surprise element out of the interview, there is other preparation which is more substantive. It *is* possible to prepare for an oral interview – in several ways:

1) Keep a copy of your application and review it carefully before the interview

This may be the only document before the oral board, and the starting point of the interview. Know what education and experience you have listed there, and the sequence and dates of all of it. Sometimes the board will ask you to review the highlights of your experience for them; you should not have to hem and haw doing it.

2) Study the class specification and the examination announcement

Usually, the oral board has one or both of these to guide them. The qualities, characteristics or knowledges required by the position sought are stated in these documents. They offer valuable clues as to the nature of the oral interview. For example, if the job involves supervisory responsibilities, the announcement will usually indicate that knowledge of modern supervisory methods and the qualifications of the candidate as a supervisor will be tested. If so, you can expect such questions, frequently in the form of a hypothetical situation which you are expected to solve. NEVER go into an oral without knowledge of the duties and responsibilities of the job you seek.

3) Think through each qualification required

Try to visualize the kind of questions you would ask if you were a board member. How well could you answer them? Try especially to appraise your own knowledge and background in each area, *measured against the job sought*, and identify any areas in which you are weak. Be critical and realistic – do not flatter yourself.

4) Do some general reading in areas in which you feel you may be weak

For example, if the job involves supervision and your past experience has NOT, some general reading in supervisory methods and practices, particularly in the field of human relations, might be useful. Do NOT study agency procedures or detailed manuals. The oral board will be testing your understanding and capacity, not your memory.

5) Get a good night's sleep and watch your general health and mental attitude

You will want a clear head at the interview. Take care of a cold or any other minor ailment, and of course, no hangovers.

What should be done on the day of the interview?

Now comes the day of the interview itself. Give yourself plenty of time to get there. Plan to arrive somewhat ahead of the scheduled time, particularly if your appointment is in the fore part of the day. If a previous candidate fails to appear, the board might be ready for you a bit early. By early afternoon an oral board is almost invariably behind schedule if there are many candidates, and you may have to wait. Take along a book or magazine to read, or your application to review, but leave any extraneous material in the waiting room when you go in for your interview. In any event, relax and compose yourself.

The matter of dress is important. The board is forming impressions about you – from your experience, your manners, your attitude, and your appearance. Give your personal appearance careful attention. Dress your best, but not your flashiest. Choose conservative, appropriate clothing, and be sure it is immaculate. This is a business interview, and your appearance should indicate that you regard it as such. Besides, being well groomed and properly dressed will help boost your confidence.

Sooner or later, someone will call your name and escort you into the interview room. *This is it.* From here on you are on your own. It is too late for any more preparation. But remember, you asked for this opportunity to prove your fitness, and you are here because your request was granted.

What happens when you go in?

The usual sequence of events will be as follows: The clerk (who is often the board stenographer) will introduce you to the chairman of the oral board, who will introduce you to the other members of the board. Acknowledge the introductions before you sit down. Do not be surprised if you find a microphone facing you or a stenotypist sitting by. Oral interviews are usually recorded in the event of an appeal or other review.

Usually the chairman of the board will open the interview by reviewing the highlights of your education and work experience from your application – primarily for the benefit of the other members of the board, as well as to get the material into the record. Do not interrupt or comment unless there is an error or significant misinterpretation; if that is the case, do not hesitate. But do not quibble about insignificant matters. Also, he will usually ask you some question about your education, experience or your present job – partly to get you to start talking and to establish the interviewing "rapport." He may start the actual questioning, or turn it over to one of the other members. Frequently, each member undertakes the questioning on a particular area, one in which he is perhaps most competent, so you can expect each member to participate in the examination. Because time is limited, you may also expect some rather abrupt switches in the direction the questioning takes, so do not be upset by it. Normally, a board member will not pursue a single line of questioning unless he discovers a particular strength or weakness.

After each member has participated, the chairman will usually ask whether any member has any further questions, then will ask you if you have anything you wish to add. Unless you are expecting this question, it may floor you. Worse, it may start you off on an extended, extemporaneous speech. The board is not usually seeking more information. The question is principally to offer you a last opportunity to present further qualifications or to indicate that you have nothing to add. So, if you feel that a significant qualification or characteristic has been overlooked, it is proper to point it out in a sentence or so. Do not compliment the board on the thoroughness of their examination – they have been sketchy, and you know it. If you wish, merely say, "No thank you, I have nothing further to add." This is a point where you can "talk yourself out" of a good impression or fail to present an important bit of information. Remember, *you close the interview yourself.*

The chairman will then say, "That is all, Mr. _____, thank you." Do not be startled; the interview is over, and quicker than you think. Thank him, gather your belongings and take your leave. Save your sigh of relief for the other side of the door.

How to put your best foot forward

Throughout this entire process, you may feel that the board individually and collectively is trying to pierce your defenses, seek out your hidden weaknesses and embarrass and confuse you. Actually, this is not true. They are obliged to make an appraisal of your qualifications for the job you are seeking, and they want to see you in your best light. Remember, they must interview all candidates and a non-cooperative candidate may become a failure in spite of their best efforts to bring out his qualifications. Here are 15 suggestions that will help you:

1) Be natural – Keep your attitude confident, not cocky

If you are not confident that you can do the job, do not expect the board to be. Do not apologize for your weaknesses, try to bring out your strong points. The board is interested in a positive, not negative, presentation. Cockiness will antagonize any board member and make him wonder if you are covering up a weakness by a false show of strength.

2) Get comfortable, but don't lounge or sprawl

Sit erectly but not stiffly. A careless posture may lead the board to conclude that you are careless in other things, or at least that you are not impressed by the importance of the occasion. Either conclusion is natural, even if incorrect. Do not fuss with your clothing, a pencil or an ashtray. Your hands may occasionally be useful to emphasize a point; do not let them become a point of distraction.

3) Do not wisecrack or make small talk

This is a serious situation, and your attitude should show that you consider it as such. Further, the time of the board is limited – they do not want to waste it, and neither should you.

4) Do not exaggerate your experience or abilities

In the first place, from information in the application or other interviews and sources, the board may know more about you than you think. Secondly, you probably will not get away with it. An experienced board is rather adept at spotting such a situation, so do not take the chance.

5) If you know a board member, do not make a point of it, yet do not hide it

Certainly you are not fooling him, and probably not the other members of the board. Do not try to take advantage of your acquaintanceship – it will probably do you little good.

6) Do not dominate the interview

Let the board do that. They will give you the clues – do not assume that you have to do all the talking. Realize that the board has a number of questions to ask you, and do not try to take up all the interview time by showing off your extensive knowledge of the answer to the first one.

7) Be attentive

You only have 20 minutes or so, and you should keep your attention at its sharpest throughout. When a member is addressing a problem or question to you, give him your undivided attention. Address your reply principally to him, but do not exclude the other board members.

8) Do not interrupt

A board member may be stating a problem for you to analyze. He will ask you a question when the time comes. Let him state the problem, and wait for the question.

9) Make sure you understand the question

Do not try to answer until you are sure what the question is. If it is not clear, restate it in your own words or ask the board member to clarify it for you. However, do not haggle about minor elements.

10) Reply promptly but not hastily

A common entry on oral board rating sheets is "candidate responded readily," or "candidate hesitated in replies." Respond as promptly and quickly as you can, but do not jump to a hasty, ill-considered answer.

11) Do not be peremptory in your answers

A brief answer is proper – but do not fire your answer back. That is a losing game from your point of view. The board member can probably ask questions much faster than you can answer them.

12) Do not try to create the answer you think the board member wants

He is interested in what kind of mind you have and how it works – not in playing games. Furthermore, he can usually spot this practice and will actually grade you down on it.

13) Do not switch sides in your reply merely to agree with a board member

Frequently, a member will take a contrary position merely to draw you out and to see if you are willing and able to defend your point of view. Do not start a debate, yet do not surrender a good position. If a position is worth taking, it is worth defending.

14) Do not be afraid to admit an error in judgment if you are shown to be wrong

The board knows that you are forced to reply without any opportunity for careful consideration. Your answer may be demonstrably wrong. If so, admit it and get on with the interview.

15) Do not dwell at length on your present job

The opening question may relate to your present assignment. Answer the question but do not go into an extended discussion. You are being examined for a *new* job, not your present one. As a matter of fact, try to phrase ALL your answers in terms of the job for which you are being examined.

Basis of Rating

Probably you will forget most of these "do's" and "don'ts" when you walk into the oral interview room. Even remembering them all will not ensure you a passing grade. Perhaps you did not have the qualifications in the first place. But remembering them will help you to put your best foot forward, without treading on the toes of the board members.

Rumor and popular opinion to the contrary notwithstanding, an oral board wants you to make the best appearance possible. They know you are under pressure – but they also want to see how you respond to it as a guide to what your reaction would be under the pressures of the job you seek. They will be influenced by the degree of poise you display, the personal traits you show and the manner in which you respond.

ABOUT THIS BOOK

This book contains tests divided into Examination Sections. Go through each test, answering every question in the margin. We have also attached a sample answer sheet at the back of the book that can be removed and used. At the end of each test look at the answer key and check your answers. On the ones you got wrong, look at the right answer choice and learn. Do not fill in the answers first. Do not memorize the questions and answers, but understand the answer and principles involved. On your test, the questions will likely be different from the samples. Questions are changed and new ones added. If you understand these past questions you should have success with any changes that arise. Tests may consist of several types of questions. We have additional books on each subject should more study be advisable or necessary for you. Finally, the more you study, the better prepared you will be. This book is intended to be the last thing you study before you walk into the examination room. Prior study of relevant texts is also recommended. NLC publishes some of these in our Fundamental Series. Knowledge and good sense are important factors in passing your exam. Good luck also helps. So now study this Passbook, absorb the material contained within and take that knowledge into the examination. Then do your best to pass that exam.

EXAMINATION SECTION

EXAMINATION SECTION
TEST 1

DIRECTIONS: Each question or incomplete statement is followed by several suggested answers or completions. Select the one that BEST answers the question or completes the statement. *PRINT THE LETTER OF THE CORRECT ANSWER IN THE SPACE AT THE RIGHT.*

1. Brick veneer has a one inch air space separating the brick face from the sheathing. The purpose of the air space is for 1.____

    A. ventilation and moisture control
    B. ventilation and control of wall thickness
    C. moisture control and control of wall thickness
    D. ventilation and insulation

2. English bond is a brick pattern consisting of 2.____

    A. alternate headers and stretchers in each course
    B. alternate courses of headers and stretchers
    C. a header course in every fifth course
    D. horizontal and vertical mortar courses

3. A 1:1:6 mortar mix consists of one part _____, one part _____, and 6 parts of _____. 3.____

    A. gypsum; lime; cement
    B. gypsum; cement; sand
    C. lime; cement; sand
    D. lime; cement; pea gravel

4. Concrete blocks are made with hollow cores to 4.____

    A. facilitate erection
    B. reduce weight
    C. increase fire resistance
    D. reduce water infiltration

5. The dimensions of a standard modular concrete block are actually 5.____

    A. 8 x 6 x 16
    B. 7 5/8 x 5 5/8 x 15 5/16
    C. 8 x 8 x 16
    D. 7 5/8 x 7 5/8 x 15 5/8

6. Brick facing for one family buildings is less frequently used primarily because brick is 6.____

    A. less durable than other facing materials
    B. less pleasing architecturally than other facing materials
    C. less resistant to water penetration than other facing materials
    D. more costly to put in place

7. Awning windows have hinges on the _____ rail of the sash and swing _____. 7.____

    A. bottom; inward
    B. top horizontal; outward
    C. bottom; outward
    D. top horizontal; inward

8.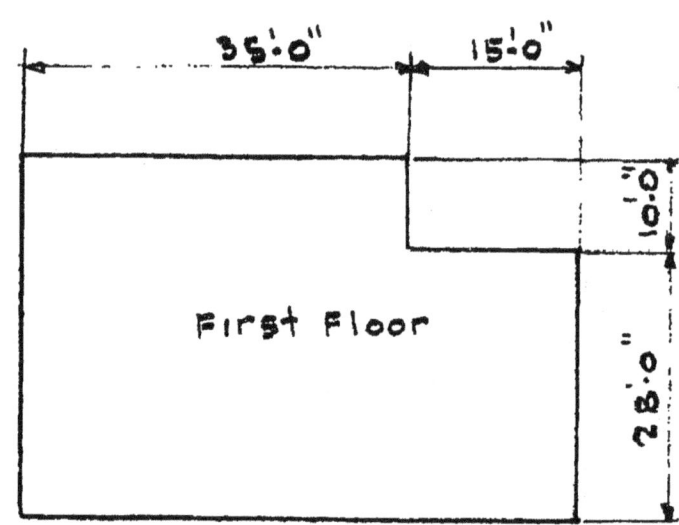

On a plot plan, the building outline is shown. The first floor area of the building is MOST NEARLY _____ sq.ft.

A. 1730   B. 1740   C. 1750   D. 1760

9. When using modular sized brick, the joint thickness should be

A. 1/8"   B. 1/2"   C. 5/8"   D. 3/4"

10. Brick laid in the position indicated in a wall is termed a _____ course.
A. stretcher
B. header
C. soldier
D. rowlock

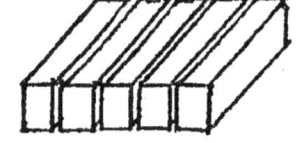

11. Arrangement of brick in common bond has a header every _____ course.

A. fourth   B. fifth   C. sixth   D. seventh

12. Of the following types of lumber, the one that is NOT used for structural purposes in a wood frame building is

A. douglas fir   B. hemlock
C. pine   D. cedar

13. Plywood comes in sheets sized

A. 3' x 6'   B. 3' x 8'   C. 4' x 6'   D. 4' x 8'

14. Gutters and leaders for one family homes are usually made of

A. aluminum   B. copper   C. plastic   D. zinc

15. Terra cotta is made PRIMARILY from

A. granite chips and neat cement paste   B. clay
C. gypsum   D. asbestos and Portland cement

16. A concrete block 3 5/8 x 5 5/8 x 15 5/8 would MOST likely be used in a   16.____

    A. beam over an opening   B. lintel over an opening
    C. jamb for a door   D. 6 inch partition

17. The area of a rhombus with one diagonal of 10", whose side is 13", is, in square inches,   17.____

    A. 100   B. 110   C. 120   D. 130

18. Of the following rolled steel shapes, the one LEAST likely to have the shape of a wide   18.____
    flange beam is

    A. W   B. S   C. C   D. HP

19. A steel member designated 6 x 6 x 1/2 is a(n)   19.____

    A. wide flange beam   B. channel
    C. angle   D. tee

20. Reinforcing steel is required in the footing under a   20.____
    continuous wall. The reinforcing steel is usually
    located _____ of the footing.
    A. at the bottom
    B. at the center
    C. at the top
    D. both at the bottom of the footing and at the
       top

21. A solid plaster wall is represented in plan by   21.____

    A. dots
    B. closely spaced 48 lines
    C. lines parallel to the face of the wall
    D. dotted lines parallel to the face of the wall

22. Gypsum lath comes in thicknesses of _____ inch.   22.____

    A. 1/4 and 3/8   B. 3/8 and 1/2
    C. 1/4 and 1/2   D. 1/2 and 5/8

23. Exterior stucco is a combination of   23.____

    A. portland cement and lime plaster
    B. gypsum plaster and portland cement
    C. gypsum plaster and lime plaster
    D. gypsum plaster and vermiculite

24. Reinforcing steel is required in concrete MAINLY because concrete is weak in   24.____

    A. compression   B. bearing
    C. tension   D. shear

25. The symbol for concrete in section is   25. ____

A. [illustration] B. [illustration] C. [illustration] D. [illustration]

KEY (CORRECT ANSWERS)

1. A
2. B
3. C
4. B
5. D

6. D
7. B
8. C
9. B
10. D

11. C
12. D
13. D
14. A
15. B

16. D
17. C
18. C
19. C
20. A

21. A
22. B
23. B
24. C
25. D

TEST 2

DIRECTIONS: Each question or incomplete statement is followed by several suggested answers or completions. Select the one that BEST answers the question or completes the statement. *PRINT THE LETTER OF THE CORRECT ANSWER IN THE SPACE AT THE RIGHT.*

1. In a 2 story wood frame dwelling, the MOST common framing system is _____ framing. 1.____
   A. braced   B. mill   C. platform   D. balloon

2. The symbol for steel in a section view is 2.____

3. The symbol for earth in a section view is 3.____

4. In architectural drafting, a quarter scale is 4.____
   A. 1/4" = 1'-0"   B. 1/4" = 3"
   C. 1" = 4'-0"   D. 3" = 1'-0"

5. Plans of houses of average size are drawn to a scale of 5.____
   A. 1/8" = 1'-0"   B. 3/16" = 1'-0"
   C. 1/4" = 1'-0"   D. 3/8" = 1'-0"

6. A soffit is 6.____
   A. the underside of an eave
   B. the face of an eave
   C. an ornamental band around a building
   D. top surface of a cornice

7. The MOST common type of roof for a one family house is 7.____
   A. hip   B. gambrel   C. gable   D. mansard

8. A note on the basement plan of a one story frame house states, *Two continuous No. 4 bars in all wall footings....* The diameter of a No. 4 bar is 8.____
   A. 3/8"   B. 1/2"   C. 5/8"   D. 3/4"

9. On the front elevation of a one story residence is a notation bibb. This refers to a 9.____
   A. faucet   B. drain
   C. electric outlet   D. catch basin

10. Fenestration refers to

    A. window arrangement
    B. room arrangement
    C. coordination of the building with landscaping
    D. minimizing the amount of material going into the building

11. Collar beams are used in wood frame buildings

    A. to reinforce the stairway openings
    B. to tie the roof rafters together
    C. in hip and valley work
    D. in dormers

12. On a one story residence, the floor plan is taken about _____ feet above the floor line.

    A. 2   B. 4   C. 6   D. 8

13. The dressed side of a 4 inch stud is usually _____ inches.

    A. 3-1/4   B. 3-1/2   C. 3-3/4   D. 3-7/8

14. If a dimension on a drawing is missing, the draftsman scales the distance to determine its value.
    This practice is

    A. *good* practice because the drawing is drawn accurately to scale
    B. *good* practice because the dimension is quickly determined
    C. *poor* practice because the scale may be too small to determine the distance accurately
    D. *poor* because architectural drawings are not meant to be scaled

15. A formula for determining the relation between tread and rise is: tread x rise = 75". If the rise is 7", the tread should be MOST NEARLY _____ inches.

    A. 10-1/2   B. 10-5/8   C. 10-3/4   D. 10-7/8

16. A stairway goes from the first to the second floor. The MINIMUM length of the stairwell in the second floor is determined by the

    A. layout of the hallway in the second floor
    B. fire code
    C. minimum height clearance on the stairway
    D. width of the stairwell

17. On a stairway run, the number of treads is usually _____ the number of risers.

    A. one more than   B. the same as
    C. one less than   D. two less than

18. In an industrial building, the steel stringers for a stairway are usually

    A. channels   B. I beams   C. H beams   D. tee sections

19. An S section differs from a W beam in that for the same depth beam the S beam has _____ flanges and ____ webs.

    A. wider; thicker
    B. narrower; thicker
    C. narrower; thinner
    D. wider; thinner

20. A blanket insulation material usually made of mineral fibers and designed to be installed between framing members is known as a

    A. batten
    B. batter
    C. batt
    D. bitt

21. If the scale of the plan of an architectural drawing is 3/16" = l'-0", the scale of the front elevation is

    A. 3/32" = l'-0"
    B. 1/8" = l'-0"
    C. 3/16" = l'-0"
    D. 1/4" = l'-0"

22. Modular measure in used in building design and construction. The basic module length is _____ inches.

    A. 3
    B. 4
    C. 5
    D. 6

23. ANSI is the abbreviation for

    A. American Numerical Standards Institute
    B. American National Standards Institute
    C. American National Safety Institute
    D. Association of National Industries

24. In architectural drafting, the heaviest weight line is the _____ line.

    A. center
    B. object
    C. dimension
    D. extension

25. In architectural drafting, the architect rarely uses

    A. cutting planes
    B. extension lines
    C. leaders
    D. hidden lines

KEY (CORRECT ANSWERS)

1.	C	11.	B
2.	D	12.	B
3.	A	13.	B
4.	D	14.	D
5.	C	15.	C
6.	A	16.	C
7.	C	17.	C
8.	B	18.	A
9.	A	19.	B
10.	A	20.	C

21. C
22. B
23. B
24. B
25. D

EXAMINATION SECTION
TEST 1

DIRECTIONS: Each question or incomplete statement is followed by several suggested answers or completions. Select the one that BEST answers the question or completes the statement. *PRINT THE LETTER OF THE CORRECT ANSWER IN THE SPACE AT THE RIGHT.*

1. What is the term for the single wood member laid on top of the foundation wall? 1.____
    A. Soffit   B. Primer   C. Jack   D. Sill

2. What is represented by the mechanical symbol shown at the right? 2.____
    A. Gauge
    C. Shower head
    B. 45° elbow
    D. Lavatory or sink

3. What is generally considered to be the MINIMUM roof pitch allowable for the use of shingles and shakes? 3.____
   _____ in 12.
    A. 1   B. 2   C. 3   D. 4

4. Approximately how many square feet of drywall can be hung by a single installer in an average work day? 4.____
    A. 200   B. 450   C. 800   D. 1150

5. Normally, the length of a nail is designated as 5.____
    A. casing   B. gauge   C. chase   D. penny

6. Approximately how many pounds of prepared drywall taping compound, or *mud,* will be required for 1000 square feet of area? 6.____
    A. 25   B. 50   C. 75   D. 100

7. What is represented by the architectural symbol shown at the right? 7.____
    A. Stone concrete
    C. Gravel
    B. Cinder concrete
    D. Rock

8. Which of the following constructions is NOT typically found in kitchen sinks? 8.____
    A. Enameled pressed steel
    C. Cast ceramic
    B. Enameled cast iron
    D. Stainless steel

9. The Uniform System separates construction specifications into _____ divisions. 9.____
    A. 4   B. 7   C. 11   D. 16

10. Which of the following structures typically requires lumber that has been pressure-treated? 10.____
    A. Mud sill   B. Joist   C. Stud   D. Rafter

11. If boards, rather than plywood, are used as the contact surface for foundation forms, how much of the board material should be calculated as waste?

    A. 5%   B. 15%   C. 25%   D. 40%

12. What is the term for the lateral bracing of floor joists?

    A. Crippling   B. Coursing   C. Fitting   D. Bridging

13. Approximately how many pounds of 8d nails will be required to install 1,000 board-feet of roof sheathing?

    A. 10   B. 25   C. 40   D. 65

14. What is represented by the electrical symbol shown at the right?

    A. Wiring in floor
    B. Circuit breaker
    C. Conduit with wires
    D. Switch and pilot light

15. Approximately how long will it take a two-person team to install a 10' length of 4" plastic soil line?

    A. 15 minutes
    B. 30 minutes
    C. 1 hour
    D. 1 1/2 hours

16. If forms are to be used for a foundation, the exterior face of the excavation should be made _____ inches beyond the wall line of the foundation.

    A. 6   B. 12   C. 18   D. 32

17. What is the MOST commonly used type of roll roofing material?

    A. Smooth
    B. Saturated felt
    C. Selvage edged
    D. Mineral surfaced

18. Approximately how many pounds of oakum are required per joint in one sewer line lead-and-oakum seal?

    A. 1/4   B. 1/2   C. 1 1/2   D. 3

19. What is the term for the construction beneath a foundation, usually of concrete, which helps distribute the imposed loads?

    A. Gasket
    B. Footing
    C. Escutcheon
    D. Sill

20. Approximately how many hours of labor are required for the installation of a single check valve in a length of water pipe?

    A. 1/4-1/2   B. 3/4-1 1/2   C. 1-3   D. 2-4

21. In an average work day, how many cubic yards of earth can be excavated by means of a backhoe?

    A. 10   B. 75   C. 125   D. 350

22. A _____ line is represented by the mechanical symbol shown at the right?   _ _ _ _ _   22.____

    A. compressed air   B. sprinkler main
    C. cold water   D. vent

23. How many floor joists would be required for a 20-foot-long span of flooring?   23.____

    A. 10   B. 15   C. 16   D. 20

24. Of the following, bathroom tubs are MOST commonly made of   24.____

    A. enameled cast iron
    B. enameled pressed steel
    C. glazed cast ceramic
    D. enameled stainless steel

25. When calculating the air conditioning needs for a building, a loss factor of _____ should be used for the exposure of walls to the exterior on all sides.   25.____

    A. 2.0   B. 3.5   C. 6.0   D. 7.5

KEY (CORRECT ANSWERS)

1.	D	11.	B
2.	A	12.	D
3.	C	13.	C
4.	C	14.	B
5.	D	15.	C
6.	C	16.	C
7.	D	17.	D
8.	C	18.	A
9.	D	19.	B
10.	A	20.	B

21. B
22. D
23. C
24. A
25. C

TEST 2

DIRECTIONS: Each question or incomplete statement is followed by several suggested answers or completions. Select the one that BEST answers the question or completes the statement. *PRINT THE LETTER OF THE CORRECT ANSWER IN THE SPACE AT THE RIGHT.*

1. Which of the following are typically drawn to a larger scale than architectural plans?

    A. Diagrams   B. Sections   C. Details   D. Elevations

2. About how many door/window openings should a workman be able to caulk or seal in an average work day?

    A. 10   B. 20   C. 30   D. 40

3. The typical residential air conditioning requirement per 1 square foot of space is about _____ British Thermal Units (BTU's).

    A. 20   B. 30   C. 40   D. 50

4. What is represented by the mechanical symbol shown at the right?
    A. Automatic expansion valve
    B. Gauge
    C. Compressor
    D. Water closet, tank type

5. In an average work day, approximately how many cubic yards of earth can be excavated by means of crew hand shoveling and truck loading?

    A. 3-7   B. 8-10   C. 12-27   D. 18-32

6. The labor for installation of bath accessories should be calculated as

    A. plumbing   B. tile
    C. common labor   D. carpentry

7. Which of the following materials, purchased for gutters, would be LEAST expensive?

    A. Zinc alloy   B. Galvanized steel
    C. Copper   D. Zinc

8. Which of the following is NOT classified as *rough* electrical work?

    A. Conduit and wiring
    B. Installation of service equipment
    C. Switch and outlet boxes
    D. Connections to motors and fans

9. Approximately how many square feet of interior acoustic duct lining can be installed in an average work day?

    A. 25-50   B. 50-75   C. 75-120   D. 100-125

10. The *R-value* of insulation material is a function of each of the following characteristics EXCEPT

    A. thickness   B. height
    C. vapor barrier   D. air space

10.____

11. Generally, finishing hardware costs will be a MINIMUM of _____% of the total job cost.

    A. .5   B. 1   C. 3   D. 7

11.____

12. Due to the *swell factor* involved in excavation, 1 cubic yard of excavated rock may measure _____% more as waste or backfill.

    A. 10   B. 20   C. 30   D. 50

12.____

13. What type of concrete masonry unit is represented by the drawing shown at the right?

    A. Partition
    B. Floor
    C. Trough
    D. Frogged brick

13.____

14. Which of the following wood floor materials would be LEAST expensive to install?

    A. Unfinished plank   B. Walnut parquet
    C. Maple strip   D. Oak parquet

14.____

15. What is generally considered to be the MAXIMUM roof pitch allowable for the use of mineral-surfaced roll roofing? _____ in 12.

    A. 1   B. 2   C. 3   D. 4

15.____

16. Most stains that are applied to interior wood finish can cover about _____ square feet per gallon.

    A. 100   B. 250   C. 350   D. 550

16.____

17. The exposed finishing hardware on windows is USUALLY made of

    A. steel   B. aluminum   C. wood   D. bronze

17.____

18. What would the calculated BM (board measure) be for a length of lumber measuring 2" x 12" x 10"?

    A. 10   B. 20   C. 48   D. 240

18.____

19. Which of the following materials, purchased as sheet metal flashing for roofing, would be LEAST expensive?

    A. Aluminum   B. Galvanized steel
    C. Copper   D. Zinc

19.____

20. Approximately how long will it take one worker to complete the lathing work for 100 square feet of a non-bearing wall?

    A. 30 minutes   B. 1 hour
    C. 90 minutes   D. Two hours

20.____

21. Sewer pipe is MOST often made of

   A. plastic
   B. copper
   C. galvanized steel
   D. cast iron

22. In an average work day, approximately how many cubic yards of earth can be backfilled by means of a man-operated pneumatic tamper?

   A. 8-10   B. 12-20   C. 30-40   D. 75

23. A _____ is used to calculate the total cost of electrical work.

   A. quantity survey
   B. lump-sum amount
   C. cost-per-square-foot estimate
   D. unit cost estimate

24. What is represented by the architectural symbol shown at the right?

   A. Plywood
   B. Wood finish
   C. Rough lumber
   D. Vertical paneling

25. For how many hours should a *C label* fire door be able to withstand continuous fire exposure?

   A. 3/4   B. 1   C. 1 1/2   D. 3

KEY (CORRECT ANSWERS)

1.	B	11.	A
2.	C	12.	D
3.	A	13.	D
4.	C	14.	C
5.	B	15.	A
6.	D	16.	D
7.	B	17.	D
8.	D	18.	B
9.	D	19.	A
10.	B	20.	D

21. D
22. C
23. A
24. A
25. A

TEST 3

DIRECTIONS: Each question or incomplete statement is followed by several suggested answers or completions. Select the one that BEST answers the question or completes the statement. *PRINT THE LETTER OF THE CORRECT ANSWER IN THE SPACE AT THE RIGHT.*

1. Exterior paints are commonly made from all of the following materials EXCEPT   1.____

   A. alkyd resin B. oleoresin
   C. full latex   D. oil latex

2. Due to the *swell factor* involved in excavation, 1 cubic yard of excavated *normal* earth may measure ____% more as waste or backfill.   2.____

   A. 10 B. 20 C. 30 D. 50

3. According to established finish-designation standards, which of the following finish materials would be ranked at the LOWEST grade?   3.____

   A. White bronze   B. Bright bronze
   C. Sanded dull black D. Cadmium-plated

4. Which plumbing component takes waste from a building to the municipal sewer?   4.____

   A. Drain line B. Soil line
   C. Clean-out   D. Trap

5. Approximately how many pounds of 6d nails will be required to install 1000 square feet of siding?   5.____

   A. 10-12 B. 15-17 C. 35-40 D. 45-50

6. Calculations for paving amounts are typically made in units of   6.____

   A. surface square feet B. surface linear feet
   C. cubic feet   D. weight

7. Which of the following types of glass will be MOST expensive?   7.____

   A. 1/4" clear plate
   B. 1/8" patterned *obscure* glass
   C. 1/4" tempered plate
   D. 1/4" wire glass

8. What type of brick masonry unit is represented by the drawing shown at the right?   8.____
   A. Modular
   B. Norwegian
   C. Roman
   D. Engineer

9. Approximately how many pounds of flooring nails are required for the installation of 1000 square feet of wood strip flooring?   9.____

   A. 10 B. 25 C. 35 D. 50

10. The cost for masonry work is typically estimated in terms of

    A. surface square feet
    B. surface linear feet
    C. cubic feet
    D. weight

11. In most newer buildings, vent piping is made of

    A. galvanized steel
    B. lead
    C. cast iron
    D. plastic

12. If 2" x 10" ceiling joists are installed with 16" of space between them, approximately how many hours of labor will it take to install joists for 100 square feet of ceiling area?

    A. 1 1/2   B. 3 1/2   C. 5 1/2   D. 7 1/2

13. What type of labor will usually be responsible for the installation of fiberglass batten insulation?

    A. Finish
    B. Roofing
    C. Common labor
    D. Carpentry

14. What is generally considered to be the MINIMUM allowable pitch of a roof that will be furnished with standing seam?
    _____ in 12.

    A. 2   B. 3   C. 4   D. 5

15. A _____ valve is represented by the mechanical symbol shown at the right?

    A. diaphragm
    B. lock and shield
    C. gate
    D. check

16. Approximately how many linear feet of galvanized steel pipe can be installed in a typical work day?

    A. 35-40   B. 50-60   C. 65-75   D. 85-100

17. Reinforcement anchor bolts are typically spaced around a building at _____ intervals.

    A. 4"-6"   B. 8"-12"   C. 1'-4'   D. 4'-6'

18. Which of the following types of wall constructions will have the GREATEST sound-dampening effect?

    A. Single-stud gypsum board
    B. Metal-stud plaster on lath
    C. Single-stud plaster on gypsum board
    D. Staggered-stud gypsum board

19. For accurate painting estimates for wall openings, such as doors and windows, the general practice is to add _____ to all height and width figures associated with the openings.

    A. 6 inches   B. 1 foot   C. 2 feet   D. 4 feet

20. In an average work day, approximately how many square feet of rock or gravel base course for paving can be laid down?

| | A. 80-100 | B. 600 | C. 1800 | D. 3000-4000 | |

21. Each of the following is a factor in the estimation of door costs EXCEPT 21.____

    A. size   B. lockset   C. type   D. finish

22. What is represented by the mechanical symbol shown at the right? 22.____
    A. Automatic expansion valve
    B. Ceiling air outlet
    C. Floor drain
    D. Reducer

23. Concrete for on-grade floor installations should typically have a compressive strength of AT LEAST _____ psi. 23.____

    A. 500   B. 1000   C. 1500   D. 2000

24. Bathroom toilets are MOST commonly made of 24.____
    A. enameled cast iron
    B. enameled pressed steel
    C. glazed cast ceramic
    D. enameled stainless steel

25. Which of the following types of windows would be LEAST expensive to install? 25.____
    A. Aluminum, horizontal sliding
    B. Wood, casement
    C. Steel, double-hung
    D. Aluminum, projected vent

KEY (CORRECT ANSWERS)

1. B		11. D	
2. C		12. B	
3. D		13. D	
4. B		14. B	
5. A		15. D	
6. A		16. C	
7. C		17. D	
8. C		18. D	
9. D		19. C	
10. A		20. D	

21. B
22. A
23. D
24. C
25. A

EXAMINATION SECTION
TEST 1

DIRECTIONS: Each question or incomplete statement is followed by several suggested answers or completions. Select the one that BEST answers the question or completes the statement. *PRINT THE LETTER OF THE CORRECT ANSWER IN THE SPACE AT THE RIGHT.*

1. Assume that a two story building measures 21'6" x 53'7". It is in a district that calls for an open space ratio of .80. The required open space on this lot must be *most nearly* square feet. 1.____

    A. 922 B. 1152 C. 1843 D. 2880

2. Assume that the elevation at the back of a lot is 127.36 ft. and the elevation at the front of the same lot is 125.49 ft. 2.____
   The difference in elevation between front and back of the lot is *most nearly*

    A. 1'10 1/8" B. 1'10 1/4" C. 1'10 3/8" D. 1'10 1/2"

3. The sketch below represents the lowest story of a new building. In order for this story to be considered a basement, the elevation of the first floor must be AT LEAST 3.____

    A. 131.09 B. 131.14 C. 131.19 D. 131.24

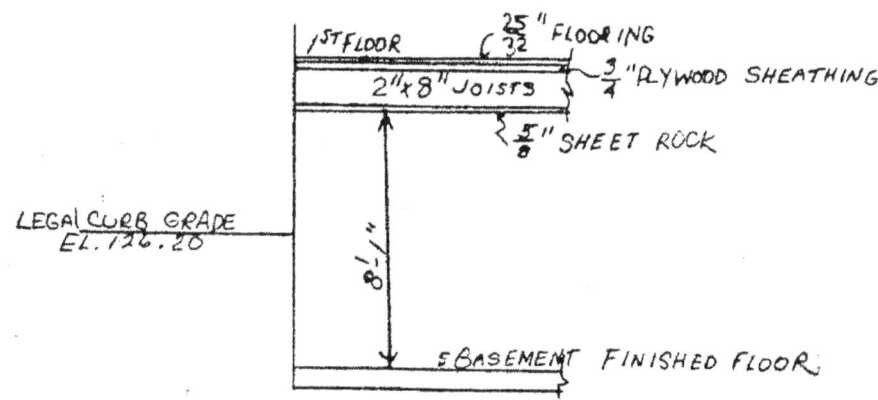

4. The MOST important requirement of a good report is that it should be 4.____

    A. properly addressed B. clear and concise
    C. verbose D. spelled correctly

5. Of the following, in determining whether a violation should be referred for court action, the MOST important item that should be considered is 5.____

    A. the amount of available time you have to process the case
    B. the availability of the inspector
    C. whether or not the owner has indicated a desire to cooperate with the department
    D. whether or not the case is important enough to warrant court action

6. In the Zoning Resolution, the size of required side yards would be found in the chapters on

   A. Use Groups
   B. Bulk Regulations
   C. Area Districts
   D. District Boundaries

7. According to the Zoning Resolution, the one of the following that is NOT considered part of the floor area of a building is a(n)

   A. basement
   B. stairwell at floor level
   C. penthouse
   D. attached garage on 1st floor

8. The one of the following that is permitted by the Zoning Resolution as a home occupation is

   A. veterinary medicine
   B. real estate broker
   C. teaching of music
   D. public relations agency

9. For the purpose of determining the number of rooms in a dwelling unit, the Zoning Resolution adds an arbitrary number to the number of *living rooms*.
   Where there are six or less living rooms, this arbitrary number is

   A. 1/2   B. 1   C. 1 1/2   D. 2

10. Assuming the following signs are all 10 square feet in area, the one that is NOT subject to the provisions of the Zoning Resolution is one indicating

    A. a freight entrance to a building
    B. a fund drive for a civic organization
    C. vacancies in an apartment building
    D. a parking area at the rear of a structure

11. On a plan, the symbol ~~~ represents

    A. earth
    B. wood
    C. metal lath
    D. marble

12. On a plan, the symbol represents

    A. cinder
    B. brick
    C. plywood
    D. rock lath and plaster

13. On a plan, the symbol represents

    A. glass
    B. asphalt shingles
    C. concrete
    D. porcelain enamel

14. A corbel is a form of

    A. cricket
    B. crown molding
    C. cantilever
    D. curtain wall

15. In balloon type framing, the second floor joists rest on a

    A. sole plate
    B. ribband
    C. header
    D. sill

16. Condensation of moisture in inadequately ventilated attics or roof spaces is usually GREATEST in

    A. summer   B. autumn   C. winter   D. spring

17. Of the following combinations of tread and riser, the one that would be acceptable for required stairs in either a new office building or a multiple dwelling is

    A. 9 1/4", 7 1/2"
    B. 9 1/2", 7 1/4"
    C. 9 1/2", 7 3/4"
    D. 10", 8"

18. A meeting rail is a common part of a

    A. door frame
    B. window sash
    C. stairwell
    D. bulkhead

19. If doors in an old building do not close, it is MOST probably an indication that the

    A. frames have shrunk
    B. building has settled
    C. hinges were not set properly
    D. wood used for the doors are of inferior grade

20. Cracks in concrete are not necessarily caused by settlement of a structure. Sometimes they are caused by

    A. shrinkage
    B. curing
    C. hydration
    D. over-troweling

KEY (CORRECT ANSWERS)

1.	C	11.	A
2.	D	12.	B
3.	A	13.	A
4.	B	14.	C
5.	C	15.	B
6.	B	16.	C
7.	D	17.	C
8.	C	18.	B
9.	C	19.	B
10.	B	20.	A

TEST 2

DIRECTIONS: Each question or incomplete statement is followed by several suggested answers or completions. Select the one that BEST answers the question or completes the statement. *PRINT THE LETTER OF THE CORRECT ANSWER IN THE SPACE AT THE RIGHT.*

1. Required exit doors from a room must open in the direction of egress when the room is occupied by more than _____ persons.

    A. 15 B. 25 C. 35 D. 50

2. A window in a masonry wall on a lot line

    A. is not permitted
    B. must have a fire resistive rating of 3/4 hour
    C. must have a fire resistive rating of 1 hour
    D. must have a fire resistive rating of 1 1/2 hours

3. Air entrained concrete is required in all cases for

    A. garage floors B. footings
    C. grade beams D. columns

4. A parapet wall or railing would be required on new non-residential structures where the height of the structure is greater than (give lowest height specified by law) _____ feet.

    A. 15 B. 19 C. 22 D. 25

5. Of the following statements, the one that is CORRECT is that wood joists may

    A. not be supported on a fire wall
    B. be supported on a fire wall only if fireproofed wall is used
    C. be supported on a fire wall only if they are separated from each other by at least 4 inches of solid masonry
    D. be supported on a fire wall only if they are separated from each other by at least 12 inches of solid masonry

6. A foundation wall below grade may be of hollow block only if the building

    A. is a residence
    B. is no more than one story high
    C. is of frame construction
    D. has no cellar or basement

7. The Building Code specifies that lintels are required to be fire-proofed when the opening is more than _____ feet.

    A. 3 B. 4 C. 5 D. 6

8. In a 12-inch brick wall, the MAXIMUM permitted depth of a chase is

    A. none B. 4" C. 6" D. 8"

9. Wood joists should clear flues and chimneys by at least

    A. 1" B. 2" C. 3" D. 4"

10. Fire retarding or enclosure in shafts of all vent ducts are required when they 10.____

   A. go through more than one floor
   B. are used for intake as well as exhaust
   C. are more than 144 square inches in area
   D. are in rooms subdivided with wood partitions

11. Assume a builder is unable to complete the pour for a continuous concrete floor slab. The slab is supported by beams and girders. 11.____
    The construction joint should be made at a point

   A. over a beam
   B. one quarter of the span length from the beam
   C. one third of the span length from the beam
   D. midway between beams

12. Under required stairs in a Class 3 building, 12.____

   A. it is unlawful to locate a closet
   B. a closet is permitted provided that the stringers are fire retarded
   C. a closet is permitted provided that the closet is completely lined with incombustible material
   D. a closet is permitted provided that fireproof wood is used to frame out the closet

13. In New York City, the exit provisions of the State Labor Law apply 13.____

   A. only to factories
   B. to factories and warehouses
   C. to factories, warehouses, and restaurants
   D. to all types of uses

14. A Class 3 building, two stories high, may have required stairs enclosed with stud partitions fire retarded with gypsum boards unless the building is used for a 14.____

   A. factory   B. storage warehouse
   C. bowling alley   D. department store

15. The one of the following rooms in a *place of assembly* that is required to be sprinklered is a 15.____

   A. performer's dressing room
   B. kitchen
   C. service pantry
   D. waiting room

16. Of the following, the FIRST operation in the demolition of a building is the 16.____

   A. shoring of the adjoining buildings
   B. erection of railings around stairwells
   C. removal of windows
   D. venting of the roof

17. As used in the Building Code, *consistency* of concrete refers to 17.____

   A. composition   B. water-cement ratio
   C. relative plasticity   D. proportion of aggregates

18. One condition that is required for a building to be considered a *Special Occupancy Structure* is that the building is used for

    A. a theater
    B. a church
    C. a restaurant
    D. motor vehicle repairs

19. A wire glass vision panel on a door opening into a fire tower is

    A. not permitted
    B. permitted if the panel has a fire rating of 3/4 hour
    C. permitted if the panel has a fire rating of 3/4 hour and is less than 100 square inches in area
    D. permitted if the panel has a fire rating of 3/4 hour, is less than 100 square inches in area, and is glazed with two thicknesses of wire glass with an air space between

20. One of the requirements that must be met before untreated wood can be used as a sub-dividing partition in a Class 1 building is that the partition

    A. be no more than 8 feet high
    B. enclose an area less than 200 square feet in size
    C. enclose office space only
    D. be made of a single thickness of wood

KEY (CORRECT ANSWERS)

1.	D	11.	D
2.	B	12.	C
3.	A	13.	A
4.	C	14.	C
5.	C	15.	A
6.	D	16.	C
7.	B	17.	C
8.	B	18.	A
9.	D	19.	A
10.	A	20.	D

TEST 3

DIRECTIONS: Each question or incomplete statement is followed by several suggested answers or completions. Select the one that BEST answers the question or completes the statement. *PRINT THE LETTER OF THE CORRECT ANSWER IN THE SPACE AT THE RIGHT.*

1. There are two criteria required for determining whether a multiple dwelling shall be classified as a *converted dwelling.*
   The FIRST is the number of families originally occupying the dwelling, and the second is the

   A. conjunctive uses
   B. date of erection of the building
   C. classification, whether Class A or B
   D. number of families now occupying the dwelling

2. According to the Multiple Dwelling Law, a *dinette* is NOT considered a living room if its area is _____ sq. ft. or less.

   A. 50   B. 55   C. 59   D. 64

3. Where a building faces only one street, the curb level used for measuring the height of the building is the

   A. lowest curb level in front of the building
   B. highest curb level in front of the building
   C. level of the curb at the center of the front of the building
   D. average of the levels of the lowest and highest curb level in front of the building

4. According to the Multiple Dwelling Code, one of the living rooms in each apartment of a newly created multiple dwelling shall have a MINIMUM floor area of _____ square feet.

   A. 59   B. 110   C. 150   D. 175

5. It is proposed to alter an old law tenement so as to increase the number of apartments. Of the following, the one that MOST completely gives the requirements to be met before the alteration can be approved is: Each new apartment must be provided a

   A. water closet
   B. water closet and a wash basin
   C. water closet, a wash basin, and a bath or shower
   D. water closet, a wash basin, a bath or shower, and centrally supplied heat

6. Gas fueled space heaters may be permitted in lieu of centrally supplied heat.
   One of the following conditions required before the use of space heaters can be permitted is that

   A. each apartment has no more than two living rooms
   B. the building is a Class A multiple dwelling
   C. all apartments are used for single room occupancy
   D. D, the gas line supplying the heater be connected directly to the main so that the tenant cannot control the flow of gas

7. An incinerator is required in all multiple

   A. dwellings
   B. dwellings four or more stories in height
   C. dwellings four or more stories in height and occupied by more than twelve families
   D. dwellings four or more stories in height occupied by more than twelve families and erected after October 1, 1951

8. Tests of required sprinkler systems in a single room occupancy building must be made

   A. monthly
   B. quarterly
   C. semi-annually
   D. annually

9. An additional apartment may be created on the first floor of a Class A frame converted dwelling provided that no more than two families will occupy this floor and

   A. the entrance hall is sprinklered
   B. the building is brick veneered
   C. there is no basement occupancy
   D. all stairs are enclosed in one hour fire partitions

10. The MAIN feature differentiating a *five tower* from a *fire stair* is the

    A. fire rating of the enclosure walls
    B. use to which the fire tower is put
    C. method of entering the fire tower from the building
    D. height of the fire tower

11. A new elevator shaft is to be built into a non-fireproof multiple dwelling.
    Of the following materials, the one that has the lowest fire resistance that would be acceptable for the enclosure walls of this shaft is

    A. 3" solid gypsum block
    B. 2" x 4" studs with 5/8" fire code 60 each side
    C. steel studs, wire mesh and 3/4" P.C. plaster
    D. 4" hollow concrete blocks, plastered both sides

12. Of the following statements, the one that is MOST complete and accurate is that a frame extension 70 sq. ft. in area added to a frame multiple dwelling is

    A. not permitted
    B. permitted only if the walls of the extension are brick filled
    C. permitted only if the walls of the extension are brick filled and the extension is to be used solely for bathrooms
    D. permitted only if the walls of the extension are brick filled, the extension is to be used solely for bathrooms and the walls are at least 3 ft. from the side lot lines

13. Assume it is proposed to extend a business use in a non-fireproof multiple dwelling by erecting an extension at the rear of the building.
    The roof the extension is required to be fireproof

    A. in all cases
    B. when the business use requires a combustible occupancy permit
    C. when there are fire escapes above the extension
    D. if the business use is a factory

14. In a Class A dwelling, two water closets may

    A. be placed in one compartment only in old law tenements
    B. be placed in one compartment in either old law or new law tenements
    C. be placed in one compartment in all types of apartment houses
    D. not be placed in one compartment

15. According to the Multiple Dwelling Law, a janitor is NOT required when the maximum number of families occupying the dwelling is

    A. 6   B. 9   C. 12   D. 15

16. The first floor above the lowest cellar in a non-fireproof multiple dwelling does NOT have to be fireproof if

    A. the cellar is used only for incombustible storage
    B. there are two means of egress from the cellar
    C. the building is no more than three stories in height
    D. the dwelling is occupied by no more than nine families

17. In a converted multiple dwelling, ventilation of a room on the top story may be obtained by

    A. a skylight
    B. a duct with a wind blown hood
    C. a duct with an electrically operated fan
    D. by a window only and no other method is acceptable

18. It is proposed to build a closet under the stairs leading to the second floor in a non-fire-proof *new law* tenement. This is

    A. not permitted
    B. permitted only if the entire closet is built of non-combustible materials
    C. permitted only if the closet is used for non-combustible storage
    D. permitted if the closet is built of fire-retarded partitions and the soffit of the stairs is also fire-retarded

19. For multiple dwellings erected after April 18, 1929, a ladder from a fire escape to a roof is NOT required when

    A. the building is three stories or less in height
    B. the roof is built of incombustible material
    C. the fire escape is on the front of the building
    D. there is no safe access from the roof to another building

20. It is proposed to convert a Class B multiple dwelling used for summer resort occupancy to year-round Class B use. This conversion is

    A. illegal
    B. legal provided the exits comply with the requirements for Class B use
    C. legal provided the exits and toilet facilities comply with the requirements for Class B use
    D. legal provided the exits, toilet facilities, and ventilation requirements comply with the requirements for Class B use

KEY (CORRECT ANSWERS)

1.	B	11.	A
2.	B	12.	A
3.	C	13.	C
4.	C	14.	A
5.	D	15.	C
6.	B	16.	C
7.	D	17.	A
8.	D	18.	A
9.	B	19.	C
10.	C	20.	A

EXAMINATION SECTION
TEST 1

DIRECTIONS: Each question or incomplete statement is followed by several suggested answers or completions. Select the one that BEST answers the question or completes the statement. *PRINT THE LETTER OF THE CORRECT ANSWER IN THE SPACE AT THE RIGHT.*

1. Forms for concrete are coated with oil because

    A. of the color that the oil imparts to the concrete
    B. they are more easily removed after the concrete sets
    C. the oil decreases the time of set
    D. the oil will not freeze in cold weather

2. Of the following, the *one* that would NOT be allowed if the temperature falls below freezing during concreting operations is to

    A. heat the water
    B. heat the aggregates
    C. heat the cement
    D. stop the work

3. The specifications call for crowning the concrete floor centering 1/4" for every 16 ft. of span.
   The *reason* for this requirement is that

    A. it allows for the deflection of the floor
    B. it will allow even expansion
    C. the centering will sag that amount when the floor is poured
    D. it will facilitate drainage

4. Of the following statements referring to brick, the *one* that is *correct* is:

    A. Salmon brick is overburned brick
    B. Brick that absorbs moisture should not be used
    C. Brick is not used where fire resistance is required
    D. Common brick should be wet before laying

5. According to the building code, the *maximum* percentage of lime to cement in a cement mortar, by volume, is

    A. 5 B. 10 C. 15 D. 20

6. A completed brick wall is *usually* washed down with a solution of

    A. lye
    B. muriatic acid
    C. oxalic acid
    D. turpentine

7. For excavation purposes, corners of a structure are located by means of

    A. slope stakes
    B. corner hubs
    C. screed boards
    D. batter boards

8. After mixing, the time of initial set of concrete *should not be less than* approximately

    A. one hour
    B. three hours
    C. twenty-four hours
    D. seven days

31

9. The term *key* in concrete work indicates the method of

   A. tying forms together
   B. uniting two succeeding days pours
   C. wiring of reinforcing rods
   D. splicing of reinforcing rods

10. Holes left in the bottoms of forms for concrete walls are *primarily* for the purpose of

    A. inspection of reinforcement
    B. placement of steel
    C. cleaning out of forms
    D. easy removal of forms

11. Of the following materials, the *one* that is *most frequently* used as a water stop at a joint in a concrete wall is

    A. stainless steel   B. copper
    C. galvanized iron   D. tin

12. A concrete mix is specified as 1:1 1/2:3.
    The *order* in which the materials are specified is:

    A. sand, gravel, cement
    B. cement, gravel, sand
    C. gravel, sand, cement
    D. cement, sand, gravel

13. Of the following kinds of lumber, the *one* that is *most likely* to be specified for finish flooring for a gymnasium is

    A. spruce   B. hemlock
    C. pine   D. maple

14. Ninety 2"x4"s, 16' long, S4S are needed.
    The *number* of board feet required is, most nearly,

    A. 840   B. 960   C. 1080   D. 1200

15. Of the following, the wood section that is NOT *commonly* used for siding is

    A. tongue and groove   B. shiplap
    C. splined plank   D. clapboard

16. Metal gutters are *most commonly* made of

    A. stainless steel   B. copper
    C. monel metal   D. brass

17. Mortar for the white or finishing coat of a three-coat plaster job consists *usually* of a mixture of:

    A. slaked lime, water, and sand
    B. slaked lime, water, sand, and plaster of paris
    C. gypsum cement, water, sand, and plaster of paris
    D. slaked lime, water, and plaster of paris

18. Of the following stones, the *one* that is NOT commonly used in building construction is   18._____

    A. granite   B. limestone
    C. sandstone   D. mica

19. Of the following, the *one* that is NOT used to support a structure directly is a   19._____

    A. combined footing   B. sheet pile
    C. grillage   D. pier

20. The top cap or top course of a wall is known as a   20._____

    A. cornice   B. corbel
    C. coping   D. fascia

21. The portion of a wall that extends above the roof line is known as a _____ wall.   21._____

    A. parapet   B. party
    C. retaining   D. spandrel

22. To prevent "honeycombing" in concrete, the   22._____

    A. forms should be well-braced
    B. concrete should be vibrated
    C. air entrained cement should not be used
    D. concrete should be retempered after the initial set

23. The *purpose* of curing concrete is that it   23._____

    A. reduces the evaporation of moisture from the concrete
    B. prevents segregation of aggregates
    C. facilitates placing of concrete
    D. prevents the use of the structure too soon

24. Curing of concrete should *begin*   24._____

    A. *just before* the concrete is poured
    B. *while* the concrete is being placed
    C. *after* the initial set
    D. *after* the forms are stripped

25. If the mix in a transit mixer is too dry to discharge readily, of the following, the BEST thing to do is to   25._____

    A. add water and sand, then mix
    B. add water and cement, then mix
    C. increase the mixing time
    D. use the concrete in another part of the job where a dry mix is desirable

26. Of the following, the *most important* item for the inspector to check when a transit mixer arrives on the job is the volume of   26._____

    A. cement added to drum
    B. aggregates added to drum
    C. cement and aggregates added to drum
    D. water added to drum

27. The inspector is required to hold a number of test cylinders of concrete brought on the job.
These cylinders will be used to test the strength of concrete in

   A. compression
   B. tension
   C. shear
   D. bond

27.____

28. A definite procedure of preparing test cylinders of concrete is specified.
Of the following, the BEST reason for specifying this procedure is that it provides

   A. a basis for comparing the strength of the concrete in the cylinders tested
   B. the strongest possible cylinders
   C. the weakest possible cylinders
   D. that the inspector use extreme care in preparing the test cylinders

28.____

29. Quicklime used in preparing plaster is lime that

   A. gives a harder finish than hydrated lime
   B. must be slaked before using
   C. sets faster than hydrated lime
   D. need not be slaked before using

29.____

30. Of the following, the one that is sometimes mixed into plaster to increase the strength is

   A. hair
   B. paint
   C. shellac
   D. glue

30.____

31. The finish coat of plaster should be trowelled after it begins to harden because

   A. this will give a harder surface
   B. it will bond better with the brown coat
   C. this will result in a stronger plaster
   D. most of the shrinkage would have taken place and cracks can be filled

31.____

32. Acoustic plaster is used where it is desired to provide

   A. soundproofing
   B. fireproofing
   C. a light weight structure
   D. a vermin proof structure

32.____

33. Keene's cement plaster is used

   A. where the plaster is not to be painted
   B. where a hard surface is desired
   C. where there is no scratch coat
   D. on perforated rock lath

33.____

34. A concrete mix consisting of sand, gravel, cement, and water is most likely to be weakened by adding additional

   A. sand
   B. gravel
   C. cement
   D. water

34.____

35. It is *important* to control the slump of concrete because

    A. the desired slump helps in properly filling the forms
    B. it enables the inspector to perform the slump test
    C. it helps the inspector in preparing test cylinders
    D. the desired slump gives the desired strength

36. *Dimension lumber* is used MAINLY for

    A. door and sash cuttings
    B. exterior trim
    C. interior trim
    D. studding

37. *Blind nailing* is the term used to describe nailing

    A. when it is not known into what material the nails are driven
    B. done with finishing nails
    C. done with assorted size nails
    D. done in such way that the heads are not visible on the face of the work

38. If two 2 x 4's are to be securely nailed to make one 4 x 4 (approximately) and the nail points are not to come through, of the following, the best size nails to use is _____ penny.

    A. 20   B. 10   C. 8   D. 6

39. Lumber used in building construction should be well-seasoned because this

    A. makes it more fire resistant
    B. helps prevent shakes
    C. prevents damage by termites
    D. prevents shrinkage and warping

40. Timber that has been pressure creosoted is *most likely* to be used as

    A. beams in buildings to support heavy loads
    B. columns in buildings to support heavy loads
    C. rafters in a roof truss
    D. piles in wet ground

41. Toe nailing is illustrated in the sketch marked:

C. 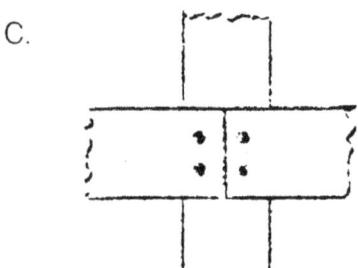   D.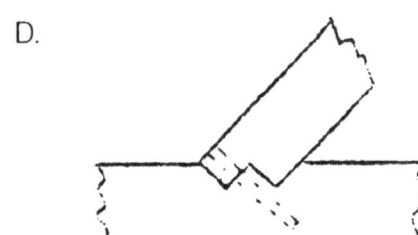

42. A piece of lumber with a cross section as shown is used in connection with: 42._____

   A. stairs
   C. doors
   B. baseboards
   D. windows

Questions 43 - 47.

Directions for answering questions 43 to 47: For each item in the sketch, shown below, labelled 43 to 47, select that letter that *most nearly* identifies the item and print that letter on your answer sheet next to the number of the item.

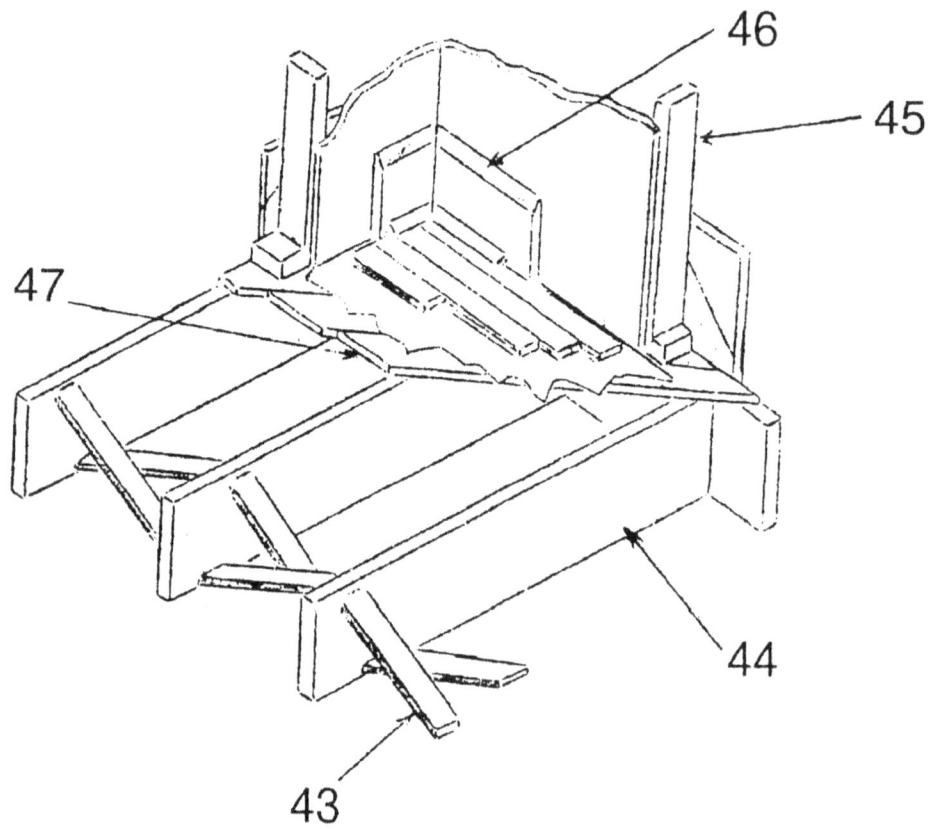

43.	A. sheathng	H. header			43.____
44.	B. finish flooring	I. sole			44.____
	C. paper	J. cap			
45.	D. sub flooring	K. bridging			45.____
46.	E. baseboard	L. wainscoting			46.____
	F. shoe	M. stud			
47.	G. joist	N. ledger			47.____

48. Of the following, the one that is NOT a *defect* of lumber is 48.____

   A. wane B. plinth
   C. check D. shake

49. A specification reads: Douglas fir shall average on either one end or the other not less 49.____
than 6 nor more than 20 annual rings per inch over a 3-inch portion of a radial line.
The *object* of this requirement is to secure lumber that is

   A. of beautiful grain B. close-grained
   C. free of knots D. chiefly heartwood

50. Of the following grades of lumber, the BEST grade is 50.____

   A. no. 1 Common B. no. 2 Common
   C. select Grade A D. select Grade B

KEY (CORRECT ANSWERS)

1.	B	11.	B	21.	A	31.	D	41.	A
2.	C	12.	D	22.	B	32.	A	42.	C
3.	A	13.	D	23.	A	33.	B	43.	K
4.	D	14.	B	24.	C	34.	D	44.	G
5.	C	15.	C	25.	D	35.	A	45.	M
6.	B	16.	B	26.	D	36.	D	46.	E
7.	D	17.	D	27.	A	37.	D	47.	D
8.	A	18.	D	28.	A	38.	B	48.	B
9.	B	19.	B	29.	B	39.	D	49.	B
10.	C	20.	C	30.	A	40.	D	50.	C

TEST 2

DIRECTIONS: Each question or incomplete statement is followed by several suggested answers or completions. Select the one that BEST answers the question or completes the statement. *PRINT THE LETTER OF THE CORRECT ANSWER IN THE SPACE AT THE RIGHT.*

1. In checking a corner of a room, the inspector marks a point 5 ft. from the corner along one wall and then he marks a point 12 ft. from the same corner along the other wall. If the corner is square, the distance between the two marked points should measure, in feet,

    A. 12 B. 13 C. 14 D. 15

2. A lot measures 60 ft. x 120 ft. and it is permissible to build on 65% of the lot. The *maximum* area that a building may occupy on that lot is, in square feet, most nearly,

    A. 7200 B. 5640 C. 4680 D. 4520

3. A wall measures 14' 3" long x 0' 6" high and has one window 5' 0" x 3' 0". The area of that wall to be painted is, in square feet, most nearly,

    A. 110 B. 115 C. 120 D. 125

4. A trench is 48 ft. long, 3 feet wide, 4' 6" deep at one end and 6' 4" deep at the other end. The volume of earth excavated is, in cubic yards, most nearly

    A. 29 B. 31 C. 27 D. 33

5. The curb on a right angle street corner is curved to a radius of 7 ft. The length of the curved portion of curb is, in feet, most nearly

    A. 9 B. 10 C. 11 D. 12

6. New plaster walls that are to be painted with an oil base paint

    A. require no sealer
    B. should be sealed with a coat of shellac
    C. should first receive a coat of primer sealer
    D. should first be brushed with turpentine

7. Of the following, the best thinner for an oil base paint is

    A. turpentine B. benzine
    C. alcohol   D. glycerine

8. A painting specification for a large job may require a different tint for each of three coats. The reason for this requirement is, most likely, that

    A. it enables the painter to get the desired shade in the final coat
    B. it is impossible to obtain the same tint in the types of paint required for the three different coats
    C. it reduces the cost of the job
    D. if a painter skimps the undercoat will show through

9. In painting new woodwork, it is best that knots and pitch streaks be

   A. sandpapered
   B. puttied
   C. shellacked
   D. given no special treatment

10. In painting new concrete masonry surfaces it is best that such surfaces first be

    A. dry-brushed   B. white-washed
    C. wet down   D. oiled

11. The letters W.C. on a building plan indicate

    A. water closet   B. wet concrete
    C. wire coil   D. workman's cloakroom

12. The letters D.S. on a building plan indicate a

    A. door saddle   B. down spout
    C. dumbwaiter shaft   D. dead space

Questions 13 - 17.

Directions for answering questions 13 to 17: For each question in the sketch below, labeled 13 to 17, select the number that most nearly identifies that item.

   I.   sub-flooring   VIII. stone facing
   II. joist   IX.   slab reinforcement
   III. beam clip   X.   bearing wall
   IV. sleeper   XI.   flashing
   V.   spandrel beam   XII. cinder fill
   VI. fireproofing concrete   XIII. plaster
   VII. screed   XIV. government anchor

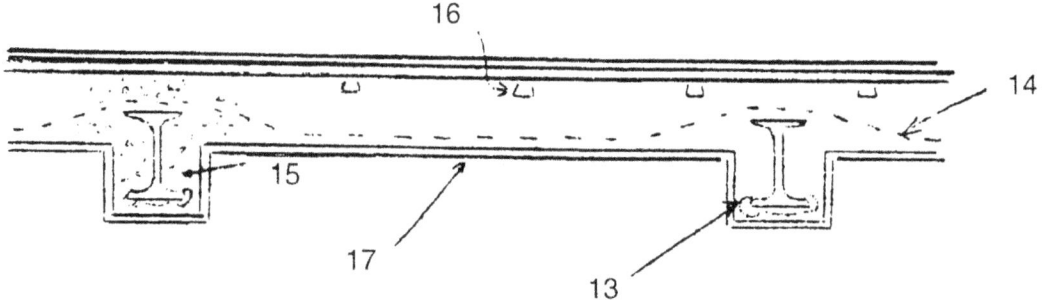

13. The CORRECT answer is:

    A. III   B. X   C. I   D. XIV

14. The CORRECT answer is:

    A. XII   B. IX   C. II   D. VII

15. The CORRECT answer is:

    A. VIII   B. XI   C. IX   D. VI

16. The CORRECT answer is:　　　　　　　　　　　　　　　　　　　　　　　　　　　　16.____

   A. II　　　　　　B. IX　　　　　　C. IV　　　　　　D. V

17. The CORRECT answer is:　　　　　　　　　　　　　　　　　　　　　　　　　　　　17.____

   A. XII　　　　　　B. XIV　　　　　　C. XIII　　　　　　D. VII

18. The symbol ____ on a building plan indicates a　　　　　　　　　　　　　　　　　　　18.____

   A. chute　　　　　　　　　　　　　B. storm window
   C. fire place　　　　　　　　　　　D. door

19. The size of moulds would be shown on the　　　　　　　　　　　　　　　　　　　　19.____

   A. plot plan　　　　　　　　　　　B. front elevation
   C. detail sheet　　　　　　　　　D. floor plan

20. The location of a partition would be shown on the　　　　　　　　　　　　　　　　20.____

   A. front elevation　　　　　　　B. plot plan
   C. floor plan　　　　　　　　　　D. detail sheet

21. Of the following, the procedure that is BEST for an inspector to follow is to　　　　　21.____

   A. check constantly with the architect
   B. observe carefully and check details
   C. allow skimping in order to expedite the work
   D. interpret vague specifications, personally

22. In making a record of an inspection, the BEST procedure for an inspector to follow is to　22.____

   A. fix in mind all important facts so that he can make out his report at the end of the day
   B. return immediately to the office to write his report while the facts are still fresh in his mind
   C. write down all important facts during the inspection
   D. dictate the facts to be recorded, to a stenographer

23. When an inspector first calls the attention of a foreman to the fact that his work does not　23.____
   comply with the specifications, the inspector should assume that the foreman

   A. did not know the specifications
   B. was guilty of deliberately violating the specifications
   C. was misinformed by a previous inspector
   D. was merely obeying orders

24. An inspector believes that the contractor would rather have another inspector on the job.　24.____
   The inspector *should*

   A. ask to be transferred
   B. disregard his feelings about the matter
   C. ask the contractor why he does not like him
   D. show special attention to the contractor to obtain his confidence

25. The inspector notifies the contractor that he is violating the specifications and the contractor disregards the inspector's notice.
    The inspector *should*

    A. report the nature of the violation to his superior with a statement that the contractor refused to comply with the specifications
    B. get his department to start legal action against the contractor
    C. instruct one of the workers to correct the work in order to avoid trouble
    D. threaten the contractor with cancellation of the contract unless he follows the specifications

26. When a contractor, because of a change in plans, is required to do work that is not covered in the contract, the inspector:

    A. Is not responsible for checking this work since it is an extra item
    B. Checks this work exactly the same way as he does any other work
    C. Is only interested in the cost of the extra work
    D. Not only checks the work the same as the rest of the job, but also keeps a record of labor and materials used on the extra work

27. It is estimated that it takes four hours to lay 100 partition tiles 12" x 12".
    If the size of the tile is changed to 8" x 12", then the time required to lay 100 tiles would be, approximately, in hours,

    A. 3   B. 4   C. 5   D. 6

28. The putty used for sealing window panes is *usually* composed of

    A. varnish and fine sand
    B. linseed oil, white lead and whiting
    C. molding clay and shellac
    D. cement and water

29. If the flange of a steel beam has been bent in handling, the beam *should*

    A. *not* be used in building construction
    B. be heated and hammered straight
    C. straightened by jacking but not heated
    D. be heated and straightened by jacking

30. In steel erection, loose rivets *should be*

    A. reheated and hammered tight
    B. tightened by additional hammering after the rivet is cooled
    C. tightened with a caulking tool
    D. cut out and replaced

31. According to the building code, soil tests are performed in order to determine the

    A. suitability of the soil for use as an aggregate in concrete or mortar
    B. safe sustaining power of the soil
    C. presence of subsurface structures
    D. height of the water table

32. The building code specifies a *minimum* weight per square yard for metal lath used in plastering.
    This weight is, in pounds,

    A. 12 B. 6 C. 3 D. 1

33. The building code specifies that splices in deformed column bars shall provide a lap of *at least* _____ times the diameter of the bars.

    A. 12 B. 24 C. 40 D. 60

34. According to the building code, all floor openings within a building used for hoisting material during construction *must*

    A. have a watchman present during working hours
    B. be completely covered at all times
    C. be guarded by a barrier between 3 ft. and 4 ft. high
    D. have a red warning light nearby

35. A non-bearing wall in skeleton construction built between columns and wholly supported at each story is a _____ wall.

    A. party   B. partition
    C. panel   D. fire

36. The part of a window that holds the glass is the

    A. jamb   B. sash
    C. casing   D. bead

37. A one-panel door has two stiles *and* _____ rails.

    A. no   B. one
    C. two   D. three

38. The vertical part of a stair step is a

    A. kick-plate   B. tread
    C. landing   D. riser

39. Sheet metal which is inserted between bricks of a chimney and extends over the roof to prevent water from penetrating down the side of the chimney is called the

    A. flashing   B. sheathing
    C. gutter   D. leader

40. Metal tubing through which electric wires of buildings are run is called

    A. insulation   B. conduit
    C. duct   D. sleeve

41. The function of a trap in a plumbing line is to prevent

    A. water hammer
    B. cross connections
    C. sewer gases from backing up
    D. leakage from a connection

42. The term *roughing in* means installing

    A. the vent lines
    B. all plumbing except the fixtures
    C. the drain pipes
    D. the soil lines

43. An expansion bolt is used to

    A. enlarge a hole
    B. fasten into hollow tile
    C. allow for expansion and contraction
    D. fasten into solid masonry

44. The purpose of the smoke test is to

    A. detect defects in plumbing installations
    B. check the operation of the boiler
    C. analyze flue gases
    D. test fire retarding materials

Questions 45 - 50.

Questions 45 to 50 refer to the plan shown on the next page.

45. The vertical bar is the bar marked

    A. I   B. II   C. III   D. IV

46. The item marked II is a(n)

    A. dowel   B. tie
    C. stirrup   D. anchor

47. The item marked VI is part of a

    A. wall   B. beam
    C. column   D. pier

48. The item marked VII is part of a

    A. wall   B. beam
    C. column   D. pier

49. 1" B.L. shown on the sketch means 1":

    A. To bare lath   B. To building line
    C. Finish as per spec. B.L.   D. Cover over reinforcing

50. In the note, "Ties - 3/8 ∅ @ 12" oc", 12" oc means 12"

    A. in compression only   B. apart
    C. long   D. all around

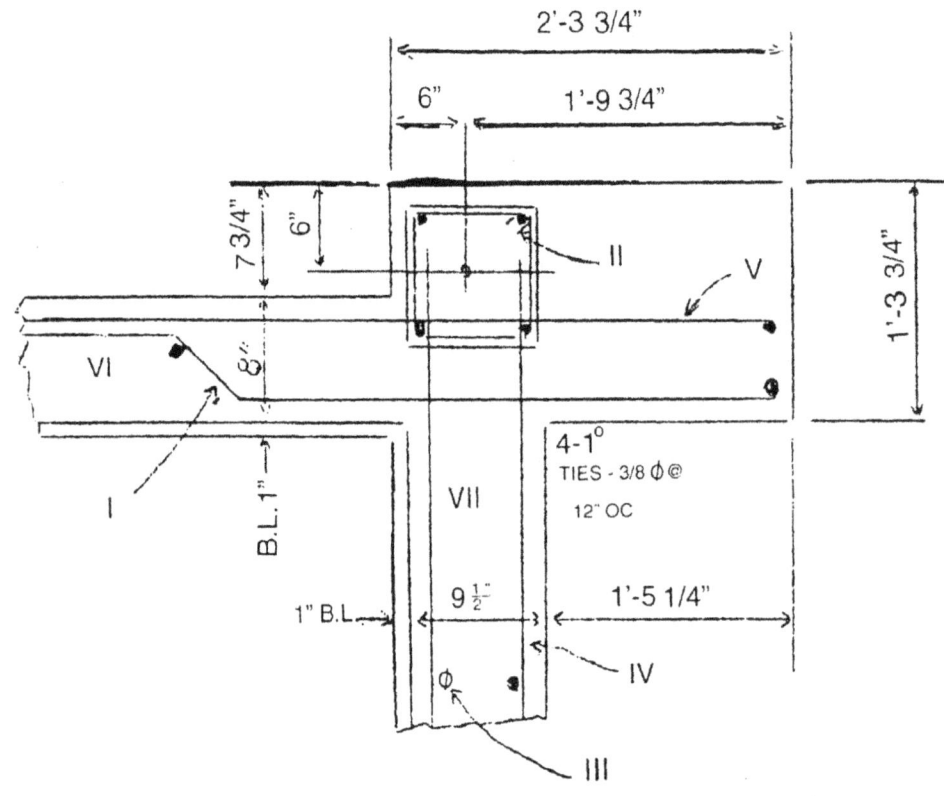

PART OF FOUNDATION PLAN OF BUILDING

KEY (CORRECT ANSWERS)

1. B	11. A	21. B	31. B	41. C
2. C	12. B	22. C	32. C	42. B
3. C	13. A	23. A	33. B	43. D
4. A	14. B	24. B	34. C	44. A
5. C	15. D	25. A	35. C	45. C
6. C	16. C	26. D	36. B	46. B
7. A	17. C	27. A	37. C	47. A
8. D	18. D	28. B	38. D	48. A
9. C	19. C	29. C	39. A	49. B
10. A	20. C	30. D	40. B	50. B

EXAMINATION SECTION
TEST 1

DIRECTIONS: Each question or incomplete statement is followed by several suggested answers or completions. Select the one that BEST answers the question or completes the statement. *PRINT THE LETTER OF THE CORRECT ANSWER IN THE SPACE AT THE RIGHT.*

1. In a stairway, the number of

    A. treads and risers is the same
    B. treads is one more than the number of risers
    C. risers is one more than the number of treads
    D. treads is two more than the number of risers

2. When constructing cellar concrete floors resting on earth, the item that should be checked MOST carefully is that

    A. the earth is dry before pouring
    B. the earth is wet before pouring
    C. all backfill is properly compacted
    D. all backfill is granular soil

3. When building the formwork for a 12" doubly reinforced concrete wall, the USUAL order of construction is: Place the

    A. formwork for both faces of the wall and then place the reinforcing steel
    B. reinforcing steel and then place the formwork for both faces of the wall
    C. formwork for one face of the wall, place the reinforcing steel, and then place the formwork for the other face of the wall
    D. formwork for one face of the wall, place the reinforcing steel for one face, place the formwork for the other face of the wall, and then place the reinforcement for the second face

4. Of the following, the BEST time to apply the final coat in a three-coat plastering job is when the second coat is _____ set and _____ dry.

    A. *completely; nearly*
    B. *completely; completely*
    C. *nearly; nearly*
    D. *nearly; completely*

5. The side forms for a 4-inch-thick sidewalk 5 feet wide are in place.
Of the following, the BEST way to see that the concrete is of proper thickness is to

    A. test the compactness of the subgrade to be certain there will be no settlement
    B. measure the depth of the side forms to the subgrade
    C. have a surveying party check the elevation of the subgrade
    D. measure the distance between the forms

6. A specification states that aluminum flashing shall be 3003 alloy with plain mill finish .032" thick material unless otherwise shown.
The thickness of the material is MOST NEARLY _____ inch.

    A. 1/64   B. 1/32   C. 3/64   D. 1/16

7. Of the following, which is the HIGHEST grade of lumber?

   A. Construction
   B. Utility
   C. Standard
   D. Run of the mill

8. Red lead paint would MOST likely be used

   A. as a prime coat on steel surfaces
   B. as a finish coat on plastered walls
   C. as a base coat for concrete surfaces
   D. where a glossy finish is desired

9. In plastering, grounds refers to strips of

   A. wire lath
   B. wood
   C. plaster
   D. rock lath

10. A specification requires that brick should be thoroughly wet before using.
    Of the following, the BEST reason for this requirement is that

    A. wetting the brick uncovers hidden flaws
    B. it is easier to shove wet brick into place
    C. this wetting cleans the pores of the brick, enabling the mortar to enter and provide stronger bond
    D. wetting prevents absorption of moisture from the mortar

11. Of the following types of glass, the one that is MOST suitable for bathroom windows, cellar windows, toilets, and lights not readily accessible for cleaning is _____ glass.

    A. rough hammered
    B. tempered
    C. single strength plate
    D. double strength sheet

Questions 12-13.

DIRECTIONS: Questions 12 and 13 are to be answered on the basis of the following statement.

Surfaces of woodwork shall be in proper condition by sanding all edges smooth to receive prime coat. The paint shall be uniformly applied and if by brush, well brushed into all cracks and crevices. Undercoat shall be well sanded before application of final enamel.

12. Of the following items, the one to which this statement MOST likely applies is

    A. finished hardware
    B. overhead clothing dryers
    C. baseboards
    D. kitchen cabinets

13. According to the statement, application of the paint by brush is

    A. optional
    B. preferable
    C. essential
    D. required if there are cracks in the wood

14. When excavating adjacent to a building on a spread footing and to a building on pile foundations, the GREATEST care must be exercised when excavating

   A. near the pile-supported building because the soil in the area is of poor quality
   B. near a building on spread footings because the concrete footings may crack
   C. for a pile-supported foundation because heavy loads are involved
   D. near a building on spread footings because of the danger of undermining the foundations

15. On a building plan, a door has a note F.P.S.C. This is an abbreviation for

   A. field painted self-contained
   B. fireproof steel covered
   C. field protected steel carbon
   D. fire protected self-closing

16. To obtain general information concerning the product of a particular major manufacturer of flooring, the BEST of the following sources of information is the

   A. ASTM
   B. Sweet's Catalogue
   C. Flooring Institute
   D. Architectural Standards

17. The final thickness of 3-coat plaster should be MOST NEARLY _____ inch(es).

   A. 1/2   B. 3/4   C. 1 1/8   D. 1 3/8

18. The specification for roofing states: Over the entire surface lay plies of coal tar felt (36 inches wide) lapping each sheet 27 1/2 inches over the preceding one, mopping with coal tar pitch, the full 27 1/2-inch lap on each sheet so that in no place shall felt touch felt. This specification is for _____ ply roofing.

   A. 2   B. 3   C. 4   D. 5

19. When constructing a tall reinforced concrete building, the pipeline system that should be built FIRST is the

   A. drainage plumbing
   B. standpipe system
   C. hot water system
   D. cold water system

20. Of the following certificates necessary at various stages during the construction of a project, the one that will usually be required FIRST is a

   A. fuel oil storage certificate
   B. gas line certificate
   C. certificate of insurance
   D. certificate of occupancy

21. A specification gives the contractor the option of using a plant mixed mortar or a semi-plant mixed mortar.
    The PRINCIPAL difference between the two mortars is that in the semi-plant mixed mortar,

   A. all the ingredients are added at the plant but the mixing is done at the job site
   B. only the dry ingredients are added at the plant, the water being added at the job site

C. the Portland cement is added at the job site
D. the lime putty is added at the job site

22. Ceramic tile is tile made of

    A. inorganic chemical plastic
    B. clay
    C. cement and sand
    D. asphalt and sand

23. If the pitch of a roof is 2 in 12, the change in elevation of the roof for a distance of 7' 6" is _____ inches.

    A. 15   B. 11   C. 7   D. 19

24. Of the following species of lumber, the one MOST likely to be used for wood formwork for concrete is

    A. pine   B. birch   C. maple   D. oak

25. Reinforcing steel for a footing resting on earth can BEST be held at the required distance above the earth by means of

    A. chairs   B. bolsters
    C. high risers   D. concrete blocks

KEY (CORRECT ANSWERS)

1. C	11. A
2. C	12. D
3. C	13. A
4. A	14. D
5. B	15. D
6. B	16. B
7. A	17. B
8. A	18. C
9. B	19. B
10. D	20. C

21. C
22. B
23. A
24. A
25. D

TEST 2

DIRECTIONS: Each question or incomplete statement is followed by several suggested answers or completions. Select the one that BEST answers the question or completes the statement. *PRINT THE LETTER OF THE CORRECT ANSWER IN THE SPACE AT THE RIGHT.*

1. Of the following, the skilled tradesman who would MOST likely do pile driving is a   1.____

    A. steelworker
    B. excavator
    C. dockbuilder
    D. carpenter

2. The following is taken from a specification for kitchen cabinets: Rails and stiles of full front frames on all cabinets shall be of hardwood 4/4 stock, maple or birch or southern poplar.   2.____
Of the following, the 4/4 stock means

    A. 4 x 4 lumber nominal size stock
    B. 1 inch thick rough stock
    C. 2 x 4 lumber nominal size stock
    D. finished four sides

3. One of the properties of tempered plate glass which affects installation is that it   3.____

    A. does not bond with putty or glazing compound
    B. cracks more easily than ordinary plate glass
    C. has a blue tint
    D. cannot be cut after the glass is tempered

4. Of the following types of piles, the one that usually requires the GREATEST care in handling prior to setting it in place for driving is a _____ pile.   4.____

    A. cast-in-place
    B. wood
    C. steel H
    D. precast concrete

5. In the city, metal door frames are USUALLY set in place by   5.____

    A. carpenters
    B. structural steel workers
    C. miscellaneous iron workers
    D. masons

6. As an inspector on the installation of wood trim, you find that one of the carpenters is leaving the round imprint of his hammer around almost every nail. Of the following, the BEST way for you to treat this situation is to   6.____

    A. recommend that this carpenter be removed
    B. recommend that the damaged trim be removed
    C. warn the carpenter that he must be more careful
    D. recommend that the specifications be changed to call for a harder wood

7. A casement window is USUALLY a window that   7.____

    A. is double hung
    B. opens inwardly only
    C. is made of wood
    D. is pivoted vertically

8. The specifications for the excavation for spread footings require that machine excavation should be within a foot of the final subgrade and the remainder of excavation shall be by hand.
   Of the following, the BEST reason for this requirement is to

   A. insure that the area in the vicinity of the footing is not excessively disturbed
   B. prevent cave-ins near the excavation
   C. cut down on the amount of fill needed
   D. prevent excavation above the subgrade

9. When structural steel beams are delivered to the job site, they USUALLY

   A. are unpainted
   B. have one shop coat of paint
   C. have two shop coats of paint
   D. are painted only on the milled surfaces

10. Of the following, it is MOST important to have a fire extinguisher on hand when

    A. burning structural steel on a steel frame building
    B. driving rivets on a steel frame building
    C. burning reinforcing steel in place in the formwork
    D. burning the heads of steel H piles

Questions 11-15.

DIRECTIONS: Questions 11 through 15 are to be answered on the basis of the following specification for a wood floor.

   I. 2" x 4" wood sleepers laid flat @ 16" o.c.
   II. 1" x 6" subflooring, laid diagonally; cut at butt joints with parallel cuts; joints at center of sleepers, well staggered, no two joints side by side. Not less than 1/8" space between boards.
   III. One layer of 15# asphalt felt on top of subfloor.
   IV. Finish floor - North Rock Maple, T & G, laid perpendicular to sleepers; 8d nails not more than 12" apart; end joints well scattered with at least 2 flooring strips between joints. Flooring 25/32" x 2 1/4" face - 1st quality.

11. It is MOST likely that such floor is to be laid

    A. directly on the ground   B. on wood joists
    C. on a concrete base   D. on steel beams

12. Of the following, the BEST reason for specifying that the subflooring be parallel cut at butt joints is that this

    A. requires less material
    B. provides more nailing surface
    C. provides staggered joints
    D. allows the joint to fall between sleepers

13. Of the following, the BEST reason for specifying a minimum space between the subfloor boards is that it   13.____

    A. saves on material   B. allows for expansion
    C. reduces creaking   D. prevents dry rot

14. Of the following, the BEST reason for speciying at least two flooring strips between joints in the finish flooring is that   14.____

    A. each board is supported by adjoining strips
    B. it is more economical
    C. each board is supported by at least two sleepers
    D. each board is supported by at least two subfloor boards

15. The dimension of this floor, from the bottom of the sleepers to the top of the finish flooring, is MOST NEARLY   15.____

    A. 3 15/16"   B. 3 3/4"   C. 3 3/16"   D. 4 15/16"

16. A foreman for a private contractor doing work for the city appears to be harsh to the employees under him. As an inspector for the city on this construction job, you should   16.____

    A. do nothing
    B. report this matter to your superior
    C. report this matter to the foreman's supervisor
    D. take this matter up with the foreman in question

17. Galvanized metal lath is coated with   17.____

    A. tin   B. zinc   C. lead   D. copper

18. In plastering, the coat that is applied to form a base sufficiently rough so that the third coat will adhere properly is known as the _____ coat.   18.____

    A. rough   B. white   C. scratch   D. brown

19. The contractor proposes to start the roofing three days after pouring the concrete roof slab.
    This proposal is   19.____

    A. *recommended* as it will speed the construction
    B. *recommended* as it will assist in curing the concrete
    C. *not recommended* in cold weather but is recommended in warm weather
    D. *not recommended* as excess water in the concrete may bulge the roofing

20. A difference between interior plaster and stucco mortar is that stucco mortar contains   20.____

    A. bitumen   B. gypsum   C. lime   D. cement

21. Safety shoes protect the feet PRIMARILY against   21.____

    A. chemical infection   B. falling objects
    C. slipping   D. punctures from nails

22. The number of days that it will take high early strength concrete to equal the 28-day strength of normal portland cement concrete is MOST NEARLY   22.____

    A. 1   B. 3   C. 7   D. 12

23. A rowlock course of brick is one in which the bricks are laid

    A. on their 2 1/4" x 8" surface
    B. in an interlocking fashion
    C. in a one header followed by one stretcher course
    D. with dowels at set intervals

24. The specifications state: Roof covering shall be 4 ply felt and pitch with slag finish not less than 200 pounds of pitch per square of roof.
    A square of roof covers an area of

    A. 1 square foot
    B. 1 square yard
    C. 10 square feet
    D. 100 square feet

25. Of the following grades, the one that MOST likely applies to brick is Grade

    A. Select Quality
    B. No. 1 Common
    C. S W
    D. A

KEY (CORRECT ANSWERS)

1. C
2. D
3. D
4. D
5. A

6. B
7. D
8. A
9. B
10. C

11. C
12. B
13. B
14. A
15. C

16. A
17. B
18. D
19. D
20. D

21. B
22. C
23. A
24. D
25. C

TEST 3

DIRECTIONS: Each question or incomplete statement is followed by several suggested answers or completions. Select the one that BEST answers the question or completes the statement. *PRINT THE LETTER OF THE CORRECT ANSWER IN THE SPACE AT THE RIGHT.*

1. The MAIN difference between sheet glass and plate glass is that plate glass

   A. is tempered while sheet glass is not tempered
   B. is thinner than sheet glass
   C. has a higher surface finish than sheet glass
   D. has a greater heat absorbing quality than sheet glass

2. Efflorescence may BEST be removed from brickwork by washing with a solution of _____ acid.

   A. muriatic   B. citric   C. carbonic   D. nitric

3. In a 2" thick solid plaster wall, the metal lath is USUALLY attached to vertical steel members which have the shape of a(n)

   A. zee   B. tee   C. angle   D. channel

4. In the specification for the stripping of formwork for concrete is the requirement that slab panels should not be stripped in less than 66 hours. Assume that a slab pour is started Monday morning and completed at 3 P.M. The EARLIEST the forms may be removed is

   A. Wednesday morning   B. Wednesday afternoon
   C. Thursday morning   D. Thursday afternoon

5. According to the building code, masonry footings shall extend at least 4' below finished grade.
   The PRIMARY reason for this is to

   A. get below the frost line
   B. utilize the higher bearing material of the lower soil strata
   C. make the foundation stronger
   D. keep water out of the basement

6. The amount of water that should be used with one sack of cement in a 1:2:5 concrete mix is, in gallons, MOST NEARLY _____ gallon(s).

   A. 1   B. 2   C. 5   D. 8

7. If there is a small amount of water on the surface of newly-laid concrete sidewalk, the recommended procedure before finishing is to

   A. allow it to evaporate
   B. remove it with a broom
   C. sprinkle some dry cement on top
   D. remove it with a pump

8. Concrete placed in forms should be placed in layers NOT more than _____ thick.

   A. 2"   B. 6"   C. 10"   D. 14"

53

9. The length of a 20 penny nail is MOST NEARLY _____ inches.

   A. 2 1/2   B. 3   C. 3 1/2   D. 4

10. Of the following outside lines, the one for which the grades must be checked and followed MOST carefully during construction is a(n)

    A. sewer line
    B. water line
    C. gas line
    D. electric cable

11. Wood sash putty USUALLY contains

    A. shellac
    B. linseed oil
    C. varnish
    D. turpentine

12. A mortar mix is 1:1:6.
    The number that is underlined is

    A. sand   B. cement   C. lime   D. gravel

13. Of the following statements relating to seams in linoleum flooring, the one that is MOST NEARLY correct is that the parts to be seamed are

    A. made by overlapping the two parts and cutting through both layers of linoleum
    B. butted against one another, cemented with a colorless paste at the joints, and rolled with a 10 pound roller
    C. dovetailed, pasted, and made integral by rolling with a 20 pound roller
    D. beveled, pasted, and rolled with a 40 pound roller

14. A backhoe is used PRIMARILY to excavate

    A. trenches
    B. foundations for spread footings
    C. foundations for pile footings
    D. for underpinning

15. Of the following, the BEST treatment for knots in woodwork that is to be painted is to coat the knots with

    A. shellac
    B. colorless stain
    C. boiled linseed oil
    D. raw linseed oil

16. Cement stored on the job site has become caked and lumpy. This cement may

    A. be used on any part of the structure if the lumps are broken
    B. be used only for foundations if the lumps are broken
    C. be used only for sidewalks
    D. not be used for concrete

17. A finished piece of lumber whose nominal dimensions are 2" x 4" is MOST NEARLY

    A. 1 7/8" x 3 7/8"
    B. 1 3/4" x 3 3/4"
    C. 1 5/8" x 3 5/8"
    D. 1 1/2" x 4 1/2"

18. Where a 2" solid laminated gypsum wallboard partition, consisting of two 1" wallboards, assembled back to back on the job, abuts a joint, the specifications require that the panel be secured to the continuous metal fins or anchors.
    Of the following, the hardware MOST likely to be specified for fastening the gypsum panel to the joint is

    A. speed clinch fasteners
    B. 1/2-inch hardened stud nails
    C. U-shaped metal joint clips
    D. 2 1/2-inch number 10 sheet metal screws

18.____

19. The difference between quicklime and hydrated lime, as far as the addition of water is concerned, is that

    A. hydrated lime requires soaking only
    B. quicklime requires soaking only
    C. hydrated lime requires soaking and slaking
    D. quicklime requires slaking only

19.____

20. A specification on carpentry for a housing project calls for the use of a nail set.
    Of the following, the BEST reason for this requirement is that

    A. certain nails are to be removed
    B. the points of certain nails are to be bent over for better anchorage
    C. the heads of certain nails are to be sunk
    D. certain nails are to be spaced at a specified interval

20.____

21. Of the following grades of lumber, the one that is MOST likely to be specified for interior finish which is to be painted is Grade

    A. No. 1 Common   B. No. 2 Common
    C. No. 1 Clear   D. D, Select

21.____

22. A note on a drawing reads: Masonry walls will be laid up in one part Portland cement, 0.15 parts lime and 3 parts sand.
    Of the following, the PRIMARY purpose in adding lime to the mix is to

    A. improve the appearance of the mortar
    B. increase the workability of the mortar
    C. increase the strength of the mortar
    D. improve the bearing capacity of the wall

22.____

23. Of the following woods, the one that is the HARDEST is

    A. Douglas Fir   B. Sitka Spruce
    C. Southern Pine   D. Hickory

23.____

24. The concrete test that will BEST determine the consistency of a concrete mix is the

    A. slump test   B. sieve analysis
    C. calorimetric test   D. water-cement ratio test

24.____

25. A riser diagram is an electrical drawing which would give information about the   25.___
    A. voltage drop in feeders
    B. size of feeders and panel loads
    C. external connections to equipment
    D. sequence of operation of devices and equipment

KEY (CORRECT ANSWERS)

1. C   11. B
2. A   12. C
3. D   13. A
4. C   14. A
5. A   15. A

6. D   16. D
7. A   17. C
8. C   18. C
9. D   19. A
10. A   20. C

21. C
22. B
23. D
24. A
25. B

EXAMINATION SECTION
TEST 1

DIRECTIONS: Each question or incomplete statement is followed by several suggested answers or completions. Select the one that BEST answers the question or completes the statement. *PRINT THE LETTER OF THE CORRECT ANSWER IN THE SPACE AT THE RIGHT.*

Questions 1-5.

DIRECTIONS: Questions 1 through 5 are to be answered on the basis of the following statement. Use ONLY the information contained in this statement in answering these questions.

No multiple dwelling shall be erected to a height in excess of one and one-half times the width of the widest street on which it faces, except that above the level of such height, for each one foot that the front wall of such dwelling sets back from the street line, three feet shall be added to the height limit of such dwelling, but such dwelling shall not exceed in maximum height three feet plus one and three-quarter times the width of the widest street on which it faces.

Any such dwelling facing a street more than one hundred feet in width shall be subject to the same height limitations as though such dwelling faced a street one hundred feet in width.

1. The MAXIMUM height of a multiple dwelling set back five feet from the street line and facing a 60 foot wide street is _____ feet.

    A. 60   B. 90   C. 105   D. 165

2. The MAXIMUM height of a multiple dwelling set back six feet from the street line and facing a 120 foot wide street is _____ feet.

    A. 198   B. 168   C. 120   D. 105

3. The MAXIMUM height of a multiple dwelling is

    A. 100 ft.   B. 150 ft.   C. 178 ft.   D. unlimited

4. The MAXIMUM height of a multiple dwelling set back 10 feet from the street line and facing a 110 foot wide street is _____ feet.

    A. 178   B. 180   C. 195   D. 205

5. The MAXIMUM height of a multiple dwelling set back eight feet from the street line and facing a 90 foot wide street is _____ feet.

    A. 135   B. 147   C. 178   D. 159

Questions 6-10.

DIRECTIONS: Questions 6 through 10 are to be answered on the basis of the following statement. Use ONLY the information contained in this statement in answering these questions.

2 (#1)

The number of persons accommodated on any story in a lodging house shall not be greater than the sum of the following components.
    a. 22 persons for each full multiple of 22 inches in the smallest clear width for each means of egress approved by the department, other than fire escapes.
    b. 20 persons for each lawful fire escape accessible from such story.

6. The MAXIMUM number of persons that may be accommodated on a story in a lodging house depends on the

    A. number of lawful fire escapes *only*
    B. number of approved means of egress *only*
    C. smallest clear width in each approved means of egress *only*
    D. number of lawful fire escapes and sum total of smallest clear widths in each approved means of egress

7. The MAXIMUM number of persons that may be accommodated on a story of a lodging house having one lawful fire escape and a sum total of 44 inches in the smallest clear widths of the two approved means of egress is

    A. 20   B. 22   C. 42   D. 64

8. The MAXIMUM number of persons that may be accommodated on a story of a lodging house having two lawful fire escapes and a sum total of 60 inches in the smallest clear width of the approved means of egress is

    A. 64   B. 84   C. 100   D. 106

9. The MAXIMUM number of persons that may be accommodated on a story of a lodging house having one lawful fire escape and a sum total of 33 inches in the smallest clear width of the approved means of egress is

    A. 42   B. 53   C. 64   D. 73

10. The MAXIMUM number of persons that may be accommodated on a story of a lodging house having two lawful fire escapes and two approved means of egress, with 40 inches and 44 inches in the smallest clear widths, respectively, is

    A. 84   B. 104   C. 106   D. 108

11. An employee of the Department of Housing and Buildings may take outside employment in private industry as a(n)

    A. architect   B. mason
    C. plumber   D. none of the above

12. The one of the following that is NOT a multiple dwelling is a

    A. college dormitory
    B. dwelling occupied by three families
    C. hospital
    D. lodging house

13. The one of the following that is a Class A multiple dwelling is a

    A. commercial building containing a janitor's apartment
    B. furnished room house

C. hotel
D. tenement

14. A dwelling occupied by one family with five transient roomers is a _____ dwelling. 14.____

   A. Class A multiple
   B. Class B multiple
   C. single family private
   D. two-family private

15. The one of the following that is deemed a living room by the multiple dwelling law is a 15.____

   A. bathroom
   B. bedroom
   C. dinette, 45 sq. ft. in area
   D. kitchenette, 45 sq. ft. in area

16. The MAXIMUM number of stories to which a new multiple dwelling may be erected without having a passenger elevator is 16.____

   A. 4   B. 5   C. 6   D. 7

17. In a new multiple dwelling, which of the following rooms are required to have windows? 17.____

   A. Bathroom
   B. Kitchen
   C. Water-closet compartment
   D. All of the above

18. New multiple dwellings three stories or more in height must have hot water supplied during 18.____

   A. the hours between 6 A.M. and Midnight *only*
   B. the hours between 8 A.M. and 8 P.M. *only*
   C. the hours between 6 A.M. and Noon and 6 P.M. and Midnight *only*
   D. all hours

19. A winding stair in a new multiple dwelling is 19.____

   A. not permitted under any circumstances
   B. permitted under all circumstances
   C. permitted only when the building is more than 6 stories high
   D. permitted only when the building is less than 6 stories high

20. All elevator shaft walls in new multiple dwellings MUST be 20.____

   A. at least 4 inches thick
   B. fireproof
   C. hollow
   D. made of gypsum plaster

21. The one of the following statements about new multiple dwellings that is NOT true is: 21.____

   A. Boiler rooms in multiple dwellings four stories or more in height must have fireproof doors
   B. Every open roof area must have a guard rail or parapet wall at least 3'6" high
   C. A new multiple dwelling may be placed on the same lot with a frame building
   D. A new multiple dwelling may be used for parking of passenger motor vehicles

22. A tenement within the meaning of the multiple dwelling law is a building erected BEFORE

    A. April 18, 1929
    B. April 6, 1948
    C. April 12, 1949
    D. March 25, 1952

23. Every entrance hall in a multiple dwelling must be provided with a light of AT LEAST _____ watts.

    A. 5   B. 10   C. 15   D. 40

24. From the entrance to the first stair, every entrance hall in a new multiple dwelling must be, in clear width, AT LEAST

    A. 3'8"   B. 4'   C. 6'   D. 8'

25. A basement in a new multiple dwelling exceeding seven stories in height MUST have AT LEAST one-half of its height _____ curb level and is _____ as a story.

    A. above; counted
    B. above; not counted
    C. below; counted
    D. below; not counted

26. The lower ends of mitred cross bridging should be nailed to the beams

    A. at the same time that the top ends are nailed
    B. before the rough flooring is placed
    C. after the plastering is complete
    D. after the flooring is placed

27. The maximum distance between lines of bridging should NOT exceed

    A. 10'0"   B. 8'0"   C. 6'6"   D. 4'6"

28. The building code states that it shall be unlawful to corbel walls less than twelve inches thick, except for fire-stopping.
    From this, it may be concluded that

    A. walls 12 inches or more in thickness shall not be corbelled
    B. if a wall is less than 12 inches thick, it is permissible to corbel provided some of the corbelling is used for fire-stopping
    C. fire-stopping shall not be considered to be corbelling
    D. corbelling and fire-stopping are the same

29. The building code states that curtain walls of solid masonry shall be at least eight inches thick for the uppermost thirteen feet and at least twelve inches thick for the next fifty-two feet or fraction thereof below and shall be increased four inches in thickness for each succeeding sixty feet or fraction thereof below.
    This means that the thickness of a solid masonry curtain wall 126 feet high should be AT LEAST

    A. 20 inches throughout its height
    B. 20 inches at the base
    C. 16 inches throughout its height
    D. 16 inches at the base

30. The term *curb cut* refers to

    A. openings in a curb
    B. tire cuts made while parking
    C. surveying marks chiseled in a curb
    D. rental for sidewalk stands

31. A bearing wall is a wall which

    A. carries its own weight *only*
    B. carries load other than its own weight
    C. bears on structural supports at each story
    D. is more than 12 feet high

32. A column is an _____ member.

    A. upright compression   B. inclined compression
    C. upright tension   D. inclined tension

33. A lintel could be broadly classified as a

    A. beam   B. column   C. footing   D. strut

34. A flat slab is MOST commonly used in _____ construction.

    A. sidewalk   B. roadway   C. conduit   D. building

35. Of the following, the member which would MOST likely be supported on a footing is the

    A. beam   B. girder   C. column   D. joist

36. A parapet wall would MOST likely support

    A. a coping   B. roof joists
    C. floor joists   D. partitions

37. Jack arches are used

    A. in ornamental iron work
    B. in fancy stairways
    C. when lintels are omitted
    D. in foundations

38. If green lumber is used for joists, shrinkage will have its MOST serious effect in _____ of joists.

    A. length   B. width   C. depth   D. weight

39. The phrase *concealed draft openings* is MOST likely to be used in connection with

    A. fireplaces   B. flues
    C. fire-stopping   D. automatic dampers

40. Of the following terms, the one which is LEAST related to the others is the

    A. jamb   B. strike plate
    C. latch bolt   D. pulley stile

Questions 41-45.

DIRECTIONS: Questions 41 through 45 are to be answered in accordance with the following sketch.

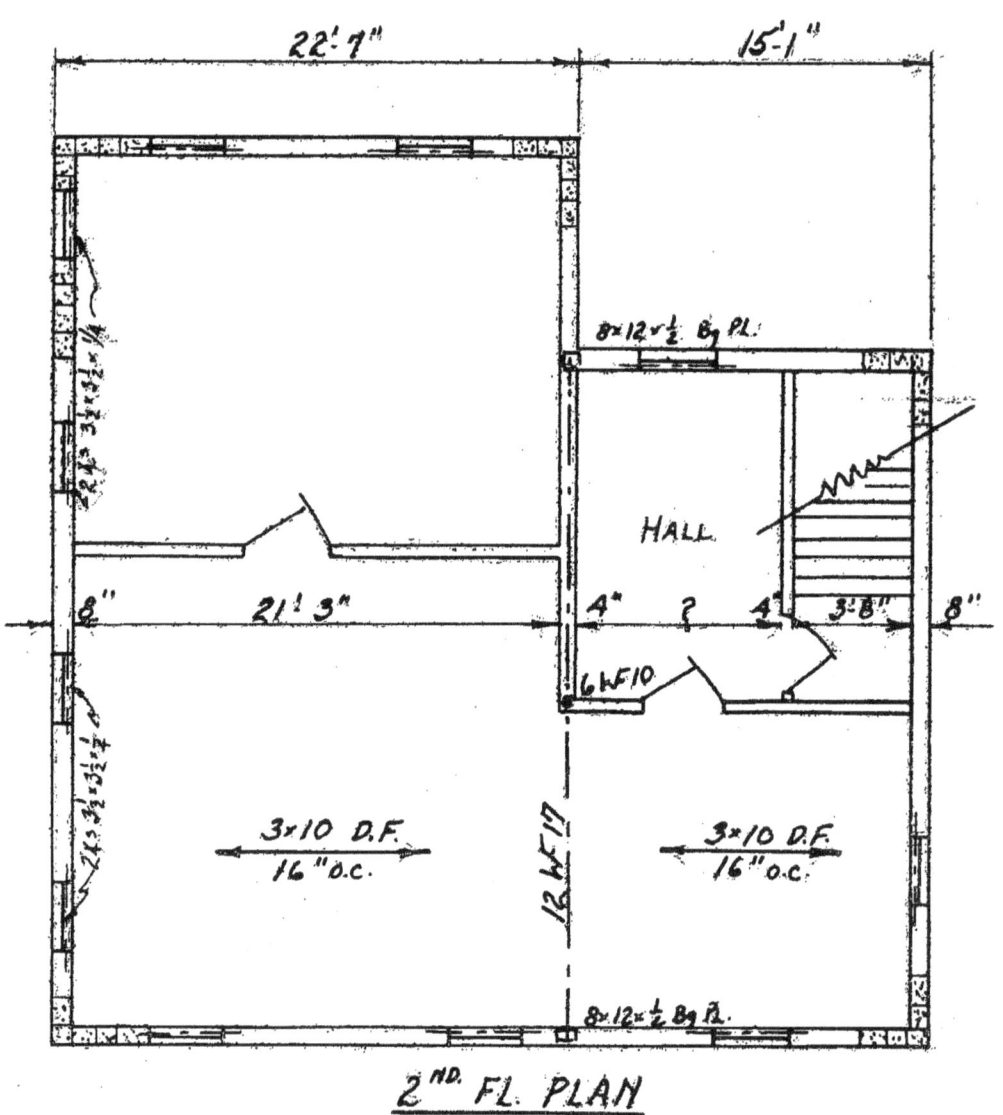

2ND. FL. PLAN

41. The one of the following statements that is CORRECT is: The building

    A. is of fireproof construction
    B. has masonry walls, with wood joists
    C. is of wood frame construction
    D. has timber posts and girders

42. The one of the following statements that is CORRECT is:

    A. The stairway from the ground floor continues through the roof
    B. There are two means of egress from the second floor of this building
    C. The door on the second floor stair landing opens in the direction of egress
    D. The entire stair is shown on this plan

43. The width of the hall is 43.____

    A. 10'3"   B. 10'5"   C. 10'7"   D. 10'9"

44. The lintels shown are 44.____

    A. angles
    B. a channel and an angle
    C. an I-beam
    D. precast concrete

45. The one of the following statements that is CORRECT is: The steel beam is 45.____

    A. supported by columns at the center and at the ends
    B. entirely supported by the walls
    C. supported on columns at the ends only
    D. supported at the center by a column and at the ends by the walls

KEY (CORRECT ANSWERS)

1. C	11. D	21. C	31. B	41. B
2. B	12. C	22. A	32. A	42. C
3. C	13. D	23. C	33. A	43. D
4. A	14. B	24. B	34. D	44. A
5. D	15. B	25. A	35. C	45. D
6. D	16. C	26. D	36. A	
7. D	17. D	27. B	37. C	
8. B	18. A	28. C	38. C	
9. A	19. A	29. B	39. C	
10. C	20. B	30. A	40. D	

EXAMINATION SECTION
TEST 1

DIRECTIONS: Each question or incomplete statement is followed by several suggested answers or completions. Select the one that BEST answers the question or completes the statement. *PRINT THE LETTER OF THE CORRECT ANSWER IN THE SPACE AT THE RIGHT.*

1. When a sidewalk shed is required in connection with the erection of a building, the Code provides that the shed must be completed before the building has risen to a height, in feet, of

    A. 12   B. 16   C. 30   D. 40

    1._____

2. Concrete for a self-supporting floor should have a slump, in inches, of about

    A. 3   B. 4   C. 7   D. 13

    2._____

3. When building material bears a distinguishing mark of the manufacturer, the inspector should

    A. ignore it
    B. ask the contractor to remove it
    C. check to see if the mark is approved by the Board
    D. ask the contractor to obtain the manufacturer's specifications

    3._____

4. The letters *A.S.T.M.* followed by letters and numbers refer to

    A. standard tests of materials
    B. paragraphs in state laws
    C. sections, text, and meaning of the Building Code
    D. the structural training manual

    4._____

5. A frame building with 2 x 4 studding has an interior partition with 2 x 6 studding. The MOST probable reason for the heavier studding is to provide

    A. heat insulation   B. sound insulation
    C. room for a soil stack   D. room for steam pipes

    5._____

6. Ties and chairs are used in construction involving

    A. plain concrete   B. reinforced concrete
    C. masonry   D. structural steel

    6._____

7. Painting of steel reinfarcing bars is

    A. *bad*, because it impairs bond
    B. *good*, because it prevents rust
    C. *bad*, because it increases costs
    D. *good*, because use of different colors permits ready identification of the various sizes

    7._____

8. An inspector picks up a brick, which has just been laid, to inspect the bedding. No mortar adhered to the brick so the furrowing of the mortar is shown clearly.
   The inspector is MOST concerned with the

   A. depth of the furrow
   B. width of the furrow
   C. depth and width of the furrow
   D. fact that no mortar adhered to the brick

9. Acoustic tile would MOST likely be used in

   A. ceilings   B. floors   C. bathrooms   D. kitchens

10. To determine the story heights of a building, you should look at the

    A. plan view   B. elevation view
    C. architect's rendition D. perspective view

11. Kalamein work is

    A. metal-sheathed wood
    B. a type of enameling
    C. woodwork using different colored woods to make a pattern
    D. used in ornamental plastering

12. The weight of all permanent construction in a building is known as _____ load.

    A. permanent   B. live   C. dead   D. design

13. A layer of plaster which is scratched both horizontally and vertically is known as a

    A. scratch coat   B. bond coat
    C. brown coat   D. plaster base

14. When steel is given two coats of paint, a different color is used for the second coat

    A. for a pleasing contrast
    B. to avoid monotony for the painter
    C. for chemical reasons
    D. to insure full coverage by the second coat

15. A certificate of occupancy is required for a new building

    A. if it is a Class A multiple dwelling
    B. if it is a multiple dwelling
    C. if it is a dwelling
    D. regardless of whether or not it is a dwelling

16. New multiple dwelling of non-fireproof construction

    A. is not allowed
    B. must be outside the fire limits
    C. must not exceed 75 feet in height
    D. must not occupy more than 70% of the lot area

17. In an elevation view, round reinforcing bars in a reinforced concrete floor would appear as

    A. circles
    B. lines
    C. either circles or line
    D. triangles

18. The columns of a building are spaced 21'0" in one direction and 28'0" in the other. The length of a diagonal of a bay is, in feet, MOST NEARLY

    A. 35.0
    B. 35.1
    C. 36.2
    D. 34.9

19. The use of peaveys or cant hooks to handle creosoted lumber in wood construction is

    A. *bad,* because it may expose untreated wood
    B. *good,* because the laborer will not get splinters in his hands
    C. *bad,* because the lumber is damaged by rolling
    D. *good,* because it is an efficient method

20. The end of a joist resting on a masonry wall is USUALLY cut on a bevel to

    A. prevent damage to the wall if the joist should fall during a fire
    B. provide circulation of air around the enclosed portion of the joist
    C. provide a larger bearing area
    D. reduce the wall opening required by the joist

21. Oiling of steel reinforcing bars for concrete is

    A. *good,* because it prevents rust
    B. *good,* because it makes handling in the forms easier
    C. *bad,* because there is a chemical reaction with the concrete
    D. *bad,* because it prevents adhesion of the concrete

22. A load-bearing cavity wall consists of a four inch wythe and an eight inch wythe with a two inch air space.
    In normal construction, the wider wythe

    A. should be the outer face of the wall
    B. should be the inner face of the wall
    C. may be either inner or outer face
    D. wastes material as the two wythes should be of equal thickness

23. Metal ties used in cavity walls sometimes have a crimp which is located in the air space when the tie is in place in the wall.
    This crimp serves to

    A. strengthen the tie
    B. add to the elasticity of the tie
    C. prevent water from traveling across the tie
    D. center the tie between the wythes

Questions 24-25.

DIRECTIONS: Questions 24 and 25 refer to the following statement and sketch.

A specification reads: *Net cross-sectional area of a masonry unit shall be taken as the gross cross-sectional area minus the area of cores or cellular space.*

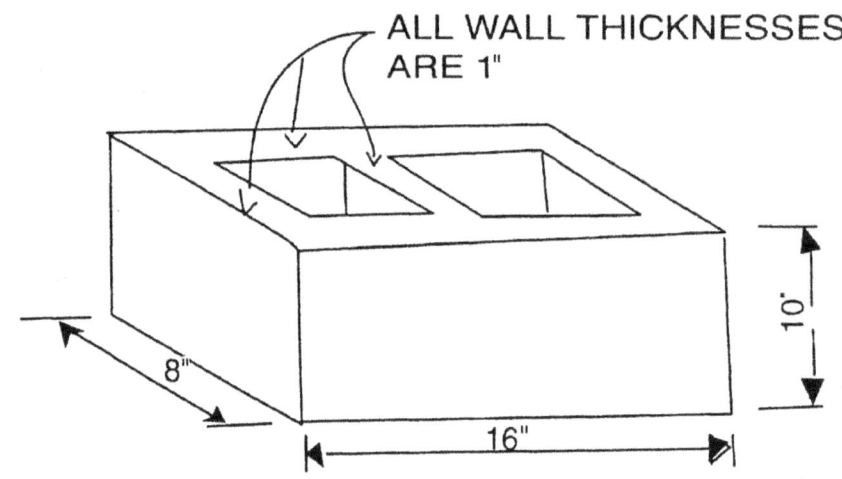

24. The gross cross-sectional area is _____ square inches.

    A. 64 B. 84 C. 128 D. 144

25. The net cross-sectional area is _____ square inches.

    A. 128 B. 112 C. 77 D. 50

26. Small wood members which are inserted in a diagonal position between floor joists for the purpose of bracing the joists and spreading loads to adjacent joists are called

    A. struts B. ties C. bridging D. ledger strips

27. A beam placed perpendicular to joists and to which joists are nailed in framing for a chimney, stairway, or other opening, is called a

    A. trimmer joist B. tail beam
    C. girder D. header

28. A narrow board let into the studding to provide added support for joists is known as a

    A. sill B. trimmer C. ribbon D. sole plate

29. In concrete construction, honeycombing is MOST likely to occur in

    A. thin floors B. thin walls
    C. heavy footing D. thick floors

30. The CHIEF objection to the use of green lumber in wood construction relates to its

    A. color
    B. strength
    C. lack of dimensional stability
    D. nailing

31. Concrete weighs 4000 pounds per cubic yard.
    A slab of concrete 4'3" wide by 7'6" long by 1'9" thick weighs, in pounds, MOST NEARLY

    A. 7550   B. 7950   C. 8000   D. 8260

32. A fire-resistive rating of an assembly is given in units of

    A. degrees centigrade
    B. degrees fahrenheit
    C. hours
    D. none of the above

33. A trimmer arch would be used in

    A. floor openings
    B. wall openings
    C. floor construction near chimneys
    D. parapet walls

34. Cracks in lumber due to contraction along annual rings are known as

    A. checks   B. pitch pockets   C. wane   D. craze

35. The length of a tenpenny nail, in inches, is

    A. 2 1/2   B. 3   C. 3 1/2   D. 4

36. When ready-mix concrete is used on a job, the PRIMARY responsibility for checking the proportioning of cement, sand, and gravel rests with

    A. the inspector on the job
    B. the engineer on the job
    C. the inspector at the batching plant
    D. none of the above

37. In plastering, coves are

    A. never required
    B. used to obtain an even finish
    C. required where floor and wall meet
    D. sometimes required where wall and ceiling meet

38. Wood bridging should

    A. be nailed top and bottom before placing the subflooring
    B. not be placed until the subflooring is placed
    C. be nailed at its upper end only before the subflooring is placed
    D. be nailed at its lower end only before the subflooring is placed

39. Cross-furring is required by the Code in

    A. walls consisting of 2 x 4 studding
    B. ceilings when lath is attached directly to the wood joists of the floor above
    C. walls using metal lath on wood studs
    D. suspended ceilings

40. Board measure is a measure of

    A. length   B. area   C. volume   D. weight

41. The consistency of concrete is measured by a _____ test.

    A. slump
    C. strength
    B. penetration
    D. time of set

42. Bricking up the space between furring at floors is done to

    A. provide corbelling
    C. stiffen the structure
    B. fire-stop the wall
    D. moisture-proof the wall

43. The dressed size of lumber is

    A. smaller than the nominal size
    B. depends upon the grade of the lumber
    C. its size as finally used on the job
    D. not related to its nominal size

44. Of the following types of joints, the one which is LEAST related to the others is

    A. raked   B. weather   C. construction   D. struck

45. A rowlock course consists of bricks

    A. set on end
    B. set on their sides
    C. set flat
    D. laid alternately as headers and stretchers

46. With respect to flooring, shrinkage in a wood joist is MOST serious in

    A. length
    C. depth
    B. width
    D. all of the above

47. Neat cement and marble chips are used

    A. as mortar in marble walls and floors
    B. to make terrazzo
    C. for stucco
    D. for ornamental ceilings

48. Cinder concrete is sometimes used in floor construction in place of stone concrete because the cinder concrete

    A. permits thinner floors
    B. provides better acoustics
    C. is more fire-resistant
    D. is lighter

49. If a subcontractor's work is unsatisfactory,

    A. inform him that his payments will be withheld
    B. make the subcontractor's foreman rip it out
    C. so inform the general contractor
    D. warn him that further unsatisfactory work will bar him from future city work

50. *Extra work* is work

    A. not called for in the contract
    B. required to correct unsatisfactory work
    C. done outside of regular hours
    D. required by inexperienced inspectors which is unnecessary

50.____

KEY (CORRECT ANSWERS)

1. D	11. A	21. D	31. D	41. A
2. B	12. C	22. B	32. C	42. B
3. C	13. A	23. C	33. C	43. A
4. A	14. D	24. C	34. A	44. C
5. C	15. D	25. D	35. B	45. B
6. B	16. C	26. C	36. C	46. C
7. A	17. C	27. D	37. D	47. B
8. D	18. A	28. C	38. C	48. D
9. A	19. A	29. B	39. D	49. C
10. B	20. A	30. C	40. C	50. A

TEST 2

DIRECTIONS: Each question or incomplete statement is followed by several suggested answers or completions. Select the one that BEST answers the question or completes the statement. *PRINT THE LETTER OF THE CORRECT ANSWER IN THE SPACE AT THE RIGHT.*

1. Aggregates used to make concrete do NOT include   1.___

    A. sand   B. gravel   C. cement   D. crushed rock

2. Careful slushing of the end joints of slip sills is PRIMARILY required to   2.___

    A. prevent displacement   B. provide water tightness
    C. maintain bond   D. prevent discoloration

3. The use of bats in brick work is justified when such use   3.___

    A. is required by the bond
    B. reduces the amount of face brick
    C. eliminates headers
    D. prevents waste of excess bats

4. In construction work, a neat line is a(n) _____ line.   4.___

    A. inside   B. outside   C. vertical   D. center

5. In acceptable concrete practice, a small w/c ratio is MOST likely to indicate that the concrete mix will   5.___

    A. be stiff
    B. produce high-strength concrete
    C. have a big slump
    D. produce low-strength concrete

6. In concrete work, wooden form spreaders should be removed   6.___

    A. as soon as the concrete is placed
    B. after the concrete has attained initial set
    C. after the concrete has attained final set
    D. after the concrete has attained full strength

7. The rounded, projecting edge of a stair tread is the   7.___

    A. coping   B. nosing   C. rising   D. stringing

8. A fire tower differs from fire stairs PRINCIPALLY in   8.___

    A. capacity
    B. location
    C. height
    D. tread and riser requirements

9. The area of a circle 2'6" in diameter is, in square feet, MOST NEARLY   9.___

    A. 4.6   B. 4.9   C. 5.3   D. 6.7

10. A cantilever beam would MOST likely be used in connection with a

    A. floor opening B. balcony
    C. warehouse floor D. roof opening

11. The Code requires various thicknesses of concrete cover for reinforcing rods used in the different elements of a building.
    That element which requires the LEAST cover is

    A. column B. beam C. girder D. flat slab

12. A specification reads: *The span length of freely supported beams shall be the clear span plus the effective depth of beam, but shall be within the distance between centers of supports.*
    According to this specification, the span length of such a beam with an effective depth of 22 inches, supported on 18 inch walls spaced 16'0" in the clear, is

    A. 17'9" B. 17'7" C. 17'6" D. 17'5"

13. Bond plaster would be used

    A. where a fine, hard finish is required
    B. on concrete surfaces
    C. between scratch and finish coats
    D. on certain types of lath

14. A concealed draft opening is MOST closely associated with

    A. ventilation B. heating
    C. fire-stopping D. air conditioning

15. In estimating the cost of a reinforced concrete structure, the contractor would be LEAST concerned with

    A. volume of concrete
    B. surface area of forms
    C. pounds of reinforcing steel
    D. type of coarse aggregate

16. A brick wall is to be plastered.
    The BEST type of joint for this surface of the wall is

    A. flush B. weathered C. concave D. raked

17. A groove is cut in the underside of a stone sill to

    A. keep water from the wall
    B. improve the bond with the wall
    C. conceal reinforcing
    D. reduce the weight of the sill

18. Joists spaced 16" o.c. on a 12'0" span support a floor which is to carry a live load of 80 pounds per square foot. The TOTAL live load carried by a single joist is, in pounds,

    A. 590 B. 920 C. 1195 D. 1280

19. Pointing up around the end of a joist resting on a brick wall is

   A. *good,* because it improves appearance
   B. *bad,* because it may cause rotting of joist
   C. *good,* because it results in a more solid wall
   D. *bad,* because it interferes with fire-stopping

20. In a roof, the LONGEST rafters are _____ rafters.

   A. common B. hip jack
   C. valley jack D. either hip or valley jack

21. The thickness of lumber used for grounds is USUALLY, in inches,

   A. 7/32   B. 3/4   C. 25/32   D. 15/32

22. The terms *plank, scantling, heavy joists,* when used in connection with lumber, refer to

   A. dimensions   B. use   C. grade   D. finish

23. The Code provides that cold bends in reinforcing bars for concrete work shall have a radius at LEAST equal to the least dimension of the bar multiplied by

   A. 1   B. 2   C. 3   D. 4

24. According to the Code, gas cutting of structural steel is NOT permitted

   A. unless the member cut is carrying stress
   B. in preparation for welding
   C. to replace the milling of surfaces
   D. under any circumstances

25. In building construction, an apron would MOST likely be installed by a

   A. carpenter   B. sheet-metal worker
   C. bricklayer   D. glazier

26. In a building with masonry walls, furring

   A. is of no advantage
   B. is of no help in preventing wetting of plaster
   C. is used only because it provides a nailing surface
   D. adds to the insulating quality of the wall

27. Oil is applied to the inside surfaces of concrete forms PRIMARILY to

   A. make form removal easier
   B. provide a smoother finish to the concrete
   C. prevent leakage of water from the concrete
   D. neutralize acids present in the wood

28. A deformed reinforcing rod is superior to an equivalent smooth rod because it

   A. permits better bond with the concrete
   B. has greater tensile strength
   C. weighs more
   D. is easier to bend

29. In the usual six-story multiple dwelling, fire escapes are   29._____
    A. supported on floor joists cantilevered out through the walls
    B. supported on a framework tied to, but otherwise independent of, the building
    C. hung from the parapet
    D. supported on brackets which are bolted to channels on the innerside of the wall

30. A building on a lot 50'0" wide by 110'0" deep has a rectangular court 37'0" long by 8'6"   30._____
    wide.
    The area of the court is the following percentage of the area of the lot:
    A. 6.4   B. 6.2   C. 5.8   D. 5.7

KEY (CORRECT ANSWERS)

1. C		16. D	
2. B		17. A	
3. A		18. D	
4. B		19. B	
5. B		20. A	
6. A		21. C	
7. B		22. A	
8. B		23. B	
9. B		24. C	
10. B		25. A	
11. D		26. D	
12. C		27. A	
13. B		28. A	
14. C		29. D	
15. D		30. D	

EXAMINATION SECTION
TEST 1

DIRECTIONS: Each question or incomplete statement is followed by several suggested answers or completions. Select the one that BEST answers the question or completes the statement. *PRINT THE LETTER OF THE CORRECT ANSWER IN THE SPACE AT THE RIGHT.*

1. Of the following, the BEST order of construction for a new room in a housing project is USUALLY

    A. 1. hardwood floor
        2. steam radiator
        3. fluorescent light fixture
        4. 3-coat plaster walls and ceiling
    B. 1. 3-coat plaster walls and ceiling
        2. hardwood floor
        3. steam radiator
        4. fluorescent light fixture
    C. 1. hardwood floor
        2. 3-coat plaster walls and ceiling
        3. fluorescent light fixture
        4. steam radiator
    D. 1. steam radiator
        2. fluorescent light fixture
        3. hardwood floor
        4. 3-coat plaster w

2. The quantity of water USUALLY required for the scratch coat of a 1:3 lime plaster is

    A. 5 1/2 gallons water per cubic foot
    B. 0.60 by weight
    C. sufficient water to make a workable mix
    D. sufficient water to give a 3-inch slump

3. Of the following, the plasterer's tool USUALLY used to force plaster into the lath is a

    A. trowel   B. screed   C. darby   D. hawk

4. If to calcined gypsum is added about one-sixth of its weight of hydrated lime to improve its plasticity and enough retarder to make it set in about two hours, the product is USUALLY known as

    A. Keene's cement   B. gypsum neat plaster
    C. plaster of paris   D. gaging plaster

5. The thickness of 3-coat plaster on metal lath is USUALLY

    A. 1/2"   B. 7/8"   C. 1 1/8"   D. 1 1/2"

6. A large crack in a plaster wall appears two years after completion of the building. The crack starts from the corner of a door and extends diagonally to the edge of the wall. The cause of this crack is PROBABLY due to

A. improper application of the scratch coat
B. precipitation of the lime in the plaster
C. improper tying of the lath to the furring
D. settlement of the building

7. According to the city building code, the MINIMUM thickness of gypsum lath should be, in inches, not less than 7._____

   A. 1/4 B. 1/4 C. 3/8 D. 1/2

8. A building specification states, "The mortar for the white finishing coat shall be a mixture of 3 parts of white lime putty, one part of plaster of paris, and the addition of a small amount of fine white sand." 8._____
   Plaster of paris is added PRIMARILY as a(n)

   A. plasticizer   B. emulsifier
   C. retarder   D. accelerator

9. Keene's Cement is manufactured from 9._____

   A. limestone   B. dolomite   C. gypsum   D. granite

10. Oversanding a plaster mix will USUALLY 10._____

    A. weaken the plaster
    B. increase the initial cost of materials
    C. increase the workability of the mix
    D. allow the mixing time to be reduced

11. A new sized brick 2 1/16 x 3 1/2 x 7 1/2 inches is being used PRIMARILY because it 11._____

    A. is more easily handled
    B. is more adaptable to modular construction
    C. presents a more pleasing appearance
    D. permits the use of narrower joints

12. Of the following, ties will be required for a brick 12._____

    A. cavity wall
    B. rolok wall
    C. wall having a common bond pattern
    D. wall having an English bond pattern

13. The type of mortar joint shown below is USUALLY defined as 13._____

    A. weather   B. struck   C. tooled   D. V joint

14. A struck joint in brickwork is USUALLY formed with 14.____

    A. the edge of a board B. a circular bar
    C. a trowel D. a concave tool

15. Bond in brickwork serves two primary functions, forming a geometric pattern for appearance and 15.____

    A. decreasing the heat conductivity of the wall
    B. binding the wall together
    C. increasing the water-tightness of the wall
    D. increasing the speed of bricklaying

16. In a 1:1:6 mortar for brickwork, the middle figure USUALLY represents the proportion of 16.____

    A. cement B. lime C. sand D. gypsum

17. A reveal in brickwork USUALLY occurs at 17.____

    A. the corners of the building
    B. windows
    C. the intersection of the brick wall and the foundation wall
    D. the intersection of the roof and parapet

18. Salmon brick are USUALLY brick that are 18.____

    A. oversized B. overburned
    C. underburned D. glazed

19. It is permissible to use bats in the face of a brick wall in order to 19.____

    A. reinforce the bond
    B. substitute for the use of ties
    C. provide imitation bond
    D. provide closure

20. At the ready mix concrete plant, the sand for the concrete mix has a greater than usual percent of moisture. 20.____
    The BEST procedure is to

    A. ignore the fact since it will have no effect on the concrete mix
    B. notify the concrete truckdrivers to reduce the amount of water to be added
    C. hold up the delivery of concrete until the excess moisture evaporates
    D. reject the sand as unfit for use as a concrete aggregate

21. A cement bag is opened, and the cement is found to be very lumpy. 21.____
    The BEST practice is to

    A. ignore the fact since this is the usual condition of the cement
    B. strain the cement through a 100 mesh sieve
    C. discard the cement
    D. use the cement only for mortar.

22. Silt is harmful to the formation of strong concrete.
Of the following ingredients of concrete, the one that is *most likely* to have the LARGEST amount of silt is

    A. cement
    B. fine aggregate
    C. coarse aggregate
    D. water

23. The slump test on a concrete mix is used PRIMARILY to determine its

    A. strength
    B. water tightness
    C. economy
    D. workability

24. If the fine aggregate is primarily of one size rather than uniformly graded in size, this will result in a concrete that is

    A. understrength
    B. unworkable
    C. inelastic
    D. uneconomical

25. Of the following ingredients in concrete, the material having the least weight per cubic foot loose, is USUALLY

    A. cement
    B. fine aggregate
    C. coarse aggregate
    D. water

26. In pouring concrete with a crane and bucket, the bucket should be kept close to the subgrade to make the height of fall of the concrete a minimum when the bucket is opened. The BEST reason for this is to

    A. prevent segregation
    B. eliminate the need for vibration
    C. avoid the dangers of splashing concrete
    D. speed the pouring of the concrete

27. If the wood formwork for concrete is not tight, it will *most likely* result in

    A. overstressing of the formwork
    B. segregation of the concrete
    C. honey combing
    D. laitance at the surface of the concrete

28. The reinforcing steel for a thin concrete wall is USUALLY placed

    A. after the formwork for both sides of the wall are in place
    B. after the formwork for one side of the wall is in place
    C. before any wall formwork is in place
    D. as the concrete is being poured

29. It is generally NOT permissible to pour concrete for a footing resting on soil when

    A. there is non-flowing water inside the formwork
    B. the temperature is under 40°F
    C. the reinforcing steel is wet
    D. the ground is frozen

Questions 30-38.

DIRECTIONS: Questions 30 to 38 refer to Drawing No. 1 at the end of the test.

30. The thickness of the slab in Panel A is, in inches, most nearly

    A. 3 1/2   B. 4   C. 4 1/2   D. 5

31. The thickness of the slab in Panel B is, in inches, *most nearly*

    A. 3 1/2   B. 4   C. 4 1/2   D. 5

32. The depth of Beam B4, that is, the distance from the top of the slab to the bottom of the beam, is, in inches, *most nearly*

    A. 18   B. 10   C. 4 1/2   D. 5

33. The diameter of an S 404 bar is, in inches,

    A. 1/2   B. 5/8   C. 3/4   D. 7/8

34. In section x-x, the dotted lines represent

    A. beam supports
    C. stirrups
    B. bent bars
    D. type 1 bars

35. Stirrup spacers are used PRIMARILY to

    A. hold the tops of the stirrups in place
    B. take some of the shear in the beams or girders
    C. keep the stirrups at the proper shear in the beams or girders
    D. insure the proper spacing of the stirrups

36. The outside walls are *most likely* composed of

    A. skeleton steel frame and brick panel walls
    B. concrete columns and brick panel walls
    C. reinforced concrete only
    D. masonry only

37. The PRIMARY difference between Girder G 1 and Girder 1a is that

    A. G 1a has greater concrete dimensions
    B. G 1a carries heavier loads
    C. G 1a has two types of stirrups
    D. G 1a has heavier reinforcing steel

38. The order of placing the reinforcing steel for the floor would *most likely* be

    A. 1. girders   2. slabs   3. beams
    B. 1. slabs   2. girders   3. beams
    C. 1. girders   2. beams   3. slabs
    D. 1. slabs   2. beams   3. girders

39. Metal lath is USUALLY fastened to an existing vertical concrete surface by means of

    A. rawl plugs
    C. special nails
    B. expansion bolts
    D. toggle bolts

40. Expanded metal lath is USUALLY specified as follows:

    A. pounds per square yard
    B. pounds per square foot
    C. gage of steel
    D. ounces per square foot

41. For city housing authority projects, the furring for 2" solid plaster walls is USUALLY

    A. 3/4" x 3/4" angles
    B. 3/4" channels
    C. 1 x 3/16 bars
    D. 3/4" I beam section

42. In the city, bars for reinforced concrete are placed by

    A. lathers
    B. concrete workers
    C. finishers
    D. carpenters

43. The type of glass USUALLY used in bathroom windows for public housing projects is _____ glass.

    A. common   B. plate   C. sheet   D. hammered

44. Of the following, the material that is NOT usually found in glazing putty is

    A. linseed oil
    B. graphite
    C. whiting
    D. white lead

45. Structural steel as it arrives on the construction site for a school building USUALLY

    A. has a coat of paint on its entire surface
    B. is painted only over areas that have been cleared of rust
    C. has 2 coats of paint on its entire surface
    D. is painted only where the surfaces are milled\

46. The vehicle for an oil paint is USUALLY

    A. soybean oil
    B. methyl alcohol
    C. linseed oil
    D. turpentine

47. Whitewash is composed PRIMARILY of

    A. lead oxide and water
    B. gypsum and water
    C. methyl alcohol and gypsum
    D. lime and water

48. In preparing a wood surface prior to painting, knots should USUALLY be

    A. removed and the space filled with putty
    B. coated with shellac
    C. sandpapered to a fine finish
    D. given no special treatment

49. Enamel is GENERALLY paint

    A. containing lithopone as a pigment
    B. having little hiding power
    C. containing organic pigments
    D. containing varnish as a vehicle

50. Of the following, the BEST reason for using wood stain on woodwork is that it   50._____

    A. bleaches the wood surface
    B. covers the defects of the wood
    C. brings out the texture of the wood
    D. etches the wood surface

51. Of the following, the finish that would *most likely* be used on a hardwood floor is   51._____

    A. enamel paint   B. wood stain
    C. gutta percha   D. shellac

52. A floor is designed as a reinforced concrete floor with a hardwood surface. A section   52._____
    through the floor would *most likely* be

    A.   B.

    hardwood floor / subfloor / sleeper / concrete

    hardwood floor / sleeper / concrete

    C.   D.

    hardwood floor / concrete

    hardwood floor / subfloor / anchor floor / concrete

53. Of the following, the saw MOST frequently employed by a carpenter is a _____ saw.   53._____

    A. keyhole   B. jig   C. crosscut   D. miter

54. Of the following, a chain saw would *most likely* be used to cut   54._____

    A. bevelled edges   B. tongue and groove joints
    C. heavy timbers   D. long thin wood members

55. Wire for other than electrical work is USUALLY specified by   55._____

    A. number of mils   B. gauge number
    C. number of circular mils   D. weight per foot

56. Lumber that has NOT been seasoned properly   56._____

    A. is brittle   B. has a tendency to rot
    C. will have pitch pockets   D. will tend to warp

Questions 57-63.

DIRECTIONS: Questions 57 to 63, inclusive, refer to Drawing No. 2

57. If the width of the masonry opening for the door is 3'6", the platform area is, in square feet, *most nearly*

    A. 21 B. 19 C. 13 D. 10.5

58. The bottom of the stairway

    A. rests on a slate bearing plate
    B. is anchored to the roof slab with anchor bolts
    C. is clipped to the roof slab
    D. is embedded in the concrete roof slab when the slab is poured

59. The platform is fastened PRIMARILY to

    A. both wythes B. cinder block
    C. concrete beam D. brickwork

60. The angle that the stair handrail makes with the horizontal is, in degrees, *most nearly*

    A. indeterminate B. 30 C. 45 D. 60

61. The maximum permissible rise on the stairway is, *most nearly*,

    A. 7 1/2 inches B. 10 inches C. 12 inches D. 9 feet

62. The vertical distance from the machine room floor to top rail of the platform is, *most nearly*,

    A. 6" B. 1'6" C. 3'0" D. 3'6"

63. The rails on the platform are removable PRIMARILY to

    A. facilitate shop fabrication
    B. facilitate field erection
    C. facilitate removal of machinery
    D. prevent damage to the masonry wall supporting the platform if the railing is struck heavily

64. The length of a line is given as 162.33 feet. The length of the line is, in feet and inches, *most nearly*

    A. 162'3.3" B. 162'4" C. 162'0.3" D. 162'3"

65. If a line is to be transferred from the floor to the ceiling of a room, the minimum equipment necessary is USUALLY a

    A. transit and plumb bob B. level and levelling rod
    C. carpenter's level D. plumb bob

66. The location of the metal base for a plaster wall is checked by the inspector with a 6 foot rule before plastering and found to be 1/16 inch horizontally out of line.
    The BEST thing for the inspector to do is to

    A. accept the location of the screed as substantially correct
    B. notify the foreman of the plasterers of the discrepancy
    C. notify the plasterer of the discrepancy
    D. recheck the measurement to determine whether he was inaccurate in his measurement

67. To check whether two walls are perpendicular to one another, a point is set 5 feet from the corner on one wall and a second point is set on the other wall 12 feet from the same corner.
If the walls are perpendicular to one another, the distance between the points should be, in feet, *most nearly*

   A. 7   B. 12.5   C. 13   D. 15

68. The number of vertical furring strips set at 16 inches center to center required for a wall 20 feet long is *most nearly*

   A. 13   B. 16   C. 19   D. 22

69. The surface of a freshly poured concrete floor that is to receive an asphalt tile finish should USUALLY be

   A. screeded only
   B. screeded and darbied
   C. screeded, darbied, and floated with no further finish
   D. screeded, darbied, floated, and troweled

70. Two days after pouring a 10' x 10' x 2' reinforced concrete footing under normal weather conditions, the contractor proposes to strip the side forms of the footing.
As an inspector, you should

   A. have the contractor wait an additional two days
   B. have the contractor wait an additional day
   C. allow the contractor to strip the forms
   D. have the contractor wait until the strength of the concrete reaches 1000 p.s.i.

71. Of the following wall materials, the one on which it is MOST difficult to secure a plaster bond is

   A. cement block   B. brick
   C. gypsum block   D. concrete

72. Of the following drawings, the one on which you would *most likely* find the length of a given reinforcing steel rod in a floor would be a

   A. reinforcing steel detail drawing
   B. floor schedule
   C. architect's floor plan
   D. reinforcing steel design drawing

73. A floor is made up of structural steel members and a reinforced concrete floor. The wood formwork for the reinforced concrete floor is USUALLY supported

   A. by the columns
   B. from the steel members of the floor above
   C. by the steel floor beams
   D. on the floor below by wood or steel shores

74. The type of wood sheathing that is USUALLY used for tight formwork is

   A. S 2 S
   B. tongue and groove
   C. dado and rabbet
   D. mortise and tenon

75. Of the following, wood formwork for an 8' x 8' rectangular reinforced concrete footing is BEST braced

   A. by stakes driven into the ground adjacent to the formwork
   B. at the corners of the formwork with vertical wooden cleats
   C. by metal form ties tieing into walers
   D. by external diagonal wood members bearing against the ground

76. The depth of formwork for a 2'0" deep footing bearing on earth should be *most nearly*

   A. 2'0"   B. 2'3"   C. 3'0"   D. 3'3"

77. Two adjacent walls are to have 1/2 inch solid expansion joint material between them. Of the following, the MOST practical method is to

   A. pour the walls, chop out 1/2 inch of concrete, and insert the expansion joint material
   B. pour one wall, anchor the expansion joint material to the poured wall, and use this as a form for the second wall
   C. nail the expansion joint material to the formwork of the first wall and pour the wall
   D. insert the expansion joint material in the space provided after the walls are poured

78. The specifications state than an 8-penny common nail is required as a fastener. Such nail should measure, in inches, *most nearly*

   A. 2   B. 2 1/2   C. 3   D. 3 1/2

79. To drill a hole 1 1/2 inches in diameter, a carpenter would *most likely* use a(n)

   A. 1 1/2" diameter drill
   B. keyhole saw
   C. expansion bit
   D. doall saw

80. A newel is part of a

   A. stairway   B. door   C. window   D. skylight

81. The area occupied by the building in the sketch, in square feet, is *most nearly*

   A. 3300
   B. 4200
   C. 15,000
   D. 4050

82. The surface of a concrete column one foot in diameter and 10 feet in height is to be rubbed. The surface to be rubbed is, in square feet, *most nearly*

    A. 40   B. 36   C. 31   D. 25

83. The weight of a 12 WF 27 steel beam 20'4" long is, in pounds, *most nearly*

    A. 244   B. 249   C. 545   D. 549

84. The inclined faces of the pedestal shown below are to be waterproofed. The area, in square feet, to be waterproofed is *most nearly*

    A. 24   B. 29   C. 34   D. 37

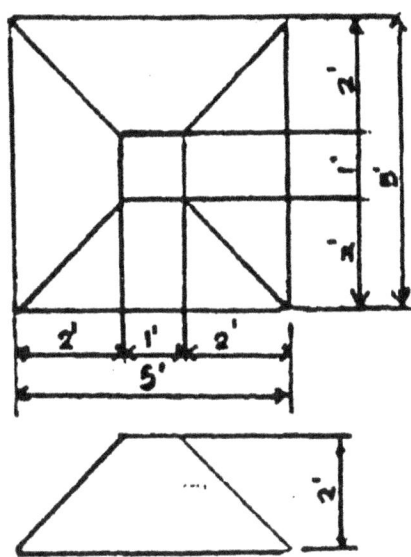

Questions 85-88.

DIRECTIONS: Questions 85 to 88, inclusive, are based on the following specification.

Holes in concrete ceiling shall be drilled not less than one inch deep with a 3/8 inch or No. 20 drill and dryer shall be secured to the ceiling with not less than No. 10 machine screws set in Rawl Taper Shields, size No. 10 x 24, or equal type, as approved. Not less than three screw fastenings shall be used for each angle. Screws and washers shall be cadmium or electro-zinc plated.

85. Of the following, it is *most likely* that this specification applies to the

    A. application of paint to a concrete surface
    B. fastening of metal lath to a concrete surface
    C. fastening of a clothes dryer to a concrete ceiling
    D. filling of holes in a concrete surface

86. The minimum diameter of the machine screws specified is, in inches, *most nearly*

   A. 1/8   B. 3/16   C. 1/4   D. 5/16

87. The taper shields specified are used

   A. to protect the screws
   B. in place of lock washers
   C. to grip the concrete by friction
   D. to provide an air space between the concrete and the angle

88. The purpose of the plating specified for the screws and washers is PRIMARILY to

   A. provide protection against corrosion
   B. increase the strength of the screws and washers
   C. provide a good surface for painting
   D. furnish a decorative appearance

Questions 89-92.

DIRECTIONS: Questions 89 to 92, inclusive, are based on the following specification.

Cap flashings shall in no case be in lengths exceeding 10 feet, and shall be shaped to lay flat against flashing. In no case shall cap flashing cover the base flashing less than 4 inches. Each joint shall be lapped 4 inches and left unsoldered.

89. The cap flashings referred to in the above specification would *most likely* be made of

   A. tarred felt   B. copper
   C. tin   D. asphalt coated linen

90. The location of the work specified is *most likely*

   A. around spandrel beams   B. over steel lintels
   C. at drain outlets   D. at parapets

91. Of the following, the BEST reason for specifying that the joints be left unsoldered is that it

   A. reduces the cost of the job
   B. allows for expansion and contraction
   C. permits the flow of hot pitch into the joints
   D. prevents hot solder from burning holes in the roofing

92. Two lengths of flashing are used to cover a certain area. One is 8'6" long, the other is 7'2" long.
    The maximum length of the area that these may cover is *most nearly*

   A. 15'0"   B. 15'4'   C. 15'8"   D. 16'0"

Questions 93-95.

DIRECTIONS: Questions 93 to 95, inclusive, are based on the following specification.

   Cellar entrance doors shall be paneled type of Northern White Pine or Idaho White Pine for painted finish. These doors shall be built up of solid stiles and rails, with mortised, tenoned, and pinned joints. Panels snail be not less than 1/2 inch thick of 3-ply construction with face veneers not less than 1/8 inch thick (after sanding) and of same materials as stiles and rails. Upper panels shall be divided with muntins with removable molds on inside for glazing. The lower panels shall be installed so as to allow for movement and shall be primed before being set in place.

93. The specification requires that the joints between adjacent members in the frame of the door should be as in   93._____

   A.

   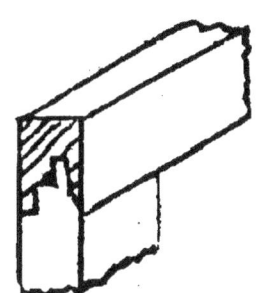

   B.

   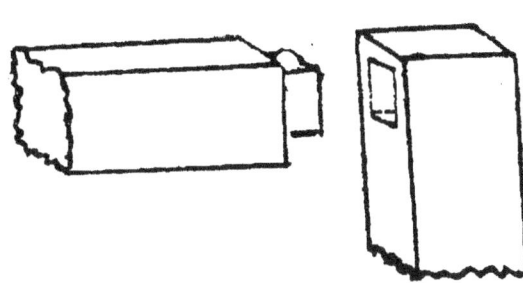

   C.

   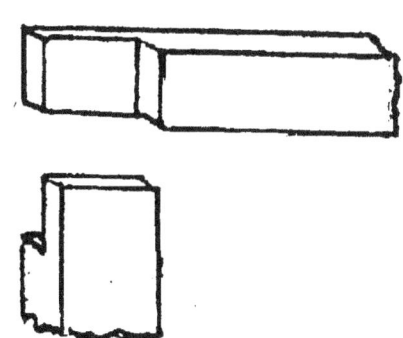

   D.

   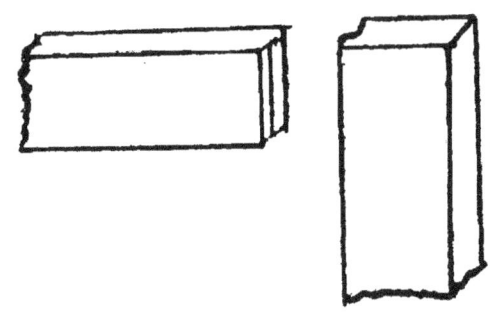

94. Of the following, the one that is *most likely* to be used for the face veneer of the panels is   94._____

   A. birch
   B. oak
   C. northern white pine
   D. hickory

95. If the 3-ply panel is 1/2 inch thick, the core must be   95._____

   A. 3/8 inch thick
   B. 1/8 inch thick
   C. not more than 1/4 inch thick
   D. not less than 1/4 inch thick

Questions 96-97.

DIRECTIONS: For questions 96 and 97, select the letter that represents the item.

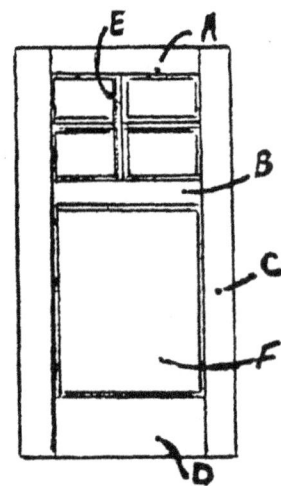

96. Stile

97. Muntin

98. Of the following, the MOST important characteristic of a good inspector is that he be

   A. observant
   B. friendly
   C. aggressive
   D. sympathetic

99. Inspectors, on being instructed in the method of writing reports, were told that: "The palest ink is better than the best memory."
    Of the following statements, the one that *most nearly* expresses the meaning of this quotation is

   A. make written reports complete; do not rely on memory
   B. a written report can not be disputed
   C. written reports are more valuable when supplemented with a good memory
   D. a report to be of value must be legible

100. In making a record of an inspection, the BEST procedure for an inspector to follow is to

   A. fix in mind all important facts so that he can make out his report at the end of the day
   B. return immediately to the office to write his report while the facts are still fresh in his mind
   C. write down all important facts during the inspection
   D. dictate the facts to be recorded to a stenographer

KEY (CORRECT ANSWERS)

1. B	21. C	41. B	61. C	81. A
2. C	22. B	42. A	62. C	82. C
3. A	23. D	43. D	63. C	83. D
4. B	24. D	44. B	64. B	84. A
5. B	25. D	45. A	65. D	85. C
6. D	26. A	46. C	66. A	86. B
7. C	27. C	47. D	67. C	87. C
8. D	28. B	48. B	68. B	88. A
9. C	29. D	49. D	69. D	89. B
10. A	30. D	50. C	70. C	90. D
11. B	31. B	51. D	71. D	91. B
12. A	32. D	52. A	72. A	92. B
13. A	33. A	53. C	73. C	93. B
14. C	34. B	54. C	74. B	94. C
15. B	35. A	55. B	75. D	95. C
16. B	36. D	56. D	76. B	96. C
17. B	37. C	57. A	77. C	97. E
18. C	38. C	58. A	78. B	98. A
19. D	39. C	59. C	79. C	99. A
20. B	40. A	60. D	80. A	100. C

FIRST FLOOR FRAMING PLAN

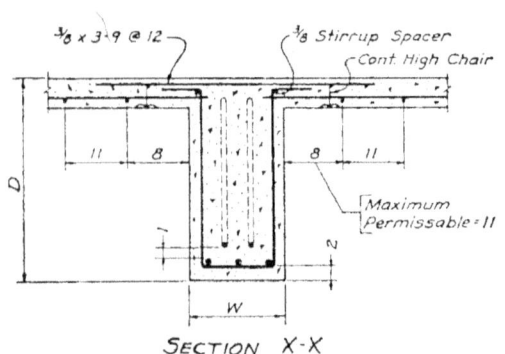

SECTION X-X

NOTES
All slabs are 4" thick unless noted otherwise.
Main slab bars to be supported in each bay by two rows of ¾" slab bolsters and two rows of continuous high chairs.
Bars over top of girders are to be supported by two rows of continuous high chairs.

ACCESSORIES REQ'D
- 85 Pcs. 2" Lower Beam Bolsters x 5'-0
- 37 Pcs. 1" Upper Beam Bolsters x 5'-0
- 690 Pcs. ¾ Slab Bolsters x 5'-0
- 85 Pcs. 3¾ Continuous High Chairs x 5'-0 (5' Slabs)
- 815 Pcs. 2¾ Continuous High Chairs x 5'-0 (4' Slabs)

DRAWING No 1

SCHEDULE

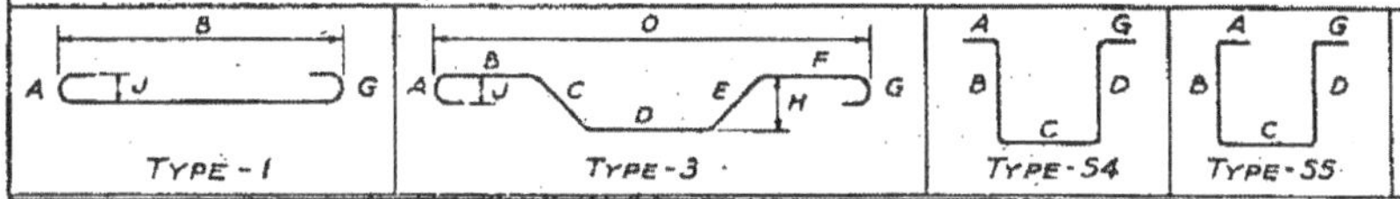

Type-1, Type-3, Type-S4, Type-S5

No.	Mark	Size W	Size D	Placing Notes	Reinforcing No	Size	Length	Mark	Sketch	Type	A	B	C	D	E	F	G	H	J	O	Bar Supports
11	G1	14	32	Bot.	3	1φ	21-6	0800	⌒	1	1-1	20-5									
				Upper Layer	3	1"	27-7	850	⌒	3	1-1	1-10	2-11½	11-3	2-11½	7-6		2-1			4-BB-2
				Top @ Cont. End	1	1¼	10-6														
				Stir. 1@2,3@6,3@9,2@10,2@12 Ea. End	22	3/8	6-7	300	⊔	S4	5	2-5	11	2-5		5					3-BBU-1
				Stir. Spacers	4	3/8	7-9		—												
1	G1a	14	32	Bot.	3	1φ	21-6	0800	⌒		See G1										
				Upper Layer	3	1"	27-7	850	⌒		See G1										
				Top @ Cont. End	1	1¼	10-6														4-BB-2
				Stir. 1@2,3@6,3@9,2@10,2@12 Wall End	11	3/8	6-7	301	⊔	S5	5	2-5	11	2-5		5					
				Stir. Same Spacing Cont. End	11	3/8	6-7	300	⊔		See G1										3-BBU-1
				Stir. Spacers	4	3/8	7-9		—												
18	G2	14	32	Bot.	3	1φ	21-4														
				Upper Layer	2	3/4	31-9	600	⌒	3		8-5	2-11½	9-0	2-11½	8-5		2-1			4-BB-2
				Top @ Cols. 11 to 16 & 21 to 26	2	1 1/8	10-6														
				Stir. 1@2, 3@12, 3@18 Ea. End	14	3/8	6-7	300	⊔		See G1										3-BBU-1
				Stir. Spacers	4	3/8	7-9		—												
5	B1	12	22	Bot.	3	1φ	21-0	0801	⌒	1	1-1	18-10					1-1				
				Upper Layer	3	7/8	21-7	700	⌒	3	10	2-0	1-10½	12-2	1-10½	2-0	10	1-4		18-10	4-BB-2
				Stir. 1@2, 1@8, 2@12 Ea. End	8	3/8	4-9	302	⊔	S4	5	1-7	9	1-7		5					3-BBU-1
				Stir. Spacers	4	3/8	3-0		—												
4	B2	12	22	Bot.	3	7/8	20-2	701	⌒	1	10	19-4									
				Upper Layer	2	1φ	25-9	0802	⌒	3	1-1	1-8	1-10½	11-2	1-10½	8-1		1-4			4-BB-2
				Top @ Cont. End	2	7/8	10-3														
				Stir. 1@2, 2@5, 2@8, 2@12 Ea. End	14	3/8	4-9	302	⊔		See B1										3-BBU-1
				Stir. Spacers	4	3/8	4-6														
11	B3	10	22	Bot.	2	7/8	21-2	702	⌒	1	10	20-4									
				Upper Layer	2	3/4	26-3	601	⌒	3	8	2-3	1-10½	11-8	1-10½	7-11		1-4			4-BB-2
				Top @ Non-Cont. End	1	3/4	4-3	602	—	1	8	3-7									
				Top @ Cont. End	1	3/4	10-0														
				Stir. 1@2, 1@9, 2@12 Ea. End	8	3/8	4-7	303	⊔	S4	5	1-7	7	1-7		5					3-BBU-1
				Stir. Spacers	4	3/8	3-0		—												
59	B4	10	22	Bot.	1	3/4	20-4														
				Bot.	2	7/8	30-4	703	⌒	3		8-7	2-1½	8-11	2-1½	8-7		1-6			4-SB-2
				Stir. 1@2, 2@12 Ea. End	6	3/8	4-7	303	⊔		See B3										
				Stir. Spacers	4	3/8	2-3		—												
13	B5	10	22	Bot.	2	7/8	20-2	701	⌒		See B2										
				Upper Layer	2	7/8	25-6	704	⌒	3	10	1-9	1-10½	11-4	1-10½	7-10		1-4			4-BB-2
				Top @ Wall End	1	3/4	4-3	602	—		See B3										
				Top @ Cont. End	1	3/4	10-0														
				Stir. 1@2, 1@9, 2@12 Ea. End	8	3/8	4-7	303	⊔		See B3										3-BBU-1
				Stir. Spacers	4	3/8	3-0		—												
1	B6	10	22	Bot.	2	1φ	21-0	0801	⌒		See B1										
				Upper Layer	2	1φ	22-1	0803	⌒	3	1-1	2-0	1-10½	12-2	1-10½	2-0	1-1	1-4		18-10	4-BB-2
				Stir. 1@2, 2@12 Ea. End	6	3/8	4-7	304	⊔	S5	5	1-7	7	1-7		5					3-BBU-1
				Stir. Spacers	4	3/8	2-3		—												
				Dwls. Into Stair Post - 4 Each	8	5/8	3-0		—												
1	B7	10	18	Bot.	2	5/8	11-2	504	⌒	1	7	10-0					7				
				Top 1 @ Each End	2	5/8	2-7	500	—	1	7	2-0					7				3-BB-2
1	B8	8	8	Bot.	2	5/8	8-4	501	⌒	1	7	7-2					7				2-BB-2
1	B8a	8	8	Bot.	2	5/8	6-10	502	⌒	1	7	5-8					7				2-BB-2
6	L1	8	12	Bot.	2	5/8	6-2	503	⌒	1	7	5-0					7				2-BB-2

SLAB BENT BARS

		Size	Length	Mark	Sketch	Type	A	B	C	D	E	F	G	H		
		½	9-9	401	⌒	1	6	9-3						3½		
		½	13-2	402	⌒	3	6	1-5	5	5-9	5	4-8	3½	3½		
		½	13-6	403	⌒	3	6	1-9	5	5-9	5	4-8	3½	3½		
		½	15-5	404	⌒	3		4-8	5	5-3	5	4-8	3½			
		½	4-0	405	⌒	3		2-0	2-0				1-3			
		3/8	6-10	305	⌒	1	4	6-6						2¾		
		3/8	8-10	306	⌒	3	4	1-1	3½	3-8	3½	3-2	2½	2¾		
		3/8	10-4	307	⌒	3		3-2	3½	3-5	3½	3-2	2½			
		3/8	7-5	308	⌒	3	4	1-2	3½	2-4	3½	3-0	2½	2¾		
		3/8	5-4	309	⌒	1	4	5-0						2¾		

(5" Slabs)
(4" Slabs)

Note:- Mark All Bent Slab Bars With Prefix "1S"
Mark All Bent Beam Bars With Prefix "1B"

STAIRS TO ELEVATOR MACHINE ROOM

DRAWING NO 2

EXAMINATION SECTION
TEST 1

DIRECTIONS: Each question or incomplete statement is followed by several suggested answers or completions. Select the one that BEST answers the question or completes the statement. *PRINT THE LETTER OF THE CORRECT ANSWER IN THE SPACE AT THE RIGHT.*

1. The material that is MOST often made from gypsum is 1._____
   A. lime
   B. mortar
   C. grout
   D. plaster of paris

2. Of the following types of utility pipes, the one for which the slope of the line is USUALLY most important is a ____ line. 2._____
   A. sewer
   B. gas
   C. water
   D. steam

3. Piles, as related to building construction, are located *most likely* in the 3._____
   A. foundation
   B. roof
   C. structural frame
   D. wall

4. The scale of a drawing is 1/8" = 1'0". A rectangle on the drawing actually measures 7 1/8" x 6 1/4". 4._____
   This represents the true area, in square feet, of *most nearly*
   A. 72
   B. 144
   C. 1375
   D. 2850

5. The architectural symbol for brick as it would appear in section is USUALLY 5._____
   A. [symbol] B. [symbol] C. [symbol] D. [symbol]

6.   6._____

   The length of AB is, in feet, *most nearly*
   A. 130
   B. 135
   C. 140
   D. 145

7. An inspector estimated that a paving job would require 30 cubic yards of concrete. The volume of the concrete actually used was 27.5 cubic yards. 7._____
   The percentage of error in the inspector's estimate is *most nearly*
   A. 4 1/2
   B. 9
   C. .08
   D. .09

8. The frame and cover of a sewer manhole is USUALLY made of 8._____
   A. stainless steel
   B. cast iron
   C. Monel metal
   D. structural steel

9. Sleeves are used around anchor bolts that bolt steel columns to footings PRIMARILY to

   A. allow for minor lateral adjustments of anchor bolts
   B. provide better bearing of base plate on the footing
   C. provide greater bond between anchor bolt and footing
   D. allow the proper setting of the column as to elevation

10.

   The weld MOST commonly used to permanently connect the end of a structural steel angle to a plate as shown above is a _____ weld.

   A. tack B. fillet C. butt D. plug

11. Cement is composed PRIMARILY of the following materials heated to fusion:

   A. Gypsum and sand
   B. Gypsum and limestone
   C. Clay and limestone
   D. Sand and clay

12. The capacity of storage batteries or its useful life is USUALLY expressed in

   A. amperes
   B. watts
   C. watt-hours
   D. ampere-hours

13. A transistor depends for its functioning on the flow of electrons through a

   A. gas B. vapor C. solid D. vacuum

14. A bi-metallic element is made up by riveting a brass and iron strip together. When subjected to high temperature, the element will

   A. vibrate
   B. bend
   C. remain the same length
   D. shorten

15. Expansion bolts would *most likely* be used to attach electric equipment to walls made of

   A. concrete B. hollow-tile C. wood D. steel

16. Of the following prefixes commonly used with electrical units, the one which would indicate one-millionth of a unit is

   A. mega B. kilo C. micro D. milli

17.

   The voltage in volts, across the 2.4 ohms resistance in the circuit shown above is *most nearly* equal to

   A. 32 B. 48 C. 60 D. 72

18. The term *bell and spigot in* plumbing refers to

    A. soil pipes
    B. faucets
    C. hot water risers
    D. overflow alarm

19. The drafting symbol —N— on a line piping diagram USUALLY indicates a _____ valve.

    A. ball B. globe C. check D. gate

20. The babbit metals are used

    A. for dies and cutting tools
    B. for high speed shafts
    C. in the manufacture of gears
    D. as bearing metals

21. The safety device that can be used instead of a fuse to protect a piece of electrical equipment in case of overload is a

    A. toggle switch
    B. circuit shunt
    C. circuit rheostat
    D. circuit breaker

22. A device that is used to convert mechanical energy into electrical energy is USUALLY called a

    A. battery
    B. generator
    C. motor
    D. transformer

23. A pitot tube is used for measuring water

    A. density
    B. velocity
    C. temperature
    D. volatility

24. $\sqrt[x]{a^y}$ is equal to

    A. $a^{\frac{y}{x}}$ B. a^{x+y} C. $a^{\frac{y}{x}}$ D. a^{y-x}

25. Of the following, an approved means of obtaining the area of an irregular figure is by means of a

    A. slide caliper
    B. micrometer
    C. planimeter
    D. pantograph

KEY (CORRECT ANSWERS)

1. D
2. A
3. A
4. D
5. B

6. B
7. B
8. B
9. A
10. B

11. C
12. D
13. C
14. B
15. A

16. C
17. D
18. A
19. C
20. D

21. D
22. B
23. B
24. C
25. C

TEST 2

DIRECTIONS: Each question or incomplete statement is followed by several suggested answers or completions. Select the one that BEST answers the question or completes the statement. *PRINT THE LETTER OF THE CORRECT ANSWER IN THE SPACE AT THE RIGHT.*

1. Of the following, the BEST reason for using vibrators in concrete construction is to 1.____

    A. increase the slump of the concrete
    B. remove excess water
    C. retard the setting of the concrete
    D. consolidate the concrete

2. Specifications state that column dowels are embedded 24 diameters in the footing. The length of embedment for a number 8 bar in the footing is, in inches, *most nearly* 2.____

    A. 6 B. 12 C. 18 D. 24

3. A *tremie* is USUALLY used to 3.____

    A. weigh large quantities of sand
    B. support precast girders
    C. deposit concrete under water
    D. measure ground elevation very accurately

4. Of the following woods, the one that is the HARDEST is 4.____

    A. Hickory B. Douglas Fir
    C. Southern Pine D. Sitka Spruce

5. The total weight of a 10 WF 45 beam 8 feet long is, in pounds, *most nearly* 5.____

    A. 45 B. 80 C. 360 D. 450

6. The thickness 17 gage steel can be BEST checked with a 6.____

    A. finely divided steel scale
    B. depth gage
    C. hermaphrodite caliper
    D. micrometer

7. A specification for mixing concrete states *the minimum time of mixing concrete shall be one minute per cubic yard after all material, including the water, has been placed in the drum and the drum shall be reversed for an additional two minutes.* 7.____
    According to the above statement, the MINIMUM time for mixing a 3 cubic yard batch of concrete is *most nearly* _____ minutes.

    A. 3 B. 5 C. 8 D. 9

8. Of the following species of lumber, the one *most likely* used for wood formwork for concrete is 8.____

    A. birch B. pine C. oak D. maple

9. Of the following, the one that is NOT a lightweight aggregate is   9._____

   A. hematite   B. perlite
   C. expanded shale   D. pumice

10. Of the following, the MOST important factor that an individual must fulfill in order to   10._____
    insure his own safety on a construction job is to

    A. work slowly
    B. be familiar with the specifications
    C. wear clothing to suit climatic conditions
    D. be alert

11. A wall alongside of a ramp is 7'6" high at one end and 12'0" high at the other end. The   11._____
    length of the wall is 32'0".
    The area of one face of the wall, in square feet, is *most nearly*

    A. 310   B. 311   C. 312   D. 313

12. The equation $x^2 + y^2 = r^2$ is that of a   12._____

    A. parabola   B. ellipse
    C. straight line   D. circle

13. A round rod with a right-handed thread is to be coupled with another rod of the same   13._____
    diameter but with a left-handed thread.
    Of the following attachments, the one which is MOST appropriate to use is a(n)

    A. turnbuckle   B. thimble
    C. clevis   D. eye bolt

14. In the two simultaneous equations   14._____
    $(3x + y = 17)$
    $(2x - y = 8)$,
    the value of y is

    A. 1   B. 2   C. 3   D. 4

15. Leaks in gas piping may be BEST located by the use of   15._____

    A. cigarette lighter   B. miner's lamp
    C. heated filament   D. soapy water solution

16. The value of x that will satisfy the equation $x^3 - x^2 - 4 = 0$ is   16._____

    A. 3   B. 2   C. 1   D. -1

17. The number of board feet in a board 24 feet long, one foot wide, and 2 inches thick is   17._____
    _____ board feet.

    A. 4   B. 12   C. 24   D. 48

18. The distinguishing characteristic of safety shoes is   18._____

    A. their color
    B. their height
    C. the use of spikes on the sole
    D. the use of a steel toe box

19. For a 20 foot ladder, the base should extend back from the face of the wall *approximately*   19.____
    A. 3'   B. 5'   C. 7'   D. 10'

20. π / 2 radian is equivalent to, in degrees,   20.____
    A. 22 1/2   B. 45   C. 90   D. 180

21. Of the following conventional cross-hatching, the one that is for brass is   21.____
    A. [hatching] B. [hatching] C. [hatching] D. [hatching]

22. The $2\sqrt{690}$ is *most nearly*   22.____
    A. 26.25   B. 26.27   C. 26.29   D. 26.30

23. The line $y = 2x + 8$ intersects the *x* axis at   23.____
    A. -4   B. +4   C. -2   D. +8

24. If the radius of the circle shown is 5", the area of the shaded area, in square inches, is *most nearly*   24.____

    A. 6.1   B. 7.1   C. 7.6   D. 8.1

25. A cone has a base whose area is A and its altitude is h. The volume of this cone is   25.____
    A. Ah   B. 1/2 Ah   C. 1/3 Ah   D. 1/4 Ah

4 (#2)

KEY (CORRECT ANSWERS)

1. D
2. D
3. C
4. A
5. C

6. D
7. B
8. B
9. A
10. D

11. C
12. D
13. A
14. B
15. D

16. B
17. D
18. D
19. B
20. C

21. A
22. B
23. A
24. B
25. C

TEST 3

DIRECTIONS: Each question or incomplete statement is followed by several suggested answers or completions. Select the one that BEST answers the question or completes the statement. *PRINT THE LETTER OF THE CORRECT ANSWER IN THE SPACE AT THE RIGHT.*

1. A street has a grade of 1 1/2%.
   The distance the street rises in 1 1/2 miles is, in feet, *most nearly*

   A. 79.20   B. 98.75   C. 103.50   D. 118.80

2. The elevation of a steel member shown above represents a

   A. tee   B. channel   C. rail   D. zee

3. A circular tank is 12 feet in diameter and 9 feet high. The depth of water in the tank is 1/3 from the top. There are 7 1/2 gallons in a cubic foot.
   The number of gallons of water in the tank is *most nearly*

   A. 4820   B. 5070   C. 5320   D. 5570

4. If log of 2 = 0.3010 and log of 3 = 0.4772, then the log of 36 equals

   A. 0.7782   B. 1.0792   C. 1.2554   D. 1.5564

5. If there are 43,560 square feet in an acre, the number of acres in a tract 2 miles long by 3.2 miles wide is *most nearly*

   A. 3750   B. 4100   C. 4350   D. 4600

6. A foundation for a building consists of 9 concrete footings 8 ft. by 6 ft. by 18 inches deep. The total number of cubic yards of concrete in the footings is *most nearly*

   A. 12   B. 24   C. 36   D. 72

7. A drawing showing the longitudinal slope in elevation of a street is known as

   A. perspective   B. plan
   C. profile   D. route

8. On a drawing showing front, rear, and side elevations, and roof plan, the projected views are *most likely*

   A. isogonic   B. orthographic
   C. isographic D. isometric

9. A note on a drawing reads *#6 bottom bars 6'0" long, 6" o.c. "* The #6 means *most nearly* _____ diameter.

   A. 6/8"   B. 0.6"   C. 6/16"   D. 6/32"

10. The signs of the sine, cosine, and tangent of an angle are all positive in Quadrant 10.____
    A. I   B. II   C. III   D. IV

11. The sum of three interior angles of a four-sided parcel of land add up to 115°, The fourth 11.____
    interior angle, in degrees, is *most nearly*
    A. 25   B. 75   C. 245   D. 295

12. Of the following print processes, the one that is LEAST like blue printing is 12.____
    A. Van Dyke   B. black and white
    C. Ozalid   D. multilith

13. Railroad curves would *most likely* be used to draw 13.____
    A. arcs of large radii
    B. ellipses
    C. circles of small radii
    D. circles of large radii

14. Concrete test cylinders are USUALLY tested in 14.____
    A. bending   B. buckling
    C. compression   D. shear

15. The invert of a sewer is the elevation of the _____ surface. 15.____
    A. bottom of the inside B. top of the outside
    C. bottom of the outside D. top of the inside

16. The symbol ++++++++++++++++ on a topographic map USUALLY represents a(n) 16.____
    A. abandoned highway   B. underground stream
    C. single track railroad D. picket fence

17. Terrazzo would *most likely* be found on a(n) 17.____
    A. interior wall   B. exterior wall
    C. ceiling   D. floor

18. Well points are USUALLY used in construction to 18.____
    A. provide water for cleaning the area under construction
    B. dewater the area under construction
    C. provide water for the concrete used in construction
    D. provide adequate drinking water where other sources are not available

19. A flexible pavement is a 19.____
    A. shoulder of compacted clay
    B. pavement containing an air entraining ingredient
    C. pavement of concrete without reinforcing
    D. pavement of graded granular materials with bitumen

20. Closely spaced contour lines on a topographic map USUALLY indicate a   20.____

    A. small contour interval B. large contour interval
    C. steep slope D. mild slope

21. If concrete weighs 150#/cubic foot, then the weight of a 15'0" long, 36" I.D. and 3" wall thickness concrete pipe is *most nearly* (I.D. - inside diameter) _____ lbs.   21.____

    A. 5300 B. 5500 C. 5700 D. 6000

22. Of the following mixes, the one that is *most likely* to be used as mortar for brickwork is cement(,)   22.____

    A. and water B. sand and water
    C. lime and water D. gypsum and water

23. The pattern of brickwork is USUALLY called the   23.____

    A. bond B. lay C. coursing D. register

24. The MOST important precaution to be observed in the storage of cement is to protect the cement against   24.____

    A. heat B. dampness
    C. corrosion D. decomposition

25. Lead was poured into the joint between two pipes. The material composition of each pipe was *most likely*   25.____

    A. cast iron B. vitrified clay
    C. asbestos cement D. concrete

KEY (CORRECT ANSWERS)

1. D
2. D
3. B
4. D
5. B

6. B
7. C
8. B
9. A
10. A

11. C
12. D
13. A
14. C
15. A

16. C
17. D
18. B
19. D
20. C

21. C
22. B
23. A
24. B
25. A

TEST 4

DIRECTIONS: Each question or incomplete statement is followed by several suggested answers or completions. Select the one that BEST answers the question or completes the statement. *PRINT THE LETTER OF THE CORRECT ANSWER IN THE SPACE AT THE RIGHT.*

1. The main danger of having oil on the surface of steel reinforcing bars is PRIMARILY that the

   A. setting time of the concrete will be too great
   B. bond between steel and concrete will be weakened
   C. concrete will be weakened
   D. steel will corrode

   1._____

2. The Brinell number of a metal is GENERALLY a measure of its

   A. hardness
   B. ductility
   C. tensile strength
   D. malleability

   2._____

3. Masonite is a

   A. gypsum product
   B. cement product
   C. wood product
   D. coal tar derivative

   3._____

4. A stairway has 9 treads. It NORMALLY would have _____ risers.

   A. 8   B. 9   C. 10   D. 11

   4._____

5. A beam projecting from a wall is called a _____ beam.

   A. dolly
   B. stringer
   C. cantilever
   D. lally

   5._____

6. In a paint mixture, the pigment is added PRIMARILY to supply

   A. hardness   B. color   C. body   D. toughness

   6._____

7. The chemical formula for sand is

   A. $CaCO_3$ B. CaO C. Al_2O_3 D. SiO_2

   7._____

8. If steel is galvanized, it is coated with

   A. copper   B. zinc   C. tin   D. lead

   8._____

9. A hod is MOST often used by a

   A. rigger
   B. plumber
   C. carpenter
   D. plasterer

   9._____

10. An engine is delivering 300 horsepower.
    The equivalent delivery, in kilowatts, is *most nearly* (1 HP = 746 watts)

    A. 175   B. 200   C. 225   D. 250

    10._____

11. Of the following drafting pencils, the one that has the SOFTEST lead is

    A. 3B   B. HB   C. H   D. F

    11._____

12. Two applications at 0.4 gallons per square yard of bituminous material on a 1/2 mile of road 18 feet wide would require *most nearly* _____ gallons.

    A. 425   B. 3,875   C. 4,225   D. 38,000

13. Rock excavation is to be paid for at a unit price of $25/cubic yard.
    Of the following, the cost of rock between Sta. 3+35 and Sta. 8+65 for a width of 45 feet and a depth of five feet is *most nearly*

    A. $75,000   B. $110,000   C. $220,000   D. $330,000

14. Three 40 foot long piles are driven so that their top elevations are 79.6', 81.7', and 80.2' before being cut off at elevation 75.5'.
    If the contract unit price is $4.50 per foot in place, then the payment to the contractor is *most nearly*

    A. $405.00   B. $472.50   C. $540.00   D. $600.00

15. To void a contract means *most nearly* to _____ it.

    A. reinstate   B. nullify   C. amend   D. redeem

16. Of the following, the MOST important characteristic of a good inspector on construction work is

    A. punctuality
    B. good penmanship
    C. superior physical strength
    D. keen observation

17. The BEST method of making assignments of technicians would be ordinarily to make them according to the technician's

    A. seniority
    B. desire to do the work
    C. ability to do the work
    D. attitude towards other employees

18. Of the following, the BEST way to correct a mistake made by your subordinate is to

    A. correct the mistake yourself and privately explain correction to subordinate
    B. correct the mistake yourself and say nothing to subordinate
    C. give it to another subordinate to correct
    D. belittle him and then have him correct the mistake

19. If a draftsman cannot possibly complete a drawing on time, then the BEST action for him to take is

    A. work during lunchtime
    B. work overtime
    C. ask an employee to assist you
    D. notify the supervisor

20. Of the following, the BEST thing for a supervisor to do when a subordinate has done a very good job is to

    A. tell him to take it easy
    B. praise his work
    C. reduce his work load
    D. say nothing because he may become conceited

21. Of the following, the method MOST often used to keep a record of progress of construction of a project is a _____ chart.

    A. bar B. pie C. polar D. Venn

22. Of the following, the BEST method of getting an employee who is not working up to his capacity to produce more work is to

    A. have another employee criticize his production
    B. privately criticize his production but encourage him to produce more
    C. criticize his production before his associates
    D. criticize his production and threaten to fire him

23. The ability of an employee to take the first step and follow through on a job is known as

    A. demeanor B. indolence
    C. initiative D. individuality

24. Of the following behavior characteristics of a supervisor, the one that is *most likely* to lower the morale of the men he supervises is

    A. diligence B. favoritism
    C. punctuality D. thoroughness

25. Of the following, the MOST important item in a good engineering report is

    A. brevity B. promptness
    C. accuracy D. good grammar

KEY (CORRECT ANSWERS)

1. B
2. A
3. C
4. C
5. C

6. B
7. D
8. B
9. D
10. C

11. A
12. C
13. B
14. B
15. B

16. D
17. C
18. A
19. D
20. B

21. A
22. B
23. C
24. B
25. C

EXAMINATION SECTION
TEST 1

DIRECTIONS: Each question or incomplete statement is followed by several suggested answers or completions. Select the one that BEST answers the question or completes the statement. *PRINT THE LETTER OF THE CORRECT ANSWER IN THE SPACE AT THE RIGHT.*

1. It is the policy of the department to hold each inspector responsible for formal work assignments given to him.
   Of the following, the BEST reason for this is that it
   A. enables division personnel to keep track of the work schedule
   B. encourages inspectors to be careful with written documents
   C. increases the speed with which inspections are carried out
   D. provides a double check on the time sheet records of inspectors

   1.____

2. Assume that you are faced with delays caused by absences of team members due to illness.
   Of the following, the BEST means of handling this problem is to
   A. have your team members keep an accurate record of their absences so that you will be able to identify anyone who is becoming accident-prone
   B. insist on prompt notification at all times when someone on your tea is absent because of illness
   C. require that your team members submit a memorandum informing you of the days on which they will be absent
   D. take over all tasks assigned to your team members when they are absent

   2.____

3. Assume that one of the men on your team tells you that he has a problem and would like to discuss it with you privately. During the course of this meeting, it becomes apparent that the man's difficulty stems from conflicts he is having with his wife.
   Of the following, the BEST course of action that you, his supervisor, should take in this situation is to
   A. advise the employee to meet with your superior, who might be able to give him more objective advice
   B. gather enough facts to advise the man about definite solutions for his problem
   C. help the man analyze what the problem is but leave the decision to him
   D. tell the man that you can talk to him only about problems that are job-related

   3.____

4. Sometimes it may be advantageous for a senior inspector to let the inspectors under his supervision participate in the development of decisions that must be made about the team's activities.
   The one of the following that is LEAST likely to result when team members participate in supervisory decisions is that the inspectors may

   4.____

A. be able to show leadership
B. have a chance to feel creative
C. require closer supervision
D. take more responsibility for minor problems

5. Of the following, the CHIEF reason that the senior inspector should take disciplinary measures as soon as possible after a subordinate inspector's violation of department rules is that
   A. delay will make the senior inspector seem lax
   B. the inspector is more likely to accept the discipline a justified
   C. the supervisor may forget about the offense
   D. there is less likelihood that other inspectors will find out about the offense

6. Assume that you have been directed to institute a new procedure for writing reports about violations encountered during the inspections conducted by the team of which you are in charge. You have heard, through the grapevine, that several of the experienced inspectors on the team have objections to this new procedure.
   Of the following, the BEST course of action for you to take FIRST in this situation is to
   A. issue a written order to put the new procedure into effect
   B. meet with all the inspectors on your team to discuss the procedure
   C. modify the procedure to make it acceptable to all of your inspectors
   D. postpone institution of the new procedure

7. Assume that the head of your unit expects to be out for a week because of illness. You are to act as head of the unit for that time.
   In determining what to do about those inspection duties that you were originally scheduled to perform and which should not be postponed, it would be MOST advisable to
   A. assign them to the inspector who needs training in this area
   B. assign them to the inspector with the most seniority
   C. attempt to do as many of them as possible yourself
   D. divide them among all inspectors who have the time and ability

8. The one of the following situations that is LEAST likely to result from poor planning and organization of an inspection unit's work is that
   A. inspectors will be uncertain about their responsibilities
   B. job performance will be poor
   C. the work will be completed at a steady monotonous pace
   D. there will be a high turnover rate in the unit's staff

9. Of the following, the BEST course of action to take in order to avoid charges of favoritism when making job assignments is to
   A. delegate the authority to make assignments to a well-liked experienced inspector
   B. keep records which may demonstrate proper distribution and rotation of assignments

C. select the oldest inspectors for the most desirable assignments
D. tell the men that, if they have any gripes about their assignments, they should see the supervising inspector

10. Of the following, the MOST important reason for a senior inspector to receive communications from the supervising inspector before they are transmitted to the inspectors is that he can
    A. avoid discussing communications with his subordinates
    B. exercises close supervision over every detail of the inspectors' assignments
    C. limit the amount of information received by his subordinates
    D. maintains his position in the chain of command

11. If an organization has rules that are clear but excessively detailed and rigid, the one of the following which is MOST likely to occur is that
    A. employees will tend to ignore the rules
    B. records of performance will be more difficult to maintain
    C. supervisors will have more difficulty in applying the rules to individual situations
    D. use of individual judgment and discretion will be decreased

12. An effective senior inspector strives to build up the feeling that he and his men are on the same team. The imposition of discipline may serious endanger the relationship built up between him and his men.
    The one of the following steps that the senior inspector may take to insure that the imposition of discipline will NOT cause any deterioration of his relationship with his subordinates is to
    A. avoid disciplinary action, except for very serious offenses
    B. delegate simple disciplinary problems to a competent, experienced inspector
    C. discipline his men in groups so that they will feel as if they were part of a team
    D. impose discipline in as impersonal way as possible

13. Suppose that one of the inspectors under the supervision of a senior inspector is repeatedly late for work. Despite the inspector's habitual lateness, he manages to complete his work assignments on schedule.
    Of the following, the MOST advisable action for the senior inspector to take in this situation is to
    A. ask one of the other inspectors to speak to him about his attendance
    B. ignore the inspector's habitual lateness as long as he does his work properly
    C. reprimand the inspector privately and follow through to see whether his attendance improves
    D. tell him in the presence of the other inspectors that he must improve his attendance record

14. Assume that you are informed by your superior that all reports prepared by your team should be checked by you when possible before their submission to a supervising inspector.
Of the following, the BEST course of action to take if you are too busy to look at all these reports and they have to be sent out right away is to
    A. delegate the responsibility for checking the reports to someone you have carefully instructed in the need for neat and accurate reports
    B. request additional staff from another unit to help you review these reports
    C. send the reports out without checking them and attach an explanatory note, telling your superior that you have not had time to look at them
    D. tell our men to review one another's reports and initial them

15. Assume that a senior inspector notices that another senior inspector divides his team's workload in what seems to him to be an inefficient manner. He decides to report this to the supervising inspector.
Of the following, an accurate evaluation of the action taken by the senior inspector in this situation is that it is GENERALLY
    A. *good* practice, mainly because the supervising inspector is the only person authorized to make this senior inspector divide the work according to standard procedure
    B. *good* practice, mainly because the senior inspector needs close supervision to adequately carry out his responsibilities
    C. *poor* practice, mainly because the senior inspector should have consulted other senior inspectors about this situation
    D. *poor* practice, mainly because the senior inspector should understand that other senior inspectors may manage their operations differently

16. Assume that you have heard a rumor that department rules are about to be changed in a manner which will make certain types of inspections more complicated.
Of the following, the BEST action for you to take in this situation is to
    A. ask the members of your staff, individually, if they have heard such a rumor
    B. call a meeting of your staff to tell them such a change is rumored
    C. make plans to change your unit's procedures to adapt to the new methods
    D. await official confirmation or denial of the rumor

17. Assume that one of the inspectors under your supervision has been doing an excellent job but no longer seems to have any interest in the work. He complains to you that he finds the work boring.
Of the following, the MOST advisable action for you to take FIRST is to
    A. ask some of his fellow inspectors to discuss the matter with him
    B. attempt to vary his assignments and give him more complex assignments
    C. remind him that his evaluation by superiors may depend in part on the interest he shows in his work
    D. suggest that the inspector be transferred to another division

18. The BEST way for you to prepare the inspectors in your unit to handle special assignments speedily and make decisions in an emergency is to
    A. follow each employee's work very carefully so you know where he is least efficient
    B. give them the freedom to make decisions in their everyday work
    C. refuse to accept work that is turned in late
    D. set deadlines ahead of the time when regularly assigned work is actually due so they will learn to work efficiently

19. Suppose you are supervising several inspectors. One of the inspectors has recently transferred to your unit. You discover that although he generally prepares his reports in a fairly correct way, he does not follow the prescribed procedure that you have taught the other inspectors.
    In this situation, the one of the following that it would be BEST for you to do is to
    A. allow him to use his own procedure if it is accurate and efficient
    B. refer him to your supervisor
    C. discuss the matter with all the inspectors and let them decide which procedure they wish to follow
    D. tell him to follow the procedure used by the other inspectors

20. Assume that you have one of your most competent inspectors working on a new type of project. As you are reviewing his work, you notice he has made some errors.
    You should
    A. correct the errors yourself, otherwise the inspector will get discouraged
    B. ignore the errors; they are probably not important, especially when the inspector is first learning the job
    C. tell the inspector about the errors; he will probably learn from them
    D. tell the inspector about the errors; then he will be aware that he is careless

21. Assume that your unit has been given a special assignment to make an original study. You plan to give this assignment to two of your most competent inspectors.
    The BEST way to start them on this work is to
    A. ask the two inspectors how they think the work can be done in a most effective way
    B. do some of the work with the inspectors to make sure they do not make any mistakes
    C. tell the inspectors they will be held directly responsible for the success of the study
    D. write up detailed instructions and give them to the inspectors who will do the work

22. Of the following steps in setting up an employee training program, the one which should PRECEDE the others is to
    A. assemble all the materials needed in the training program
    B. decide what training methods would be most effective
    C. determine what facilities are available for training purposes
    D. outline the areas that would be covered in the training program

22.____

23. Assume that you find it necessary to retrain an older, experienced inspector because you are giving this inspector a different kind of assignment.
    Of the following, the problem that is MOST likely to arise when retraining such a staff member is that the
    A. instructor will have disciplinary problems with this employee
    B. instructor will know less than this staff member
    C. employee at this status often lacks motivation to be retrained
    D. younger men will be unable to keep up with the performance of this employee

23.____

24. Assume that an inspector has recently been transferred from another unit and is now on your team.
    Of the following, the BEST method for you to use to determine whether this man needs any additional instruction or training is to
    A. ask him whether he is having difficulty with the work you assign to him
    B. ask the man's former supervisor whether he was a competent inspector
    C. review the way he handles the various tasks that you assign to him
    D. send this man into the field with one of your inspectors and have him evaluate the newly assigned inspector

24.____

25. Instituting a program of on-the-job training may sometimes present problems for the supervisor because, when first initiated, such training
    A. does not take place under actual working conditions
    B. is less instructive than formal training sessions
    C. may result in a decrease in the authority of the supervisor
    D. may slow down the unit's work

25.____

26. Suppose that you are approached by a newly appointed inspector who asks you to make an inspection visit with him because he is unsure of the procedure.
    The one of the following that you should do FIRST is to
    A. agree to make the visit with him
    B. refer him to the supervisor for help
    C. report him to the supervisor for incorrect behavior
    D. tell him to do the best he can and offer to help him write up the report

26.____

27. Suppose that you are writing up your inspection reports in your office on a particular day. A fellow inspector, who has left his identification at home, asks if he may use your identification card and badge in order to perform his scheduled inspections.

27.____

Of the following, you should
- A. allow him to use your identification since he is an inspector
- B. offer to perform the inspections for him if he will write the reports
- C. refuse his request and suggest he explain the situation to the supervisor
- D. tell him you need your identification for yourself

28. Assume that you are assigned to handle telephone complaints. After you have attempted to handle a complaint from a belligerent caller, the caller asks your name, saying that he is going to report you to your superior for being insolent to him.
It would be BEST for you to
- A. give the caller a false name so he will stop bothering you
- B. give the caller your name and explain the circumstances to your superior afterwards
- C. refuse to give the caller your name
- D. tell the caller that you have not been insolent to him

28.____

29. As a senior inspector, you are permitted to hold an outside job as long as it is NOT
- A. dangerous
- B. in conflict with the performance of your inspection duties
- C. mentally or physically taxing
- D. paid at a rate higher than your inspector job

29.____

30. Of the following, the MOST important reason that graphs and charts are used in reports to present material that can be treated statistically is that such material
- A. is easier to understand when it is presented in graph or chart form
- B. looks more impressive when it is presented in graph or chart form
- C. requires less time to prepare when it is presented in a graph or chart form instead of written out
- D. take up less space in graph or chart form than when it is written out

30.____

KEY (CORRECT ANSWERS)

1.	A	11.	D	21.	A
2.	B	12.	D	22.	D
3.	C	13.	C	23.	C
4.	C	14.	A	24.	C
5.	B	15.	D	25.	D
6.	B	16.	D	26.	B
7.	D	17.	B	27.	C
8.	C	18.	B	28.	B
9.	B	19.	D	29.	B
10.	D	20.	C	30.	A

TEST 2

DIRECTIONS: Each question or incomplete statement is followed by several suggested answers or completions. Select the one that BEST answers the question or completes the statement. *PRINT THE LETTER OF THE CORRECT ANSWER IN THE SPACE AT THE RIGHT.*

1. If an inspector finds a discrepancy between the plans and specifications, he should
   A. always follow the plans
   B. ask for an interpretation
   C. always follow the specifications
   D. follow the plans if the difference is in dimensions

   1._____

2. In performing field inspectional work, an inspector is the contact man between the public and the agency, and it is his job to secure compliance through the maximum utilization of persuasion and education and the minimum application of coercion.
   According to this statement, an inspector performing inspectional duties should
   A. seek to obtain voluntary compliance and use coercion only as a last resort
   B. be conciliatory on all issues of non-compliance and not take an attitude of firmness and authority
   C. maintain a strictly impersonal attitude in the exercise of his duties at all times
   D. use the threat of legal action to secure conformance with specified requirements

   2._____

3. The BEST way for a supervising inspector to determine whether a new inspector is learning his work properly is to
   A. ask the other men how this man is making out
   B. question him directly on details of the work
   C. assume that if he asks no questions, he knows the work
   D. inspect and follow up on the work which is assigned to him

   3._____

4. In assigning his men to various jobs, the BEST principle for a supervising inspector to follow is to
   A. study the men's abilities and assign them accordingly
   B. rotate a man from job to job until you find one which he can do well
   C. assign each of them to a job and let them adjust to it in their own way
   D. assume that men appointed to the position can do all parts of the work equally well

   4._____

5. Good inspection methods require that the inspector
   A. be observant and check all details
   B. constantly check with the engineer who designed the job
   C. apply specifications according to his interpretations
   D. permit slight job variation to establish good public relations

   5._____

6. An inspector inspecting a large job under construction inspected plumbing at 9 A.M., heating at 10 A.M., and ventilation at 11 A.M., and did his officework in the afternoon. He followed the same pattern daily for months.
This procedure is
   A. *bad*, because not enough time is devoted to plumbing
   B. *bad*, because the tradesmen know when the inspections will occur
   C. *good*, because it is methodical and he does not miss any of the trades
   D. *good*, because it gives equal amount of time to the important trades

7. The BEST way to evaluate the overall state of completion of a construction project is to check the progress estimate against the
   A. inspection worksheet
   B. construction schedule
   C. inspector's checklist
   D. equipment maintenance schedule

8. When a contractor fails to adhere to an approved progress schedule, he should
   A. revise the schedule without delay
   B. ask for an extension of time on account of delays
   C. adopt such additional means and methods of construction as will make up for time lost
   D. take no immediate action with the hope that sufficient time will be available later on that will assure the completion in accordance with the schedule

9. The usual contract for agency work includes a section entitled instructions to bidders, which states that the
   A. contractor agrees that he has made his own examination and will make no claim for damages on account of errors or omissions
   B. contractor shall not make claims for damages of any discrepancy, error or omission in any plans
   C. estimates of quantities and calculations are guaranteed by the agency to be correct and are deemed to be a representation of the conditions affecting the work
   D. plans, measurement, dimensions, and conditions under which the work is to be performed are guaranteed by the agency

10. A lump sum type of contract may require the contractor to submit a schedule of unit price.
The BEST reason for this is that it
    A. prevents the lump sum from being too high
    B. simplifies the selection of the lowest bidder
    C. enables the estimators to check the total cost
    D. provides a means of making equitable partial payments

11. A contractor on a large construction project USUALLY receives partial payments based on
    A. estimates of completed work
    B. actual cost of materials delivered and work completed
    C. estimates of material delivered and not paid for by the contractor
    D. the breakdown estimate submitted after the contract was signed and prorated over the estimated duration of the contract

11.____

12. In order to avoid disputes over payments for extra work in a contract for construction, the BEST procedure to follow would be to
    A. have contractor submit work progress reports daily
    B. insert a special clause in the contract specifications
    C. have a representative on the job at all times to verify conditions
    D. allocate a certain percentage of the cost of the job to cover such expenses

12.____

13. A fixed amount of money is generally withheld from the contractor for a definite period after the completion of construction.
    The BEST reason for this is
    A. that the money will be available for taxes due
    B. to penalize the contractor for poor work
    C. that it is a security for the repair of any defective work
    D. that the money will be available for modifications in the design of the structure

13.____

14. Prior to the installation of equipment called for in the specifications, the contractor is USUALLY required to submit for approval
    A. sets of shop drawings
    B. a set of revised specifications
    C. a detailed description of the methods of work to be used
    D. a complete list of skilled and unskilled tradesmen he proposes to use

14.____

15. During the actual construction work, the CHIEF value of a construction schedule is to
    A. insure that the work will be done on time
    B. reveal whether production is falling behind
    C. show how much equipment and material is required for the project
    D. furnish data as to the methods and techniques of construction operations

15.____

16. Of the following items, the one which should NOT be included in a proposed work schedule is
    A. a schedule of hourly wage rates and supplementary benefits
    B. an estimated time required for delivery of materials and equipment
    C. the anticipated commencement and completion of the various operations
    D. the sequence and inter-relationship of various operations with those of related contracts

16.____

17. The frequency with which job reports are submitted should depend MAINLY on   17.____
    A. how comprehensive the report has to be
    B. the amount of information in the report
    C. the availability of an experienced man to write the report
    D. the importance of changes in the information included in the report

18. The CHIEF purpose in preparing an outline for a report is usually to insure that   18.____
    A. the report will be grammatically correct
    B. every point will be given equal emphasis
    C. principal and secondary points will be properly integrated
    D. the language of the report will be of the same level and include the same technical terms

19. The MAIN reason for requiring written job reports is to   19.____
    A. avoid the necessity of oral orders
    B. develop better methods of doing the work
    C. provide a permanent record of what was done
    D. increase the amount of work that can be done

20. Assume you are recommending in a report to your superior that a radical change in a standard maintenance procedure should be adopted.   20.____
    Of the following, the MOST important information to be included in this report is
    A. a list of the reasons for making this change
    B. the names of others who favor the change
    C. a complete description of the present procedure
    D. amount of training time needed for the new procedure

KEY (CORRECT ANSWERS)

1.	B	11.	A
2.	A	12.	C
3.	B	13.	C
4.	A	14.	A
5.	A	15.	B
6.	B	16.	A
7.	B	17.	D
8.	C	18.	C
9.	A	19.	C
10.	D	20.	A

READING COMPREHENSION
UNDERSTANDING AND INTERPRETING WRITTEN MATERIAL
EXAMINATION SECTION
TEST 1

DIRECTIONS: Each question or incomplete statement is followed by several suggested answers or completions. Select the one that BEST answers the question or completes the statement. *PRINT THE LETTER OF THE CORRECT ANSWER IN THE SPACE AT THE RIGHT.*

Questions 1-3.

DIRECTIONS: Questions 1 through 3, inclusive, are to be answered in accordance with the following paragraph.

All cement work contracts, more or less, in setting. The contraction in concrete walls and other structures causes fine cracks to develop at regular intervals. The tendency to contract increases in direct proportion to the quantity of cement in the concrete. A rich mixture will contract more than a lean mixture. A concrete wall which has been made of a very lean mixture and which has been built by filling only about one foot in depth of concrete in the form each day will frequently require close inspection to reveal the cracks.

1. According to the above paragraph,

    A. shrinkage seldom occurs in concrete
    B. shrinkage occurs only in certain types of concrete
    C. by placing concrete at regular intervals, shrinkage may be avoided
    D. it is impossible to prevent shrinkage

2. According to the above paragraph, the one of the factors which reduces shrinkage in concrete is the

    A. volume of concrete in wall
    B. height of each day's pour
    C. length of wall
    D. length and height of wall

3. According to the above paragraph, a rich mixture

    A. pours the easiest
    B. shows the largest amount of cracks
    C. is low in cement content
    D. need not be inspected since cracks are few

Questions 4-6.

DIRECTIONS: Questions 4 through 6, inclusive, are to be answered SOLELY on the basis of the following paragraph.

It is best to avoid surface water on freshly poured concrete in the first place. However, when there is a very small amount present, the recommended procedure is to allow it to evaporate before finishing. If there is considerable water, it is removed with a broom, belt, float, or by other convenient means. It is never good practice to sprinkle dry cement, or a mixture of cement and fine aggregate, on concrete to take up surface water. Such fine materials form a layer on the surface that is likely to dust or hair check when the concrete hardens.

4. The MAIN subject of the above passage is

   A. surface cracking of concrete
   B. evaporation of water from freshly poured concrete
   C. removing surface water from concrete
   D. final adjustments of ingredients in the concrete mix

4.____

5. According to the above passage, the sprinkling of dry cement on the surface of a concrete mix would MOST LIKELY

   A. prevent the mix from setting
   B. cause discoloration on the surface of the concrete
   C. cause the coarse aggregate to settle out too quickly
   D. cause powdering and small cracks on the surface of the concrete

5.____

6. According to the above passage, the thing to do when considerable surface water is present on the freshly poured concrete is to

   A. dump the concrete back into the mixer and drain the water
   B. allow the water to evaporate before finishing
   C. remove the water with a broom, belt, or float
   D. add more fine aggregate but not cement

6.____

Questions 7-9.

DIRECTIONS: Questions 7 through 9, inclusive, are to be answered ONLY in accordance with the information given in the paragraph below.

Before placing the concrete, check that the forms are rigid and well braced and place the concrete within 45 minutes after mixing it. Fill the forms to the top with the wearing-course concrete. Level off the surfaces with a strieboard. When the concrete becomes stiff but still workable (in a few hours), finish the surface with a wood float. This fills the hollows and compacts the concrete and produces a smooth but gritty finish. For a non-gritty and smoother surface (but one that is more slippery when wet), follow up with a steel trowel after the water sheen from the wood-troweling starts to disappear. If you wish, slant the tread forward a fraction of an inch so that it will shed rain water.

7. Slanting the tread a fraction of an inch gives a surface that will

   A. have added strength
   B. not be slippery when wet
   C. shed rain water
   D. not have hollows

7.____

8. In addition to giving a smooth but gritty finish, the use of a wood float will tend to   8._____

    A. give a finish that is slippery when wet
    B. compact the concrete
    C. give a better wearing course
    D. provide hollows to retain rain water

9. Which one of the following statements is most nearly correct?   9._____

    A. Having checked the forms, one may place the concrete immediately after mixing same.
    B. One must wait at least 15 minutes after mixing the concrete before it may be placed in the forms.
    C. A gritty compact finish and one which is more slippery when wet will result with the use of a wood float.
    D. A steel trowel used promptly after a wood float will tend to give a non-gritty smooth finish.

Questions 10-11.

DIRECTIONS: Questions 10 and 11 are to be answered SOLELY on the basis of information contained in the following paragraph.

Tools and plastering methods have changed very little over the years. Most of the changes are mere improvements of the basic tools. The tools formerly made by hand are now machine-made and are *rigidly* constructed of light, but strong, materials in contrast to the clumsy constructions of the early types. The power-driven mixers and hoisting equipment used on large plastering jobs today produce better mortars and lighten the tasks involved.

10. According to the above paragraph, present day tools used for plastering   10._____

    A. have made plastering much more complicated than it used to be
    B. are heavier than the old-fashioned tools they replaced
    C. produce poorer results but speed up the job
    D. are lighter and stronger than the hand-made tools of the past

11. As used in the above paragraph, the word *rigidly* means MOST NEARLY   11._____

    A. feeble   B. weakly   C. firmly   D. flexibly

Questions 12-18.

DIRECTIONS: Questions 12 through 18 are to be answered in accordance with the following paragraphs.

SURFACE RENEWING OVERLAYS

A surface renewing overlay should consist of material which can be constructed in very thin layers. The material must fill surface voids and provide an impervious skid-resistant surface. It must also be sufficiently resistant to traffic abrasion to provide an economical service life.

Materials meeting these requirements are:
- a. Asphalt concrete having small particle size
- b. Hot sand asphalts
- c. Surface seal coats

Fine-graded asphalt concrete or hot sand asphalt can be constructed in layers as thin as one-half inch and fulfill all requirements for surface renewing overlays. They are recommended for thin resurfacing of pavements having high traffic volumes, as their service lives are relatively long when constructed properly. They can be used for minor leveling, they are quiet riding, and their appearance is exceptionally pleasing. Seal coats or slurry seals may fulfill surface requirements for low traffic pavements.

12. A surface renewing overlay must fill surface voids, provide an impervious skid-resistant surface, and

    A. be resistant to traffic abrasion
    B. have small particle size
    C. be exceptionally pleasing in appearance
    D. be constructed in half-inch layers

13. An *impervious skid-resistant surface* means a surface that is

    A. rough to the touch and fixed firmly in place
    B. waterproof and provides good gripping for tires
    C. not damaged by skidding vehicles
    D. smooth to the touch and quiet riding

14. The number of types of materials that can be constructed in very thin layers and are also suitable for surface renewing overlays is

    A. 1   B. 2   C. 3   D. 4

15. The SMALLEST thickness of asphalt concrete or hot sand asphalt that can fulfill all requirements for surface renewing overlays is _____ inch(es).

    A. ¼   B. ½   C. 1   D. 2

16. The materials that are recommended for thin resurfacing of pavements having high traffic volumes are

    A. those that have relatively long service lives
    B. asphalt concretes with maximum particle size
    C. surface seal coats
    D. slurry seals with voids

17. Fine-graded asphalt concrete and hot sand asphalt are quiet riding and are also

    A. recommended for low traffic pavements
    B. used as slurry seal coats
    C. suitable for major leveling
    D. exceptionally pleasing in appearance

18. The materials that may fulfill surface requirements for low traffic pavements are 18.____

    A. fine-graded asphalt concretes
    B. hot sand asphalts
    C. seal coats or slurry seals
    D. those that can be used for minor leveling

Questions 19-25.

DIRECTIONS: Questions 19 through 25 are to be answered SOLELY on the basis of the paragraphs below.

OPEN-END WRENCHES

Solid, non-adjustable wrenches with openings in one or both ends are called open-end wrenches. Wrenches with small openings are usually shorter than wrenches with large openings. This proportions the lever advantage of the wrench to the bolt or stud and helps prevent wrench breakage or damage to the bolt or stud.

Open-end wrenches may have their jaws parallel to the handle or at angles anywhere up to 90 degrees. The average angle is 15 degrees. This angular displacement variation permits selection of a wrench suited for places where there is room to make only a part of a complete turn of a nut or bolt. Handles are usually straight, but may be curved. Those with curved handles are called S-wrenches. Other open-end wrenches may have offset handles. This allows the head to reach nut or bolt heads that are sunk below the surface.

There are a few basic rules that you should keep in mind when using wrenches. They are:
    I. ALWAYS use a wrench that fits the nut properly. Otherwise, the wrench may slip, or the nut may be damaged.
    II. Keep wrenches clean and free from oil. Otherwise, they may slip, resulting in possible serious injury to you or damage to the work.
    III. Do NOT increase the leverage of a wrench by placing a pipe over the handle. Increased leverage may damage the wrench or the work.

19. Open-end wrenches 19.____

    A. are adjustable
    B. are solid
    C. always have openings at both ends
    D. are always S-shaped

20. Wrench proportions are such that wrenches with _____ openings have _____ handles. 20.____

    A. larger; shorter   B. smaller; longer
    C. larger; longer   D. smaller; thicker

21. The average angle between the jaws and the handle of a wrench is _____ degrees. 21.____

    A. 0   B. 15   C. 22   D. 90

22. Offset handles are intended for use MAINLY with 22.____

   A. offset nuts
   B. bolts having fine threads
   C. nuts sunk below the surface
   D. bolts that permit limited swing

23. The wrench which is selected should fit the nut properly because this 23.____

   A. prevents distorting the wrench
   B. insures use of all wrench sizes
   C. avoids damaging the nut
   D. overstresses the bolt

24. Oil on wrenches is 24.____

   A. *good* because it prevents rust
   B. *good* because it permits easier turning
   C. *bad* because the wrench may slip off the nut
   D. *bad* because the oil may spoil the work

25. Extending the handle of a wrench by slipping a piece of pipe over it is considered 25.____

   A. *good* because it insures a tight nut
   B. *good* because less effort is needed to loosen a nut
   C. *bad* because the wrench may be damaged
   D. *bad* because the amount of tightening can not be controlled

KEY (CORRECT ANSWERS)

1. D	11. C
2. B	12. A
3. B	13. B
4. C	14. C
5. D	15. B
6. C	16. A
7. C	17. D
8. B	18. C
9. A	19. B
10. D	20. C

21. B
22. C
23. C
24. C
25. C

TEST 2

DIRECTIONS: Each question or incomplete statement is followed by several suggested answers or completions. Select the one that BEST answers the question or completes the statement. *PRINT THE LETTER OF THE CORRECT ANSWER IN THE SPACE AT THE RIGHT.*

Questions 1-3.

DIRECTIONS: Questions 1 through 3 are to be answered SOLELY on the basis of the following passage.

    A utility plan is a floor plan which shows the layout of a heating, electrical, plumbing, or other utility system. Utility plans are used primarily by the persons reponsible for the utilities, but they are important to the craftsman as well. Most utility installations require the leaving of openings in walls, floors, and roofs for the admission or installation of utility features. The craftsman who is, for example, pouring a concrete foundation wall must study the utility plans to determine the number, sizes, and locations of the openings he must leave for piping, electric lines, and the like.

1. The one of the following items of information which is LEAST likely to be provided by a utility plan is the

    A. location of the joists and frame members around stairwells
    B. location of the hot water supply and return piping
    C. location of light fixtures
    D. number of openings in the floor for radiators

1.____

2. According to the passage, the persons who will *most likely* have the GREATEST need for the information included in a utility plan of a building are those who

    A. maintain and repair the heating system
    B. clean the premises
    C. paint housing exteriors
    D. advertise property for sale

2.____

3. According to the passage, a repair crew member should find it MOST helpful to consult a utility plan when information is needed about the

    A. thickness of all doors in the structure
    B. number of electrical outlets located throughout the structure
    C. dimensions of each window in the structure
    D. length of a roof rafter

3.____

Questions 4-9.

DIRECTIONS: Questions 4 through 9 are to be answered SOLELY on the basis of the following passage.

    The basic hand-operated hoisting device is the tackle or purchase, consisting of a line called a fall, reeved through one or more blocks. To hoist a load of given size, you must set up a rig with a safe working load equal to or in excess of the load to be hoisted. In order to do this, you must be able to calculate the safe working load of a single part of line of given size, the safe working load of a given purchase which contains a line of given size, and the minimum size of hooks or shackles which you must use in a given type of purchase to hoist a given load. You must also be able to calculate the thrust which a given load will exert on a gin pole or a set of shears inclined at a given angle, the safe working load which a spar of a given size used as a gin pole or as one of a set of shears will sustain, and the stress which a given load will set up in the back guy of a gin pole or in the back guy of a set of shears inclined at a given angle.

4. The above passage refers to the lifting of loads by means of

   A. erected scaffolds
   B. manual rigging devices
   C. power-driven equipment
   D. conveyor belts

5. It can be concluded from the above passage that a set of shears serves to

   A. absorb the force and stress of the working load
   B. operate the tackle
   C. contain the working load
   D. compute the safe working load

6. According to the above passage, a spar can be used for a

   A. back guy   B. block   C. fall   D. gin pole

7. According to the above passage, the rule that a user of hand-operated tackle MUST follow is to make sure that the safe working load is AT LEAST

   A. equal to the weight of the given load
   B. twice the combined weight of the block and falls
   C. one-half the weight of the given load
   D. twice the weight of the given load

8. According to the above passage, the two parts that make up a tackle are

   A. back guys and gin poles
   B. blocks and falls
   C. rigs and shears
   D. spars and shackles

9. According to the above passage, in order to determine whether it is safe to hoist a particular load, you MUST

   A. use the maximum size hooks
   B. time the speed to bring a given load to a desired place
   C. calculate the forces exerted on various types of rigs
   D. repeatedly lift and lower various loads

Questions 10-15.

DIRECTIONS: Questions 10 through 15 are to be answered SOLELY on the basis of the following set of instructions.

PATCHING SIMPLE CRACKS IN A BUILT-UP ROOF

If there is a visible crack in built-up roofing, the repair is simple and straightforward:

1. With a brush, clean all loose gravel and dust out of the crack, and clean three or four inches around all sides of it.
2. With a trowel or putty knife, fill the crack with asphalt cement and then spread a layer of asphalt cement about 1/8 inch thick over the cleaned area.
3. Place a strip of roofing felt big enough to cover the crack into the wet cement and press it down firmly.
4. Spread a second layer of cement over the strip of felt and well past its edges.
5. Brush gravel back over the patch.

10. According to the above passage, in order to patch simple cracks in a built-up roof, it is necessary to use a

    A. putty knife and a drill
    B. knife and pliers
    C. tack hammer and a punch
    D. brush and a trowel

11. According to the above passage, the size of the area that should be clear of loose gravel and dust before the asphalt cement is first applied should

    A. be the exact size of the crack itself
    B. extend three or four inches on all sides of the crack
    C. be 1/8 inch greater than the size of the crack itself
    D. extend the length of the roofing strip

12. According to the above passage, loose gravel and dust in the crack should be removed with a

    A. brush   B. felt pad   C. trowel   D. dust mop

13. Assume that both layers of asphalt cement needed to patch the crack are of the same thickness.
    The total thickness of asphalt cement used in the patch should be MOST NEARLY _____ inch.

    A. 1/2   B. 1/3   C. 1/4   D. 1/8

14. According to the instructions in the above passage, how large should the strip of roofing felt be cut?

    A. Three of four inches square
    B. Smaller than the crack and small enough to be surrounded by cement on all sides of the strip
    C. Exactly the same size and shape of the area covered by the wet cement
    D. Large enough to completely cover the crack

15. The final or finishing action to be taken in patching a simple crack in a built-up roof is to

    A. clean out the inside of the crack
    B. spread a layer of asphalt a second time
    C. cover the crack with roofing felt
    D. cover the patch of roofing felt and cement with gravel

Questions 16-17.

DIRECTIONS: Questions 16 and 17 are to be answered SOLELY on the basis of the information given in the following paragraph.

Supplies are to be ordered from the stockroom once a week. The standard requisition form, Form SP21, is to be used for ordering all supplies. The form is prepared in triplicate, one white original and two green copies. The white and one green copy are sent to the stockroom, and the remaining green copy is to be kept by the orderer until the supplies are received.

16. According to the above paragraph, there is a limit on the

    A. amount of supplies that may be ordered
    B. day on which supplies may be ordered
    C. different kinds of supplies that may be ordered
    D. number of times supplies may be ordered in one year

17. According to the above paragraph, when the standard requisition form for supplies is prepared,

    A. a total of four requisition blanks is used
    B. a white form is the original
    C. each copy is printed in two colors
    D. one copy is kept by the stock clerk

Questions 18-21.

DIRECTION: Questions 18 through 21 are to be answered SOLELY on the basis of the following passage.

The Oil Pollution Act for U. S. waters defines an *oily mixture* as 100 parts or more of oil in one million parts of mixture. This mixture is not allowed to be discharged into the prohibited zone. The prohibited zone may, in special cases, be extended 100 miles out to sea but, in general, remains at 50 miles offshore. The United States Coast Guard must be contacted to report all *oily mixture* spills. The Federal Water Pollution Control Act provides for a fine of $10,000 for failure to notify the United States Coast Guard. An employer may take action against an employee if the employee causes an *oily mixture* spill. The law holds your employer responsible for either cleaning up or paying for the removal of the oil spillage.

18. According to the Oil Pollution Act, an *oily mixture* is defined as one in which there are _____ parts or more of oil in _____ parts of mixture.

    A. 50; 10,000   B. 100; 10,000
    C. 100; 1,000,000   D. 10,000; 1,000,000

19. Failure to notify the proper authorities of an *oily mixture* spill is punishable by a fine. Such fine is provided for by the

    A. United States Coast Guard
    B. Federal Water Pollution Control Act
    C. Oil Pollution Act
    D. United States Department of Environmental Protection

20. According to the law, the one responsible for the removal of an *oily mixture* spilled into U.S. waters is the

    A. employer
    B. employee
    C. U.S. Coast Guard
    D. U.S. Pollution Control Board

21. The *prohibited zone,* in general, is the body of water

    A. within 50 miles offshore
    B. beyond 100 miles offshore
    C. within 10,000 yards of the coastline
    D. beyond 10,000 yards from the coastline

Questions 22-25.

DIRECTIONS: Questions 22 through 25 are to be answered SOLELY on the basis of the following paragraph.

Synthetic detergents are materials produced from petroleum products or from animal or vegetable oils and fats. One of their advantages is the fact that they can be made to meet a particular cleaning problem by altering the foaming, wetting, and emulsifying properties of a cleaner. They are added to commonly used cleaning materials such as solvents, water, and alkalies to improve their cleaning performance. The adequate wetting of the surface to be cleaned is paramount in good cleaning performance. Because of the relatively high surface tension of water, it has poor wetting ability, unless its surface tension is decreased by addition of a detergent or soap. This allows water to flow into crevices and around small particles of soil, thus loosening them.

22. According to the above paragraph, synthetic detergents are made from all of the following EXCEPT

    A. petroleum products   B. vegetable oils
    C. surface tension oils   D. animal fats

23. According to the above paragraph, water's poor wetting ability is related to

    A. its low surface tension
    B. its high surface tension
    C. its vegetable oil content
    D. the amount of dirt on the surface to be cleaned

24. According to the above paragraph, synthetic detergents are added to all of the following EXCEPT

    A. alkalines   B. water   C. acids   D. solvents

25. According to the above paragraph, altering a property of a cleaner can give an advantage in meeting a certain cleaning problem.
The one of the following that is NOT a property altered by synthetic detergents is the cleaner's

   A. flow ability
   B. foaming property
   C. emulsifying property
   D. wetting ability

25.____

KEY (CORRECT ANSWERS)

1. A
2. A
3. B
4. B
5. A

6. D
7. A
8. B
9. C
10. D

11. B
12. A
13. C
14. D
15. D

16. D
17. B
18. C
19. B
20. A

21. A
22. C
23. B
24. C
25. A

BASIC FUNDAMENTALS OF
DRAWINGS AND SPECIFICATIONS

A building project may be broadly divided into two major phases: (1) the DESIGN phase, and (2) the CONSTRUCTION phase. In accordance with a number of considerations, of which the function and desired appearance of the building are perhaps the most important, the architect first conceives the building in his mind's eye, as it were, and then sets his concept down on paper in the form of PRESENTATION drawings. Presentation drawings are usually done in PERSPECTIVE, by employing the PICTORIAL drawing techniques.

Next the architect and the engineer, working together, decide upon the materials to be used in the structure and the construction methods which are to be followed. The engineer determines the loads which supporting members will carry and the strength qualities the members must have to bear the loads. He also designs the mechanical systems of the structure, such as the lighting, heating, and plumbing systems. The end-result of all this is the preparation of architectural and engineering DESIGN SKETCHES. The purpose of these sketches is to guide draftsmen in the preparation of CONSTRUCTION DRAWINGS.

The construction drawings, plus the SPECIFICATIONS to be described later, are the chief sources of information for the supervisors and craftsman responsible for the actual work of construction. Construction drawings consist mostly of ORTHOGRAPHIC views, prepared by draftsmen who employ the standard technical drawing techniques, and who use the symbols and other designations

You should make a thorough study of symbols before proceeding further with this chapter. Figure 1 illustrates the conventional symbols for the more common types of material used on structures. Figure 2 shows the more common symbols used for doors and windows.

Before you can interpret construction drawings correctly, you must also have some knowledge of the structure and of the terminology for common structural members.

I. STRUCTURES

The main parts of a structure are the LOAD-BEARING STRUCTURAL MEMBERS, which support and transfer the loads on the structure while remaining in equilibrium with each other. The places where members are connected to other members are called JOINTS. The sum total of the load supported by the structural members at a particular instant is equal to the total DEAD LOAD plus the total LIVE LOAD.

The total dead load is the total weight of the structure, which gradually increases, of course, as the structure rises, and remains constant once it is completed. The total live load is the total weight of movable objects (such as people, furniture, bridge traffic or the like) which the structure happens to be supporting at a particular instant.

The live loads in a structure are transmitted through the various load-bearing structural members to the ultimate support of the earth as follows. Immediate or direct support for the live loads is provided by HORIZTONAL members; these are in turn supported by VERTICAL members; which in turn are supported by FOUNDATIONS and/or FOOTINGS; and these are, finally, supported by the earth.

The ability of the earth to support a load is called the SOIL BEARING CAPACITY; it is determined by test and measured in pounds per square foot. Soil bearing capacity varies considerably with different types of soil, and a soil of given bearing capacity will bear a heavier load on a wide foundation or footing than it will on a narrow one.

VERTICAL STRUCTURAL MEMBERS

Vertical structural members are high-strength columns; they are sometimes called PILLARS in buildings. Outside wall columns and inside bottom-floor columns, usually rest directly on footings. Outside-wall columns usually extend from the footing or foundation to the roof line. Inside bottom-floor columns extend upward from footings or foundations to horizontal members which in turn support the

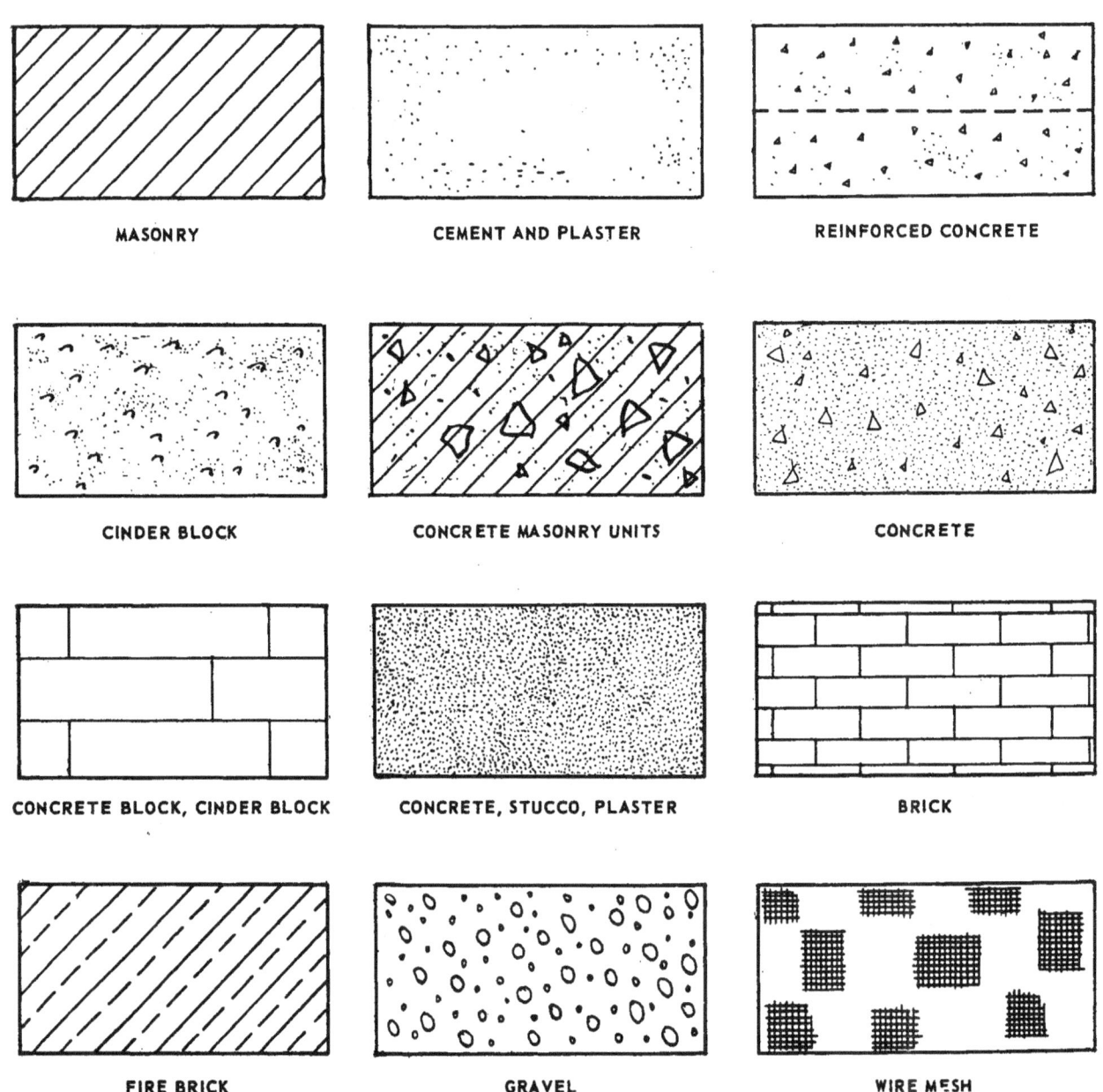

Figure 1.—Material symbols.

first floor. Upper floor columns usually are located directly over lower floor columns.

A PIER in building construction might be called a short column. It may rest directly on a footing, or it may be simply set or driven in the ground. Building piers usually support the lowermost horizontal structural members.

In bridge construction a pier is a vertical member which provides intermediate support for the bridge superstructure.

The chief vertical structural members in light frame construction are called STUDS. They are supported on horizontal members called SILLS or SOLE PLATES, and are topped by horizontal members called TOP PLATES or RAFTER PLATES. CORNER POSTS are enlarged studs, as it were, located at the building corners. In early FULL-FRAME construction a corner post was usually a solid piece of larger timber. In most modern construction BUILT-UP

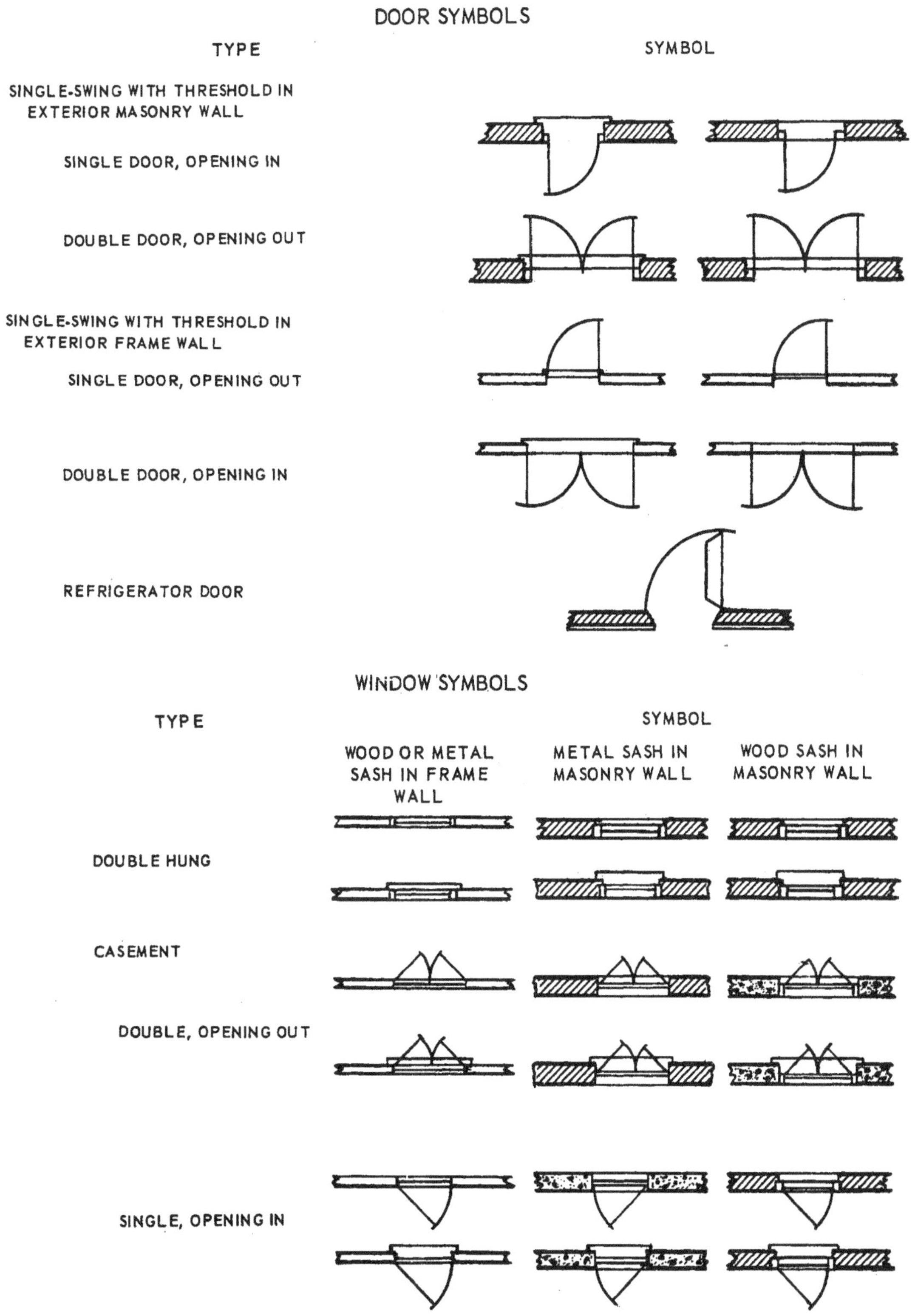

DOOR SYMBOLS

TYPE	SYMBOL
SINGLE-SWING WITH THRESHOLD IN EXTERIOR MASONRY WALL SINGLE DOOR, OPENING IN	
DOUBLE DOOR, OPENING OUT	
SINGLE-SWING WITH THRESHOLD IN EXTERIOR FRAME WALL SINGLE DOOR, OPENING OUT	
DOUBLE DOOR, OPENING IN	
REFRIGERATOR DOOR	

WINDOW SYMBOLS

TYPE	SYMBOL		
	WOOD OR METAL SASH IN FRAME WALL	METAL SASH IN MASONRY WALL	WOOD SASH IN MASONRY WALL
DOUBLE HUNG			
CASEMENT DOUBLE, OPENING OUT			
SINGLE, OPENING IN			

Figure 2 —Architectural symbols (door and windows).

corner posts are used, consisting of various numbers of ordinary studs, nailed together in various ways.

HORIZONTAL STRUCTURAL MEMBERS

In technical terminology, a horizontal load-bearing structural member which spans a space, and which is supported at both ends, is called a BEAM. A member which is FIXED at one end only is called a CANTILEVER. Steel members which consist of solid pieces of the regular structural steel shapes are called beams, but a type of steel member which is actually a light truss is called an OPEN-WEB STEEL JOIST or a BAR STEEL JOIST.

Horizontal structural members which support the ends of floor beams or joists in wood frame construction are called SILLS, GIRTS, or GIRDERS, depending on the type of framing being done and the location of the member in the structure. Horizontal members which support studs are called SILL or SOLE PLATES. Horizontal members which support the wall-ends of rafters are called RAFTER PLATES. Horizontal members which assume the weight of concrete or masonry walls above door and window openings are called LINTELS.

TRUSSES

A beam of given strength, without intermediate supports below, can support a given load over only a certain maximum span. If the span is wider than this maximum, intermediate supports, such as a column must be provided for the beam. Sometimes it is not feasible or possible to install intermediate supports. When such is the case, a TRUSS may be used instead of a beam.

A beam consists of a single horizontal member. A truss, however, is a framework, consisting of two horizontal (or nearly horizontal) members, joined together by a number of vertical and/or inclined members. The horizontal members are called the UPPER and LOWER CHORDS; the vertical and/or inclined members are called the WEB MEMBERS.

ROOF MEMBERS

The horizontal or inclined members which provide support to a roof are called RAFTERS. The lengthwise (right angle to the rafters) member which support the peak ends of the rafters in a roof is called the RIDGE. (The ridge may be called the Ridge board, the Ridge PIECE, or the Ridge pole.) Lengthwise members other than ridges are called PURLINS. In wood frame construction the wall ends of rafters are supported on horizontal members called RAFTER PLATES, which are in turn supported by the outside wall studs. In concrete or masonry wall construction, the wall ends of rafters may be anchored directly on the walls, or on plates bolted to the walls.

II. CONSTRUCTION DRAWINGS

Construction drawings are drawings in which as much construction information as possible is presented GRAPHICALLY, or by means of pictures. Most construction drawings consist of ORTHOGRAPHIC views. GENERAL drawings consist of PLANS AND ELEVATIONS, drawn on a relatively small scale. DETAIL drawings consist of SECTIONS and DETAILS, drawn on a relatively large scale.

PLANS

A PLAN view is, as you know, a view of an object or area as it would appear if projected onto a horizontal plane passed through or held above the object or area. The most common construction plans are PLOT PLANS (also called SITE PLANS), FOUNDATION PLANS, FLOOR PLANS, and FRAMING PLANS.

A PLOT PLAN shows the contours, boundaries, roads, utilities, trees, structures, and any other significant physical features pertaining to or located on the site. The locations of proposed structures are indicated by appropriate outlines or floor plans. By locating the corners of a proposed structure at given distances from a REFERENCE or BASE line (which is shown on the plan and which can be located on the site), the plot plan provides essential data for those who will lay out the building lines. By indicating the elevations of existing and proposed earth surfaces (by means of CONTOUR lines), the plot plan provides essential data for the graders and excavators.

A FOUNDATION PLAN (fig. 3) is a plan view of a structure projected on a horizontal plane passed through (in imagination, of course) at the level of the tops of the foundations. The plan shown in figure 3 tells you that the main foundation of this structure will consist of a rectangular 12-in. concrete block wall, 22 ft

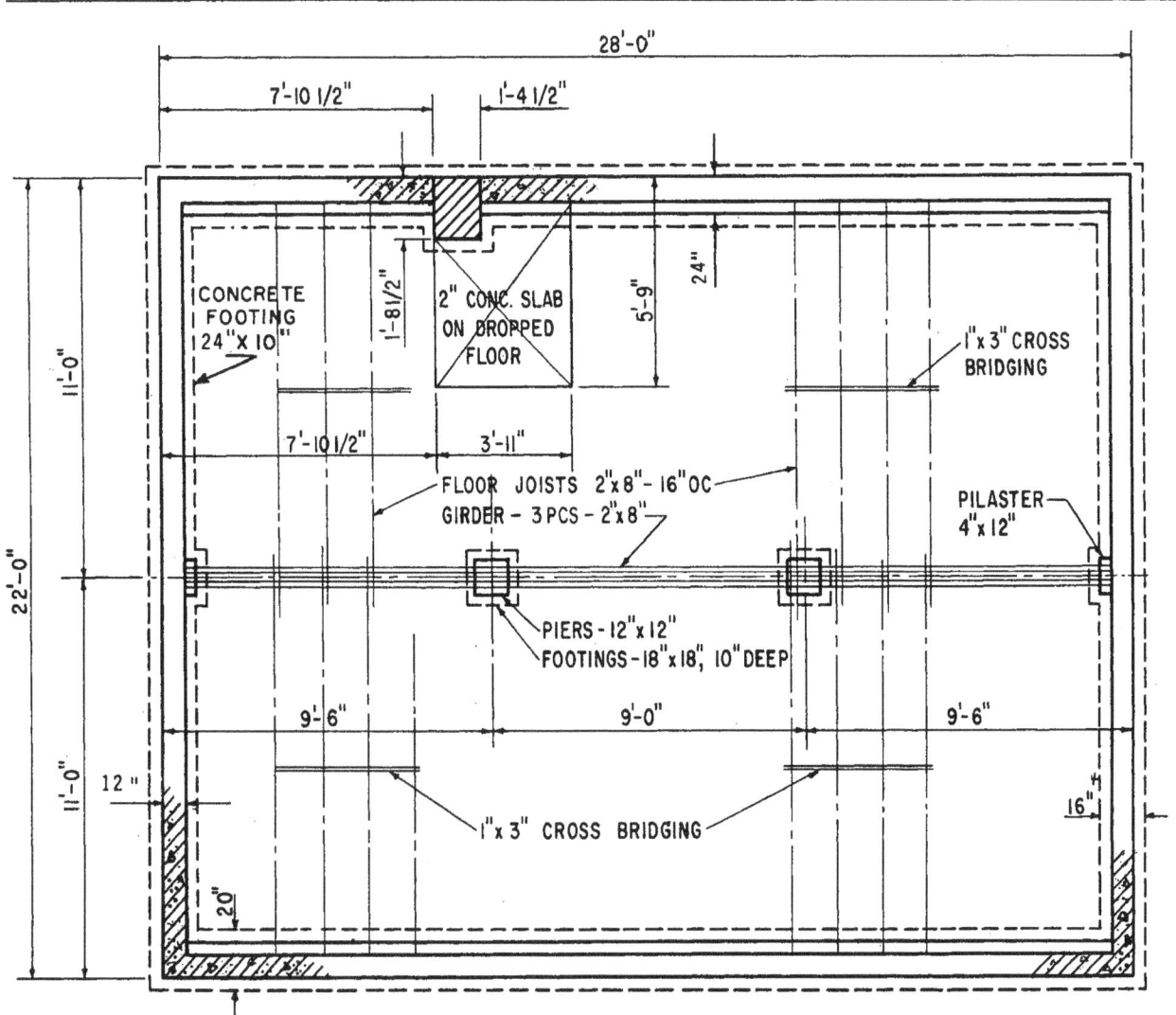

Figure 3.—Foundation plan.

wide by 28 ft long, centered on a concrete footing 24 in. wide. Besides the outside wall and footing, there will be two 12-in. square piers, centered on 18-in. square footings, and located on center 9 ft 6 in. from the end wall building lines. These piers will support a ground floor center-line girder.

A FLOOR PLAN (also called a BUILDING PLAN) is developed as shown in figure 4. Information on a floor plan includes the lengths, thicknesses, and character of the building walls at that particular floor, the widths and locations of door and window openings, the lengths and character of partitions, the number and arrangement of rooms, and the types and locations of utility installations. A typical floor plan is shown in figure 5.

FRAMING PLANS show the dimensions, numbers, and arrangement of structural members in wood frame construction. A simple FLOOR FRAMING PLAN is superimposed on the foundation plan shown in figure 3. From this foundation plan you learn that the ground-floor joists in this structure will consist of 2 x 8's, lapped at the girder, and spaced 16 in. O. C. The plan also shows that each row of joists is to be braced by a row of 1 x 3 cross bridging. For a more complicated floor framing problem, a framing plan like the one shown in figure 2-6 would be required. This plan

  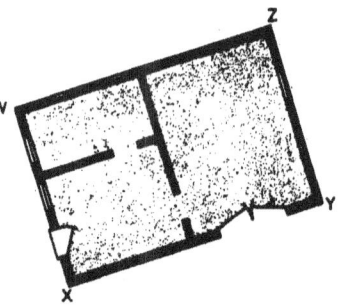

PERSPECTIVE VIEW OF A BUILDING SHOWING CUTTING PLANE WXY

PREVIOUS PERSPECTIVE VIEW AT CUTTING PLANE WXYZ, TOP REMOVED

DEVELOPED FLOOR PLAN WXYZ

Figure 4.—Floor plan development.

shows, among other things, the arrangement of joists and other members around stair wells and other floor openings.

A WALL FRAMING PLAN gives similar information with regard to the studs, corner posts, bracing, sills, plates, and other structural members in the walls. Since it is a view on a vertical plane, a wall framing plan is not a plan in the strict technical sense. However, the practice of calling it a plan has become a general custom. A ROOF FRAMING PLAN gives similar information with regard to the rafters, ridge, purlins, and other structural members in the roof.

A UTILITY PLAN is a floor plan which shows the layout of a heating, electrical, plumbing, or other utility system. Utility plans are used primarily by the ratings responsible for the utilities, but they are important to the Builder as well. Most utility installations require the leaving of openings in walls, floors, and roofs for the admission or installation of utility features. The Builder who is placing a concrete foundation wall must study the utility plans to determine the number, sizes, and locations of the openings he must leave for utilities.

Figure 7 shows a heating plan. Figure 8 shows an electrical plan.

ELEVATIONS

ELEVATIONS show the front, rear, and sides of a structure projected on vertical planes parallel to the planes of the sides. Front, rear, right side, and left side elevations of a small building are shown in figure 9.

As you can see, the elevations give you a number of important vertical dimensions, such as the perpendicular distance from the finish floor to the top of the rafter plate and from the finish floor to the tops of door and window finished openings. They also show the locations and characters of doors and windows. Dimensions of window sash and dimensions and character of lintels, however, are usually set forth in a WINDOW SCHEDULE.

A SECTION view is a view of a cross-section, developed as indicated in figure 10. By general custom, the term is confined to views of cross-sections cut by vertical planes. A floor plan or foundation plan, cut by a horizontal plane, is, technically speaking, a section view as well as a plan view, but it is seldom called a section.

The most important sections are the WALL sections. Figure 11 shows three wall sections for three alternate types of construction for the building shown in figures 3, 5, 7 and 8. The angled arrows marked "A" in figure 5 indicate the location of the cutting plane for the sections.

The wall sections are of primary importance to the supervisors of construction and to the craftsmen who will do the actual building. Take the first wall section, marked "masonry construction," for example. Starting at the bottom, you learn that the footing will be concrete, 2 ft wide and 10 in. high. The vertical distance of the bottom of the footing below FINISHED GRADE (level of the finished earth surface around the house) "varies"—meaning that it will depend on the soil-bearing capacity at the particular site. The foundation wall will consist of

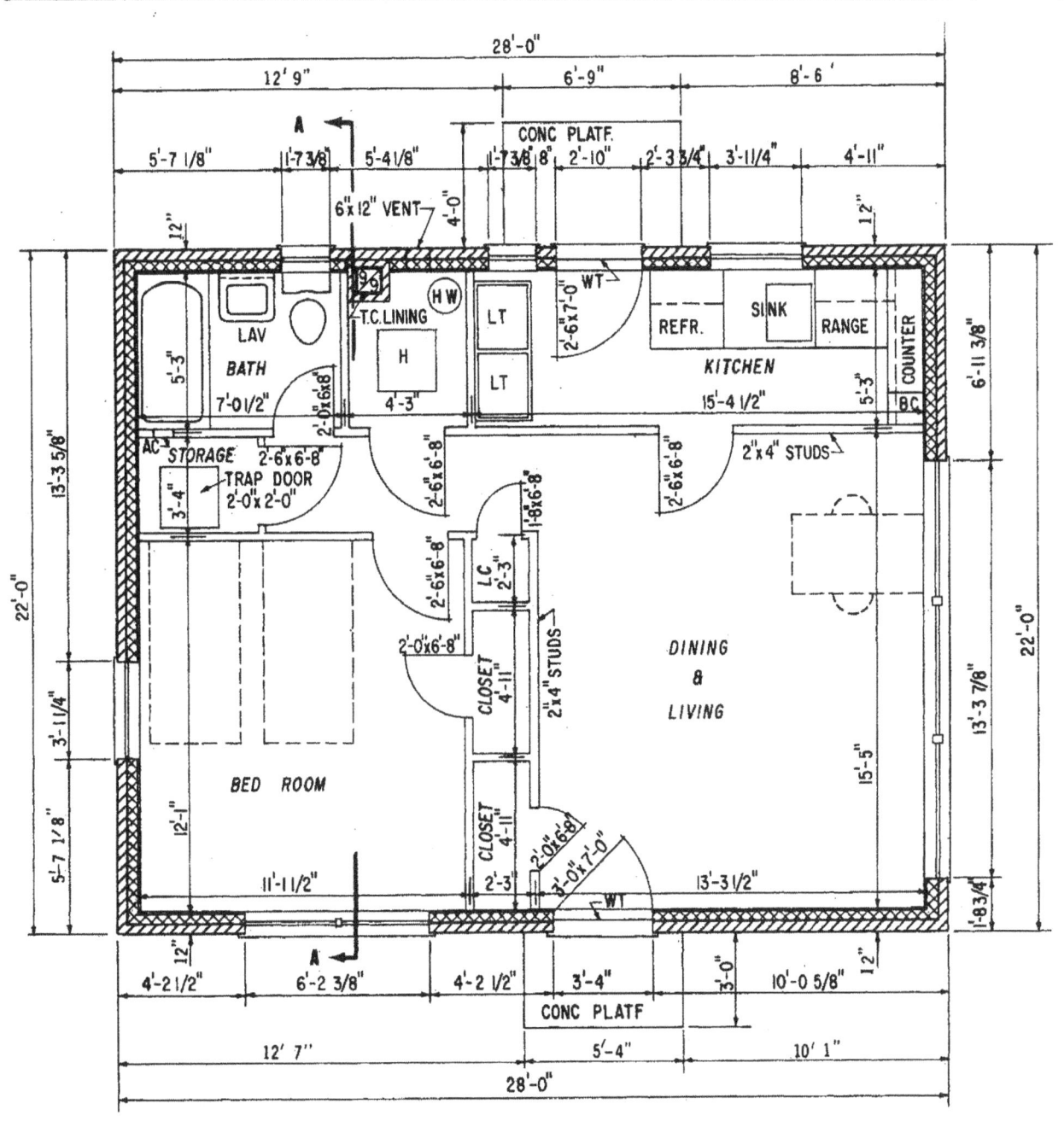

Figure 5.—Floor plan.

12-in. CMU, centered on the footing. Twelve-inch blocks will extend up to an unspecified distance below grade, where a 4-in. brick FACING (dimension indicated in the middle wall section) begins. Above the line of the bottom of the facing, it is obvious that 8-in. instead of 12-in. blocks will be used in the foundation wall.

The building wall above grade will consist of a 4-in. brick FACING TIER, backed by a BACKING TIER of 4-in. cinder blocks. The floor joists, consisting of 2 x 8's placed 16 in. O.C., will be anchored on 2 x 4 sills bolted to the top of the foundation wall. Every third joist will be additionally secured by a 2 x 1/4 STRAP ANCHOR embedded in the cinder block backing tier of the building wall.

The window (window B in the plan front elevation, fig. 9) will have a finished opening

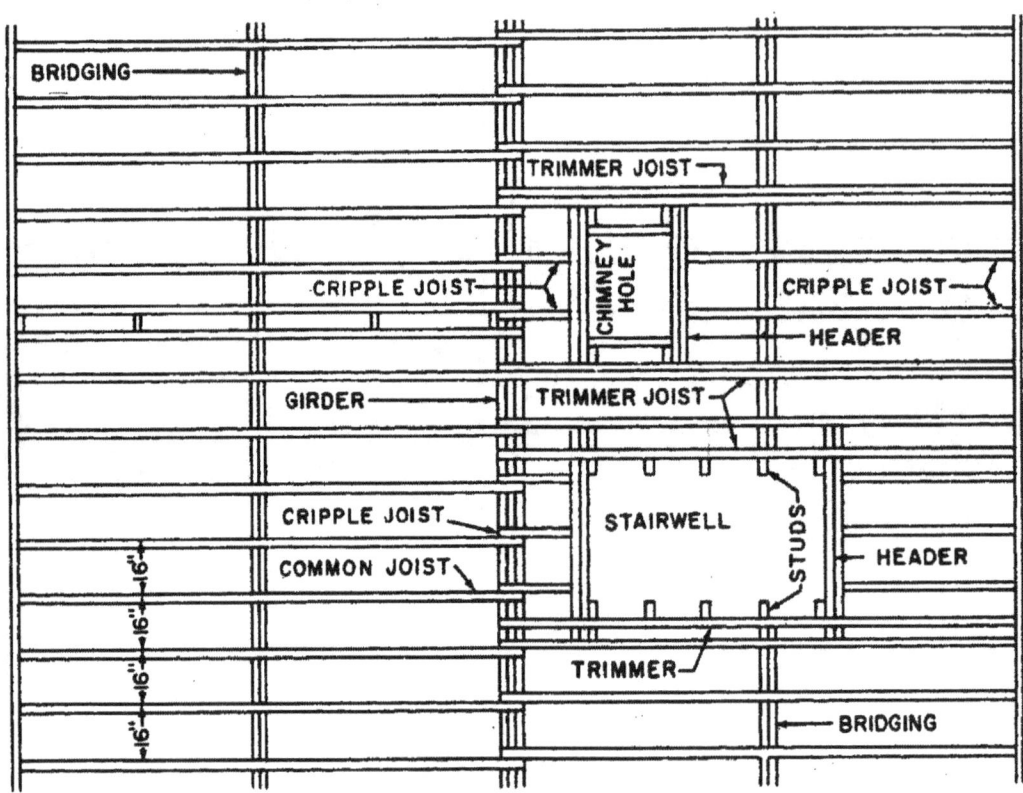

Figure 6.—Floor framing plan.

4 ft 2-5/8 in. high. The bottom of the opening will come 2 ft 11-3/4 in. above the line of the finished floor. As indicated in the wall section, (fig. 11) 13 masonry COURSES (layers of masonry units) above the finished floor line will amount to a vertical distance of 2 ft 11-3/4 in. As also indicated, another 19 courses will amount to the prescribed vertical dimension of the finished window opening.

Window framing details, including the placement and cross-sectional character of the lintel, are shown. The building wall will be carried 10-1/4 in., less the thickness of a 2 x 8 RAFTER PLATE, above the top of the window finished opening. The total vertical distance from the top of the finished floor to the top of the rafter plate will be 8 ft 2-1/4 in. Ceiling joists and rafters will consist of 2 x 6's, and the roof covering will consist of composition shingles laid on wood sheathing.

Flooring will consist of a wood finisher floor laid on a wood subfloor. Inside walls will be finished with plaster on lath (except on masonry wall which would be with or without lath as directed). A minimum of 2 vertical feet of crawl space will extend below the bottoms of the floor joists.

The middle wall section in figure 2-11 gives you similar information for a similar building constructed with wood frame walls and a DOUBLE-HUNG window. The third wall section shown in the figure gives you similar information for a similar building constructed with a steel frame, a casement window, and a concrete floor finished with asphalt tile.

DETAILS

DETAIL drawings are drawings which are done on a larger scale than that of the general drawings, and which show features not appearing at all, or appearing on too small a scale, on the general drawings. The wall sections just described are details as well as sections, since

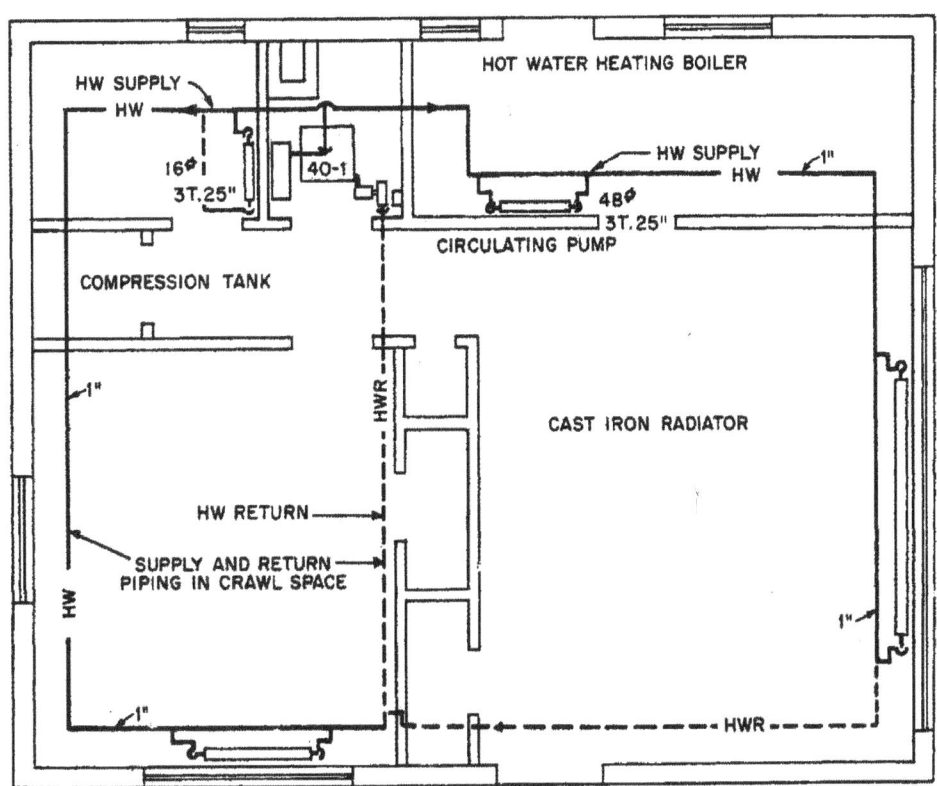

Figure 7.—Heating plan.

they are drawn on a considerable larger scale than the plans and elevations. Framing details at doors, windows, and cornices, which are the most common types of details, are practically always sections.

Details are included whenever the information given in the plans, elevations, and wall sections is not sufficiently "detailed" to guide the craftsmen on the job. Figure 12 shows some typical door and window wood framing details, and an eave detail for a very simple type of CORNICE. You should study these details closely to learn the terminology of framing members.

III. SPECIFICATIONS

The construction drawings contain much of the information about a structure which can be presented GRAPHICALLY (that is, in drawings). A very considerable amount of information can be presented this way, but there is more information which the construction supervisors and artisans must have and which is not adaptable to the graphic form of presentation. Information of this kind includes quality criteria for materials (maximum amounts of aggregate per sack of cement, for example), specified standards of workmanship, prescribed construction methods, and the like.

Information of this kind is presented in a list of written SPECIFICATIONS, familiarly known as the "SPECS." A list of specifications usually begins with a section on GENERAL CONDITIONS. This section starts with a GENERAL DESCRIPTION of the building, including the type of foundation, type or types of windows, character of framing, utilities to be installed, and the like. Next comes a list of DEFINITIONS of terms used in the specs, and next certain routine declarations of responsibility and certain conditions to be maintained on the job.

SPECIFIC CONDITIONS are grouped in sections under headings which describe each of the major construction phases of the job. Separate specifications are written for each phase, and the phases are then combined to more or less follow the usual order of construction sequences on the job. A typical list of sections under "Specific Conditions" follows:

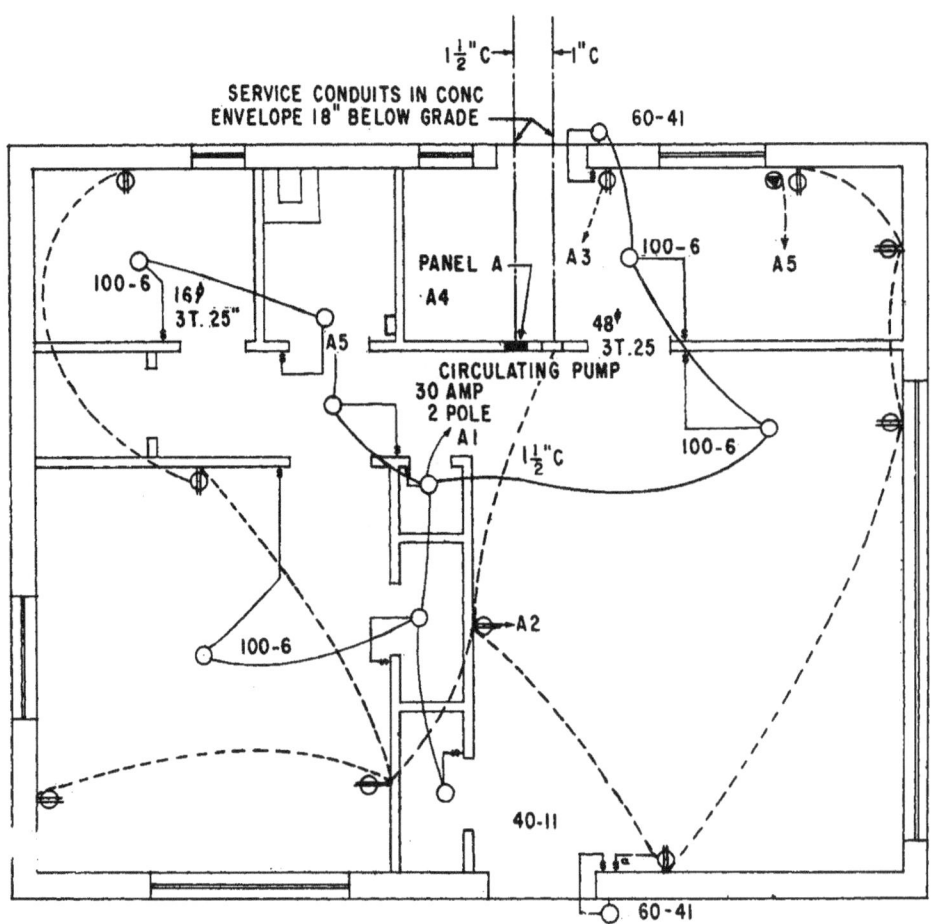

Figure 8.—Electrical plan.

2.—EARTHWORK 3.—CONCRETE 4.—MASONRY 5.—MISCELLANEOUS STEEL AND IRON 6.—CARPENTRY AND JOINERY 7.—LATHING AND PLASTERING 8.—TILE WORK 9.—FINISH FLOORING 10.—GLAZING 11.—FINISHING HARDWARE 12.—PLUMBING 13.—HEATING 14.—ELECTRICAL WORK 15.—FIELD PAINTING.

A section under "Specific Conditions" usually begins with a subsection of GENERAL REQUIREMENTS which apply to the phase of construction being considered. Under Section 6, CARPENTRY AND JOINERY, for example, the first section might go as follows:

6-01. GENERAL REQUIREMENTS. All framing, rough carpentry, and finishing woodwork required for the proper completion of the building shall be provided. All woodwork shall be protected from the weather, and the building shall be thoroughly dry before the finish is placed. All finish shall be dressed, smoothed, and sandpapered at the mill, and in addition shall be hand smoothed and sandpapered at the building where necessary to produce proper finish. Nailing shall be done, as far as practicable, in concealed places, and all nails in finishing work shall be set. All lumber shall be S4S (meaning, "surfaced on 4 sides"); all materials for millwork and finish shall be kiln-dried; all rough and framing lumber shall be air- or kiln-dried. Any cutting, fitting, framing, and blocking necessary for the accommodation of other work shall be provided. All nails, spikes, screws, bolts, plates, clips, and other fastenings and rough hardware necessary for the proper completion of the building shall be provided.

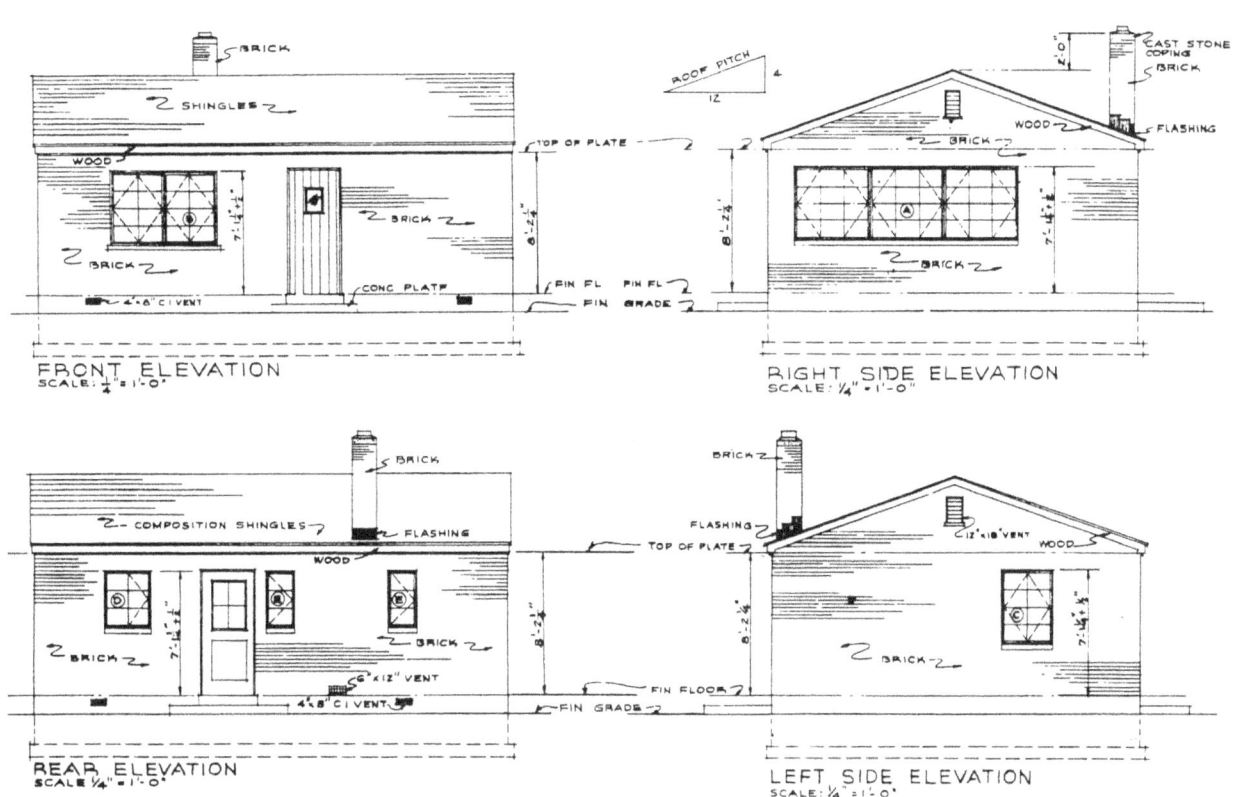

Figure 2-9.—Elevations.

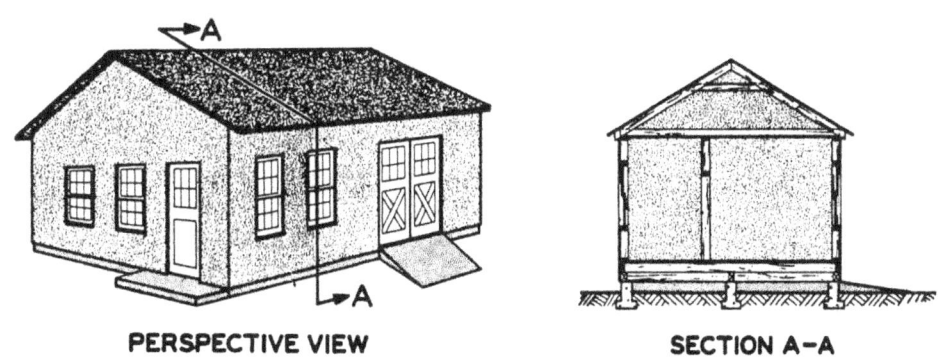

Figure 10.—Development of a section view.

All finishing hardware shall be installed in accordance with the manufacturers' directions. Calking and flashing shall be provided where indicated, or where necessary to provide weathertight construction.

Next after the General Requirements for Carpentry and Joinery, there is generally a subsection on "Grading," in which the kinds and grades of the various woods to be used in the structure are specified. Subsequent subsections

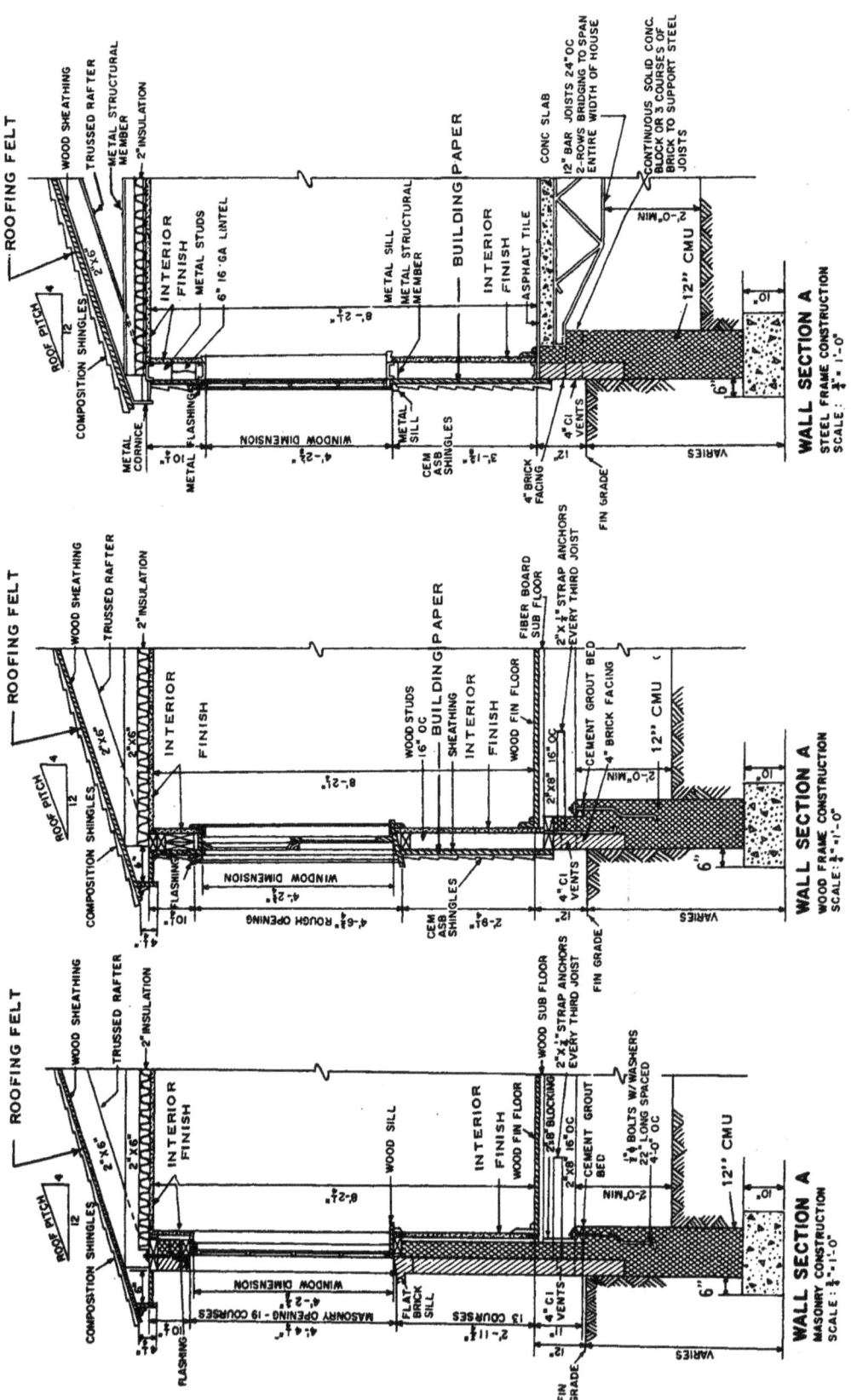

Figure 11.—Wall sections

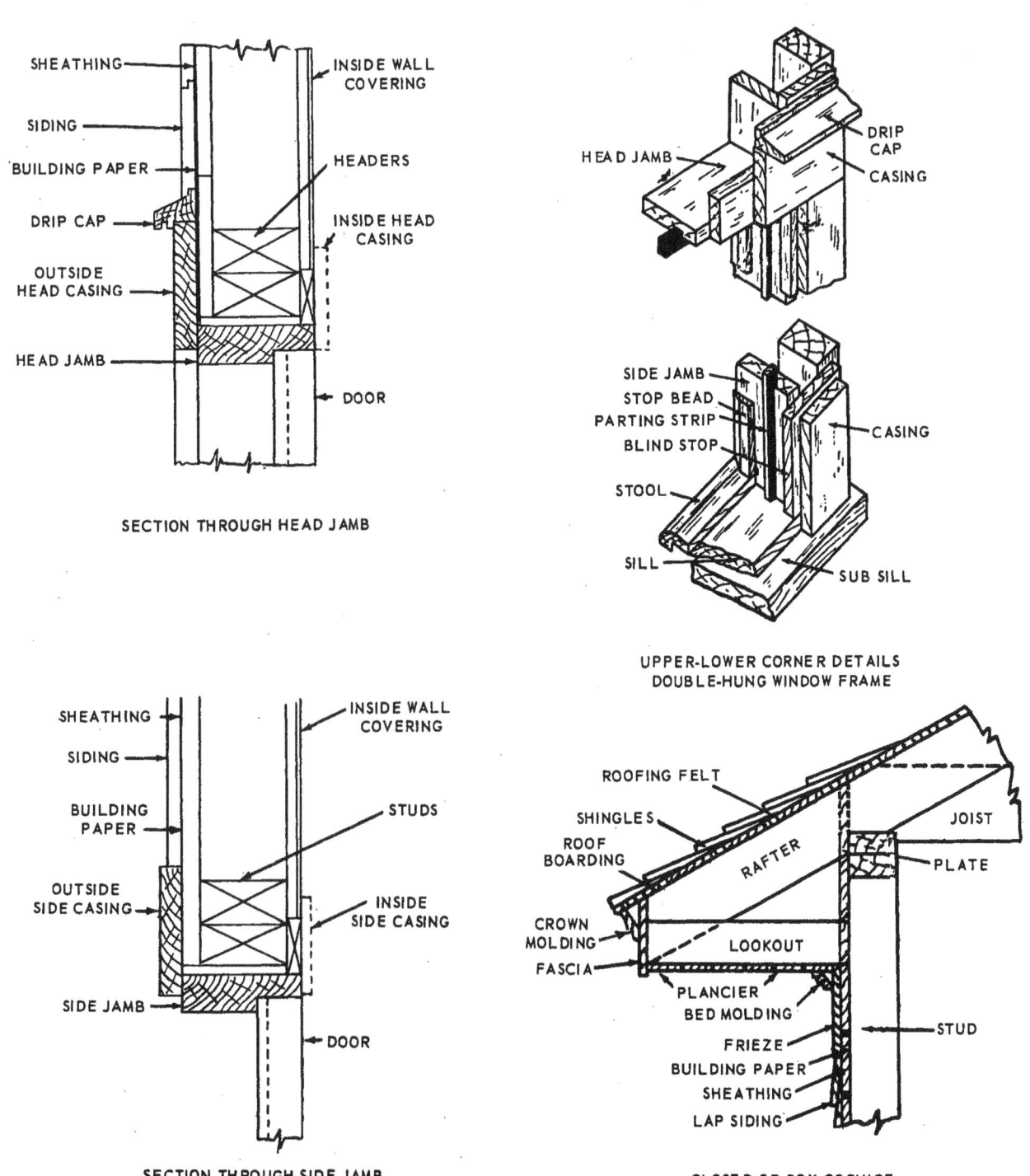

Figure 12.—Door, window and eave details.

specify various quality criteria and standards of workmanship for the various aspects of the rough and finish carpentry work, under such headings as FRAMING; SILLS, PLATES, AND GIRDERS; FLOOR JOISTS AND ROOF RAFTERS; STUDDING; and so on. An example of one of these subsections follows:

STUDDING for walls and partitions shall have doubled plates and doubled stud caps. Studs shall be set plumb and not to exceed 16-in. centers and in true alignment; they shall be bridged with one row of 2 x 4 pieces, set flatwise, fitted tightly, and nailed securely to each stud. Studding shall be doubled around openings and the heads of openings shall rest on the inner studs. Openings in partitions having widths of 4 ft and over shall be trussed. In wood frame construction, studs shall be trebled at corners to form posts.

From the above samples, you can see that a knowledge of the relevant specifications is as essential to the construction supervisor and the construction artisan as a knowledge of the construction drawings.

It is very important that the proper spec be used to cover the material requested. In cases in which the material is not covered by a Government spec, the ASTM (American Society for Testing Materials) spec or some other approved commercial spec may be used. It is EXTREMELY IMPORTANT in using specifications to cite all amendments, including the latest changes.

As a rule, the specs are provided for each project by the A/E (ARCHITECT-ENGINEERS). These are the OFFICIAL guidelines approved by the chief engineer or his representative for use during construction. These requirements should NOT be deviated from without prior approval from proper authority. This approval is usually obtained by means of a change order. When there is disagreement between the specifications and drawings, the specifications should normally be followed; however, check with higher authority in each case.

IV. BUILDER'S MATHEMATICS

The Builder has many occasions for the employment of the processes of ordinary arithmetic, and he must be thoroughly familiar with the methods of determining the areas and volumes of the various plane and solid geometrical figures. Only a few practical applications and a few practical suggestions, will be given here.

RATIO AND PROPORTION

There are a great many practical applications of ratio and proportion in the construction field. A few examples are as follows:

Some dimensions on construction drawings (such as, for example, distances from base lines and elevations of surfaces) are given in ENGINEER'S instead of CARPENTER's measure. Engineer's measure is measure in feet and decimal parts of a foot, or in inches and decimal parts of an inch, such as 100.15 ft or 11.14 in. Carpenter's measure is measure in yards, feet, inches, and even-denominator fractions of an inch, such as 1/2 in., 1/4 in., 1/16 in., 1/32 in., and 1/64 in.

You must know how to convert an engineer's measure given on a construction drawing to a carpenter's measure. Besides this, it will often happen that calculations you make yourself may produce a result in feet and decimal parts of a foot, which result you will have to convert to carpenter's measure. To convert engineer's to carpenter's measure you can use ratio and proportion as follows:

Let's say that you want to convert 100.14 ft to feet and inches to the nearest 1/16 in. The 100 you don't need to convert, since it is already in feet. What you need to do, first, is to find out how many twelfths of a foot (that is, how many inches) there are in 14/100 ft. Set this up as a proportional equation as follows: x:12::14:100.

You know that in a proportional equation the product of the means equals the product of the extremes. Consequently, $100x = (12 \times 14)$, or 168. Then $x = 168/100$, or 1.68 in. Next question is, how many 16ths of an in. are there in 68/100 in.? Set this up, too, as a proportional equation, thus: x:16::68:100. Then $100x = 1088$, and $x = 10\ 88/100$ sixteenths. Since 88/100 of a sixteenth is more than one-half of a sixteenth, you ROUND OFF by calling it 11/16. In 100.14 ft, then, there are 100 ft 1 11/16 in. For example:

A. $\underbrace{x:12::14:100}_{\text{Extremes}}$ means

Product of extremes = product of means:

$$100\ x = 168$$
$$x = 1.68 \text{ IN.}$$

B. $x:16::68:100$

$$100\ x = 1088$$

$$x = 10.88$$

$$x = 10\frac{88}{100} \text{ sixteenths}$$

Rounded off to 11/16

Another way to convert engineer's measurements to carpenter's measurements is to multiply the decimal portion of a foot by 12 to get inches; multiply the decimal by 16 to get the fraction of an inch.

There are many other practical applications of ratio and proportion in the construction field. Suppose, for example, that a table tells you that, for the size and type of brick wall you happen to be laying, 12,321 bricks and 195 cu ft of mortar are required per every 1000 sq ft of wall. How many bricks and how much mortar will be needed for 750 sq ft of the same wall? You simply set up equations as follows; for example:

Brick: $x:750::12,321:1000$
Mortar: $x:750::195:1000$

Brick: $\dfrac{X}{750} = \dfrac{12,321}{1000}$ Cross multiply

$$1000\ X = 9,240,750 \quad \text{Divide}$$
$$X = 9,240.75 = 9241 \text{ Brick.}$$

Mortar: $\dfrac{X}{750} = \dfrac{195}{1000}\cdot$ Cross multiply

$$1000\ X = 146,250 \quad \text{Divide}$$
$$X = 146.25 = 146\ 1/4 \text{ cu ft}$$

Suppose, for another example, that the ingredient proportions by volume for the type of concrete you are making are 1 cu ft cement to 1.7 cu ft sand to 2.8 cu ft coarse aggregate. Suppose you know as well, by reference to a table, that ingredients combined in the amounts indicated will produce 4.07 cu ft of concrete. How much of each ingredient will be required to make a cu yd of concrete?

Remember here, first, that there are not 9, but 27 (3 ft x 3 ft x 3 ft) cu ft in a cu yd. Your proportional equations will be as follows:

Cement: $x:27::1:4.07$

Sand: $x:27::1.7:4.07$

Coarse aggregate: $x:27::2.8:4.07$

Cement: $x:27::1:4.07$

$$\frac{x}{27} = \frac{1}{4.07}$$

$$4.07\ x = 27$$

$$x = 6.63 \text{ cu ft Cement}$$

Sand: $x:27::1.7:4.07$

$$\frac{x}{27} = \frac{1.7}{4.07}$$

$$4.07\ x = 45.9$$

$$x = 11.28 \text{ cu ft Sand}$$

Coarse aggregate: $x:27::2.8:407$

$$\frac{x}{27} = \frac{2.8}{4.07}$$

$$4.07\ x = 75.6$$

$$x = 18.57 \text{ cu ft Coarse aggregate}$$

ARITHMETICAL OPERATIONS

The formulas for finding the area and volume of geometric figures are expressed in algebraic equations which are called formulas. A few of the more important formulas and their mathematical solutions will be discussed in this section.

To get an area, you multiply 2 linear measures together, and to get a volume you multiply 3 linear measures together. The linear measures you multiply together must all be expressed in the SAME UNITS; you cannot, for example, multiply a length in feet by a width in inches to get a result in square feet or in square inches.

Dimensions of a feature on a construction drawing are not always given in the same units. For a concrete wall, for example, the length and height are usually given in feet and the thickness in inches. Furthermore, you may want to get a result in units which are different from any shown on the drawing. Concrete volume, for example, is usually expressed in cubic yards, while the dimensions of concrete work are given on the drawings in feet and inches.

You can save yourself a good many steps in calculating by using fractions to convert the original dimension units into the desired end-result units. Take 1 in., for example. To express 1 in. in feet, you simply put it over 12, thus: 1/12 ft. To express 1 in. in yards, you simply put it over 36, thus: 1/36 yd. In the same manner, to express 1 ft in yards you simply put it over 3, thus: 1/3 yd.

Suppose now that you want to calculate the number of cu yd of concrete in a wall 32 ft long by 14 ft high by 8 in. thick. You can express all these in yards and set up your problem thus:

$$\frac{32}{3} \times \frac{14}{3} \times \frac{8}{36}$$

Next you can cancel out, thus:

$$\frac{\cancel{32}^{16}}{3} \times \frac{\cancel{14}}{3} \times \frac{8}{\cancel{36}_{\cancel{18}_9}} = \frac{896}{81}$$

Dividing 896 by 81, you get 11.06 cu yds of concrete in the wall.

The right triangle is a triangle which contains one right (90°) angle. The following letters will denote the parts of the triangle indicated in figure 2-13—a = altitude, b = base, c = hypotenuse.

In solving a right triangle, the length of any side may be found if the lengths of the other two sides are given. The combinations of 3-4-5 (lengths of sides) or any multiple of these combinations will come out to a whole number. The following examples show the formula for finding

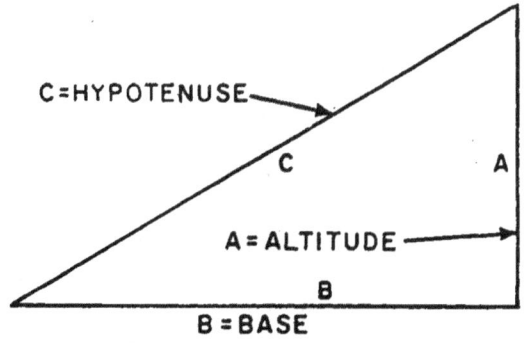

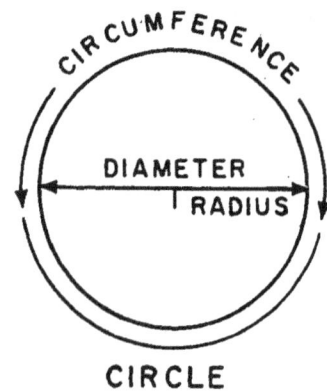

Figure 13.—Right triangle and circle.

each side. Each of these formulas is derived from the master formula $c^2 = a^2 + b^2$.

(1) Find c when a = 3, and b = 4.

$$c = \sqrt{a^2 + b^2} = \sqrt{3^2 + 4^2} = \sqrt{9 + 16} = \sqrt{25} = 5$$

(2) Find a when b = 8, and c = 10.

$$a = \sqrt{c^2 - b^2} = \sqrt{10^2 - 8^2} = \sqrt{100 - 64} = \sqrt{36} = 6$$

(3) Find b when a = 9, and c = 15.

$$b = \sqrt{c^2 - a^2} = \sqrt{15^2 - 9^2} = \sqrt{225 - 81} = \sqrt{144} = 12.$$

There are tables from which the square roots of numbers may be found; otherwise, they may be found arithmetically as explained later in this chapter.

Areas And Volumes Of Geometric Figures

This section on areas and volumes of geometric figures will be limited to the most commonly used geometric figures. Reference books, such as Mathematics, Vol. 1, are available for additional information if needed. Areas are expressed in square units and volumes in cubic units.

1. A circle is a plane figure bounded by a curved line every point of which is the same distance from the center.
    a. The curved line is called the circumference.
    b. A straight line drawn from the center to any point on the circumference is called a radius. (r = 1/2 the diameter.)
    c. A straight line drawn from one point of the circumference through the center and terminating on the opposite point of the circumference is called a diameter. (d = 2 times the radius.) See figure 2-13.
    d. The area of a circle is found by the following formulas: $A = \pi r^2$ or $A = .7854 d^2$. (π is pronounced pie = 3.1416 or 3 1/7, .7854 is 1/4 of π.) Example: Find the area of a circle whose radius is 7". $A = \pi r^2 = 3\ 1/7 \times 7^2 = 22/7 \times 49 = 154$ sq in. If you use the second formula you obtain the same results.
    e. The circumference of a circle is found by multiplying π times the diameter or 2 times π times the radius. Example: Find the circumference of a circle whose diameter is 56 inches. $C = \pi d = 3.1415 \times 56 = 175.9296$ inches.

2. The area of a right triangle is equal to one-half the product of the base by the altitude. (Area = 1/2 base x altitude.) Example: Find the area of a triangle whose base is 16" and altitude 6". Solution:

$$A = 1/2\ bh = 1/2 \times 16 \times 6 = 48 \text{ sq in.}$$

3. The volume of a cylinder is found by multiplying the area of the base times the height. ($V = 3.1416 \times r^2 \times h$). Example: Find the volume of a cylinder which has a radius of 8 in. and a height of 4 ft. Solution:

$$8 \text{ in} = \frac{2}{3} \text{ ft and } \left(\frac{2}{3}\right)2 = \frac{4}{9} \text{ sq ft.}$$

$$V = 3.1416 \times \frac{4}{9} \times 4 = \frac{50.2656}{9} = 5.59 \text{ cu ft.}$$

4. The volume of a rectangular solid equals the length x width x height. (V = lwh.) Example: Find the volume of a rectangular solid which has a length of 6 ft, a width of 3 ft, and a height of 2 ft. Solution:

$$V = lwh = 6 \times 3 \times 2 = 36 \text{ cu ft.}$$

5. The volume of a cone may be found by multiplying one-third times the area of the base times the height.

$$\left(V = \frac{1}{3} \pi r^2 h\right)$$

Example: Find the volume of a cone when the radius of its base is 2 ft and its height is 9 ft. Solution:

$$\pi = 3.1416, r = 2, 2^2 = 4$$

$$V = \frac{1}{3} r^2 h = \frac{1}{3} \times 3.1416 \times 4 \times 9 = 37.70 \text{ cu ft.}$$

Powers And Roots

1. Powers—When we multiply several numbers together, as 2 x 3 x 4 = 24, the numbers 2, 3, and 4 are factors and 24 the product. The operation of raising a number to a power is a special case of multiplication in which the factors are all equal. The power of a number is the number of times the number itself is to be taken as a factor. Example: 2^4 is 16. The second power is called the square of the number, as 3^2. The third power of a number is called the cube of the number, as 5^3. The exponent of a number is a number placed to the right and above a base to show how many times the base is used as a factor. Example:

$$4^3 \leftarrow \text{exponent} = \\ \leftarrow \text{base}$$

$$4 \times 4 \times 4 = 64.$$

2. Roots—To indicate a root, use the sign $\sqrt{\ }$, which is called the radical sign. A small figure, called the index of the root, is placed in the opening of the sign to show which root is to be taken. The square root of a number is one of the two equal factors into which a number is

divided. Example: $\sqrt{81} = \sqrt{9 \times 9} = 9$. The cube root is one of the three equal factors into which a number is divided. Example: $\sqrt[3]{125} = \sqrt[3]{5 \times 5 \times 5} = 5$.

Square Root

1. The square root of any number is that number which, when multiplied by itself, will produce the first number. For example; the square root of 121 is 11 because 11 times 11 equals 121.

2. How to extract the square root arithmetically:

```
                    95.
   √9025     √90'25.

            : -81

       180 : 925
       +5  : -925

       185 : 000
```

a. Begin at the decimal point and divide the given number into groups of 2 digits each (as far as possible), going from right to left and/or left to right.
b. Find the greatest number (9) whose square is contained in the first or left hand group (90). Square this number (9) and place it under the first pair of digits (90), then subtract.
c. Bring down the next pair of digits (25) and add it to the remainder (9).
d. Multiply the first digit in the root by 20 and use it as a trial divisor (180). This trial divisor (180) will go into the new dividend (925) five times. This number, 5 (second digit in the root), is added back to the trial divisor, obtaining the true divisor (185).
e. The true divisor (185) is multiplied by the second digit (5) and placed under the remainder (925). Subtract and the problem is solved.
f. If there is still a remainder and you want to carry the problem further, add zeros (in pairs) and continue the above process.

Coverage Calculations

You will frequently have occasion to estimate the number of linear feet of boards of a given size, or the number of tiles, asbestos shingles, and the like, required to cover a given area. Let's take the matter of linear feet of boards first.

What you do here is calculate, first, the number of linear feet of board required to cover 1 sq ft. For boards laid edge-to-edge, you base your calculations on the total width of a board. For boards which will lap each other, you base your calculations on the width laid TO THE WEATHER, meaning the total width minus the width of the lap.

Since there are 144 sq in. in a sq ft, linear footage to cover a given area can be calculated as follows. Suppose your boards are to be laid 8 in. to the weather. If you divide 8 in. into 144 sq in., the result (which is 18 in., or 1.5 ft) will be the linear footage required to cover a sq ft. If you have, say, 100 sq ft to cover, the linear footage required will be 100 x 1.5, or 150 ft.

To estimate the number of tiles, asbestos shingles, and the like required to cover a given area, you first calculate the number of units required to cover a sq ft. Suppose, for example, you are dealing with 9 in. x 9 in. asphalt tiles. The area of one of these is 9 in. x 9 in. or 81 sq in. In a sq ft there are 144 sq in. If it takes 1 to cover 81 sq in., how many will it take to cover 144 sq in.? Just set up a proportional equation, as follows.

$$1:81::x:144$$

When you work this out, you will find that it takes 1.77 tiles to cover a sq ft. To find the number of tiles required to cover 100 sq ft, simply multiply by 100. How do you multiply anything by 100? Just move the decimal point 2 places to the right. Consequently, it takes 177 9 x 9 asphalt tiles to cover 100 sq ft of area.

Board Measure

BOARD MEASURE is a method of measuring lumber in which the basic unit is an abstract volume 1 ft long by 1 ft wide by 1 in. thick. This abstract volume or unit is called a BOARD FOOT.

There are several formulas for calculating the number of board feet in a piece of given dimensions. Since lumber dimensions are most frequently indicated by width and thickness in inches and length in feet, the following formula is probably the most practical.

$$\frac{\text{Thickness in in. x width in in. x length in ft}}{12}$$

= board feet

Suppose you are calculating the number of board feet in a 14-ft length of 2 x 4. Applying the formula, you get:

$$\frac{\overset{1}{\cancel{2}} \times \overset{2}{\cancel{4}} \times 14}{\underset{\underset{3}{\cancel{6}}}{\cancel{12}}} = \frac{28}{3} = 9\ 1/3\ \text{bd ft}$$

The chief practical use of board measure is in cost calculations, since lumber is bought and sold by the board foot. Any lumber less than 1 in. thick is presumed to be 1 in. thick for board measure purposes. Board measure is calculated on the basis of the NOMINAL, not the ACTUAL, dimensions of lumber.

The actual size of a piece of dimension lumber (such as a 2 x 4, for example) is usually less than the nominal size.

CONSTRUCTION PRINT READING

Section I. WORKING DRAWINGS

1. Introduction

a. Working drawings plus specifications are the main sources of information for supervisors and technicians responsible for the actual work of construction. The construction working drawing gives a complete graphic description of the structure to be erected, the construction site, the materials to be used, and the construction method to be followed. Most construction drawings consist of orthographic views (right angles and perpendicular lines). A set of working drawings includes both general and detail drawings. General drawings consist of plans and elevations, while detail drawings consist of sections and detail views.

b. Site plans, elevations, floor plans, sections, and details are described in this section together with the most common architectural symbols and material conventions in military use.

2. Architectural Symbols and Material Conventions

a. Architectural Symbols. Architectural symbols on construction plans show the type and location of doors, windows, and other features. They have the same general shape as the feature itself and show any motion that is supposed to occur. Figure 1 shows several of these symbols.

b. Material Conventions. Material conventions are symbols that show the type of material used in the structure. Appendix B illustrates those for the more common types of materials. The symbol selected normally represents the material in some way where possible. For example, the symbol for wood shows the grains in the wood. It is not always possible to use a common characteristic of the material for the symbol. The carpenter should know all these symbols for materials to help him read a construction print. A symbol should always be checked if there is any doubt about its meaning.

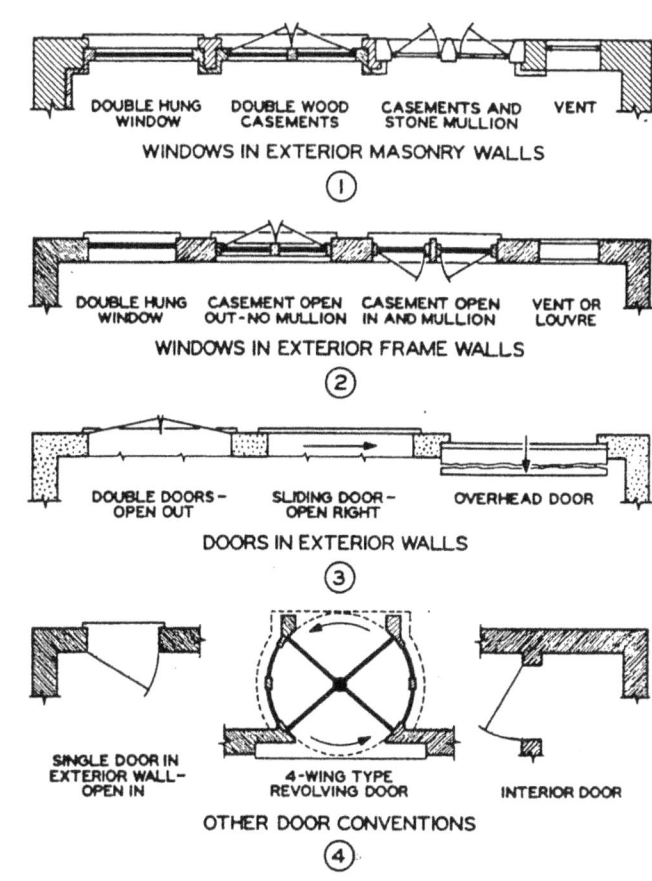

Figure 1. Window, door, and wall symbols.

3. Site Plans

a. A site plan (also called plot plan) shows all necessary property lines and locations, contours and profiles, building lines, location of structures to be constructed, existing structures, approaches, finished grades, existing and new utilities such as sewer, water, gas, and the like. Figure 2 shows a typical site plan. Appropriate outlines show the location of the new facility. The site plan has a north-pointing arrow to indicate site north (not magnetic north). Each facility has a number (or code letter) to identify it in the schedule

155

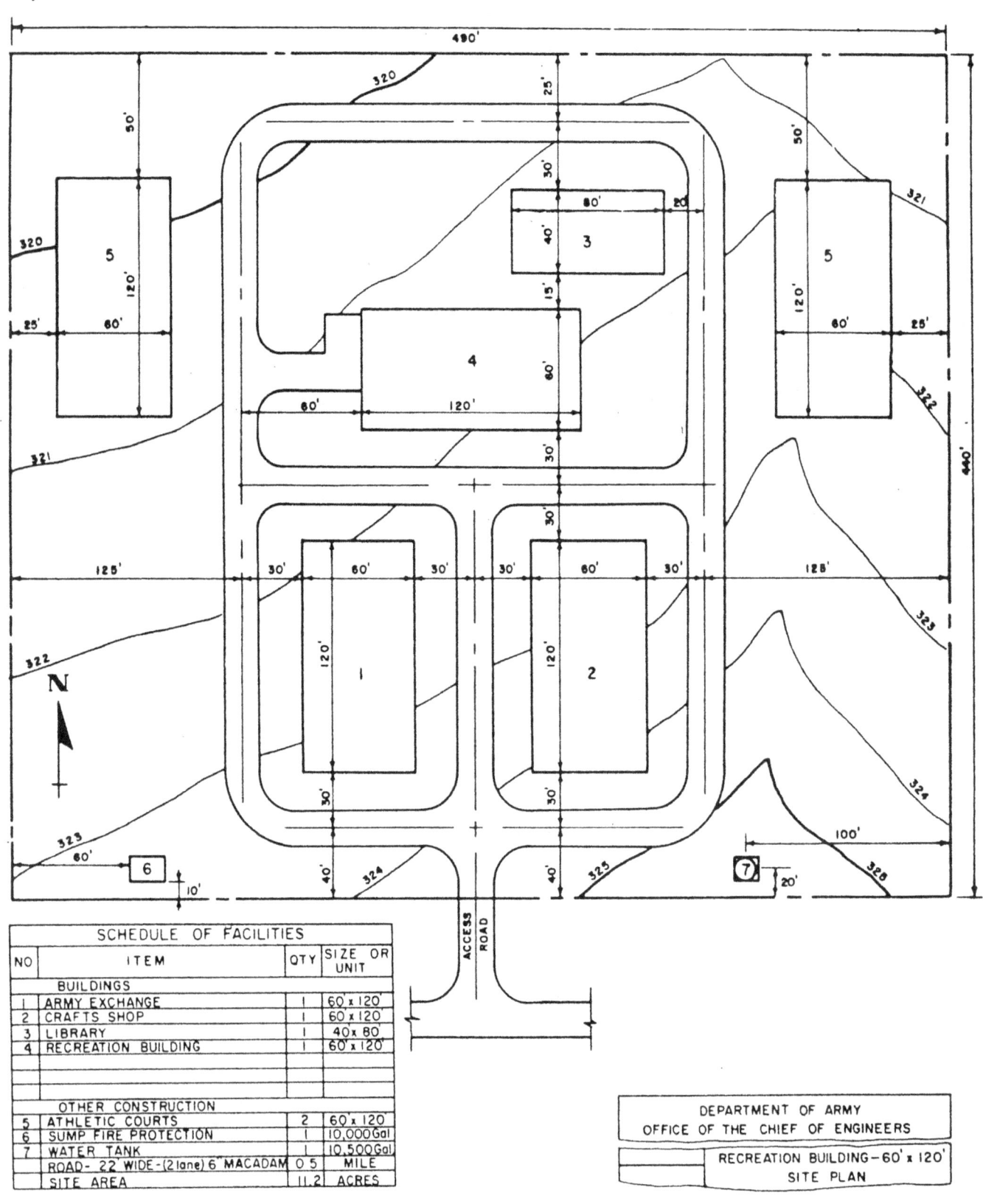

Figure 2. Typical site plan.

of facilities. The contour lines show the elevation of the earth surfaces; all points on a contour have the same elevation. Distances are given between principal details and reference lines. (The coordinate reference lines on figure 2 are centerlines of the roads surrounding the area.) All distances in a plan view simply give the horizontal measurement between two points and do not show terrain irregularities. The sizes of proposed facilities are given in the schedule of facilities.

b. Examine the site plan shown in figure 2 to see what information can be obtained from it. For example, the contour lines show that the ground surface of the site area slopes. The plan locates and identifies each facility. Most of the facilities are spaced at least 60 feet apart, while the library (facility No. 3) and the recreation building (facility No. 4) must be only 15 feet apart. Besides being the smallest of the four buildings, the library is closest to the road; that is, the east wall of the library is 20 feet from the centerline of the road, while the other buildings are 30 or 60 feet from the centerline.

4. Elevations

a. Elevations are drawings that show the front, rear, or side view of a building or structure. Sample elevation views are given in figure 3. Construction materials may be shown on the elevation. It may also show the ground level surrounding the structure, called the grade. When more than one view is shown on a drawing sheet, each view is given a title. If any view has a scale different from that shown in the title block, the scale is given beneath the title of that view.

b. The centerline symbol of alternate long and short dashes in an elevation shows finished floor lines. Foundations below the grade line are shown by the hidden line symbol of short, evenly spaced dashes. Note in figure 3 that the footings are shown below grade.

c. Elevations show the locations and kind of doors and windows. Each different type window shown in the elevations is marked (in figure 3, the three types of windows are marked W-1, W-2, and W-3). These identifying marks refer to a particular size window whose dimensions are given in a table known as the window schedule. In some cases, the rough opening dimensions of

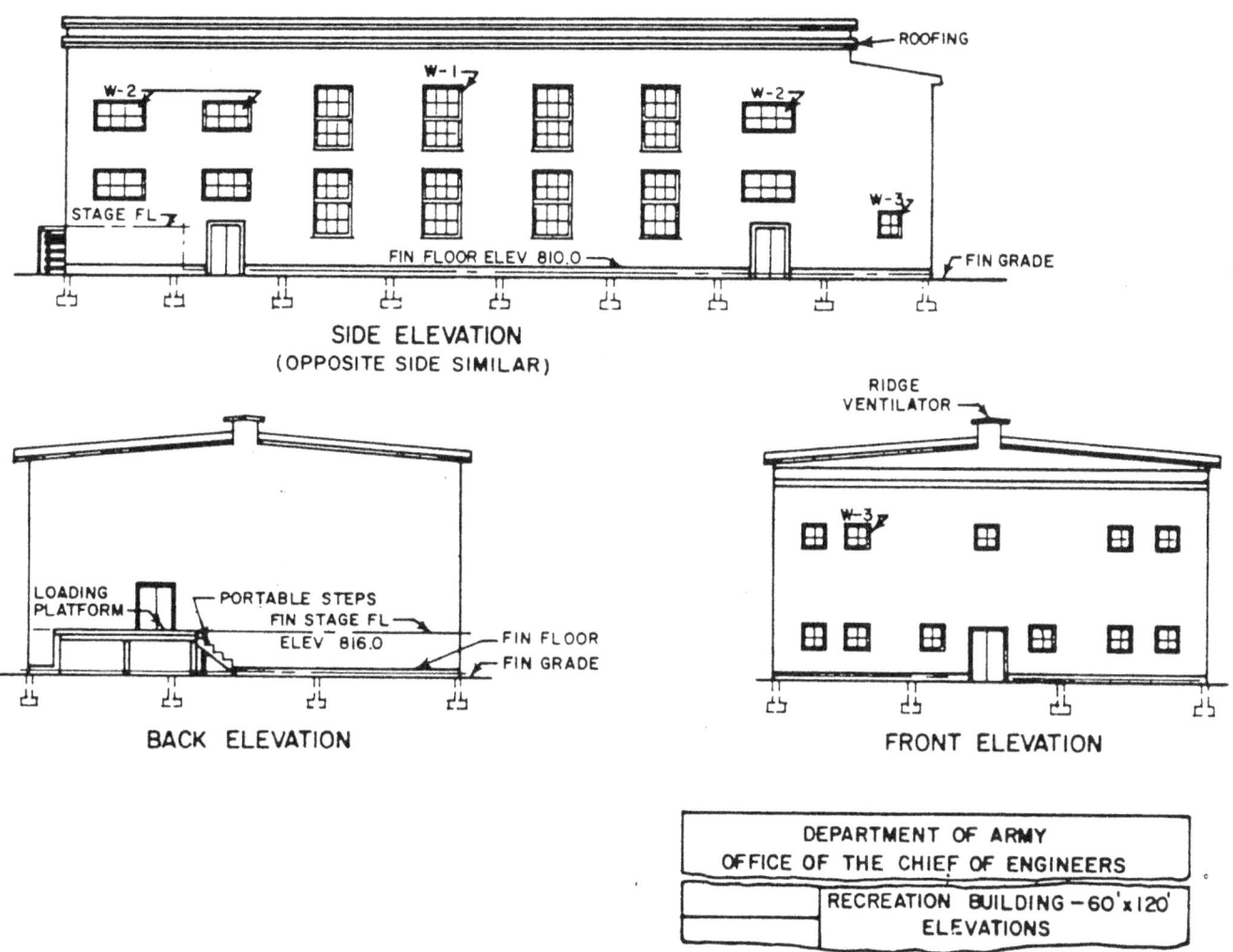

Figure 3. Elevation views.

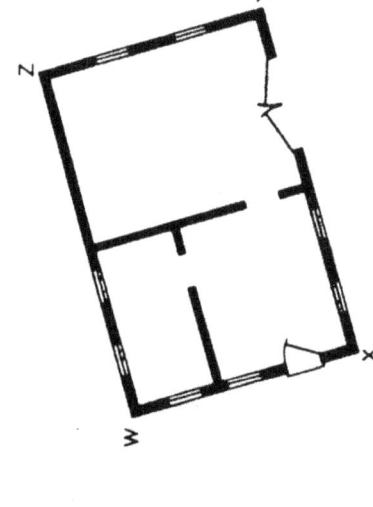

DEVELOPED FLOOR PLAN ABCD

DEVELOPED FLOOR PLAN WXYZ

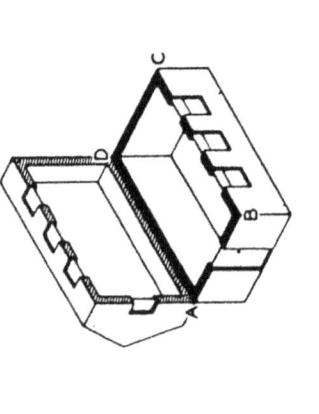
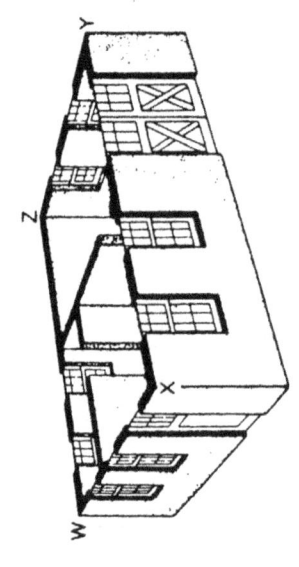

PREVIOUS PERSPECTIVE VIEW AT CUTTING PLANE ABCD, HINGED AND TOP LAID BACK

PREVIOUS PERSPECTIVE VIEW AT CUTTING PLANE WXYZ, TOP REMOVED

PLAN DEVELOPMENT – SIMPLE BUILDING (1)

PLAN DEVELOPMENT – TYPICAL T.O. BUILDING (2)

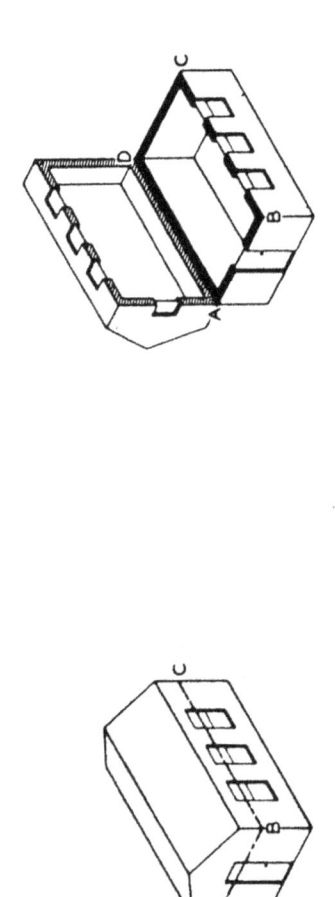

PERSPECTIVE VIEW OF A SIMPLE BUILDING SHOWING CUTTING PLANE ABC

PERSPECTIVE VIEW OF A TYPICAL T/O BUILDING SHOWING CUTTING PLANE WXY

Figure 4. Floor plan development.

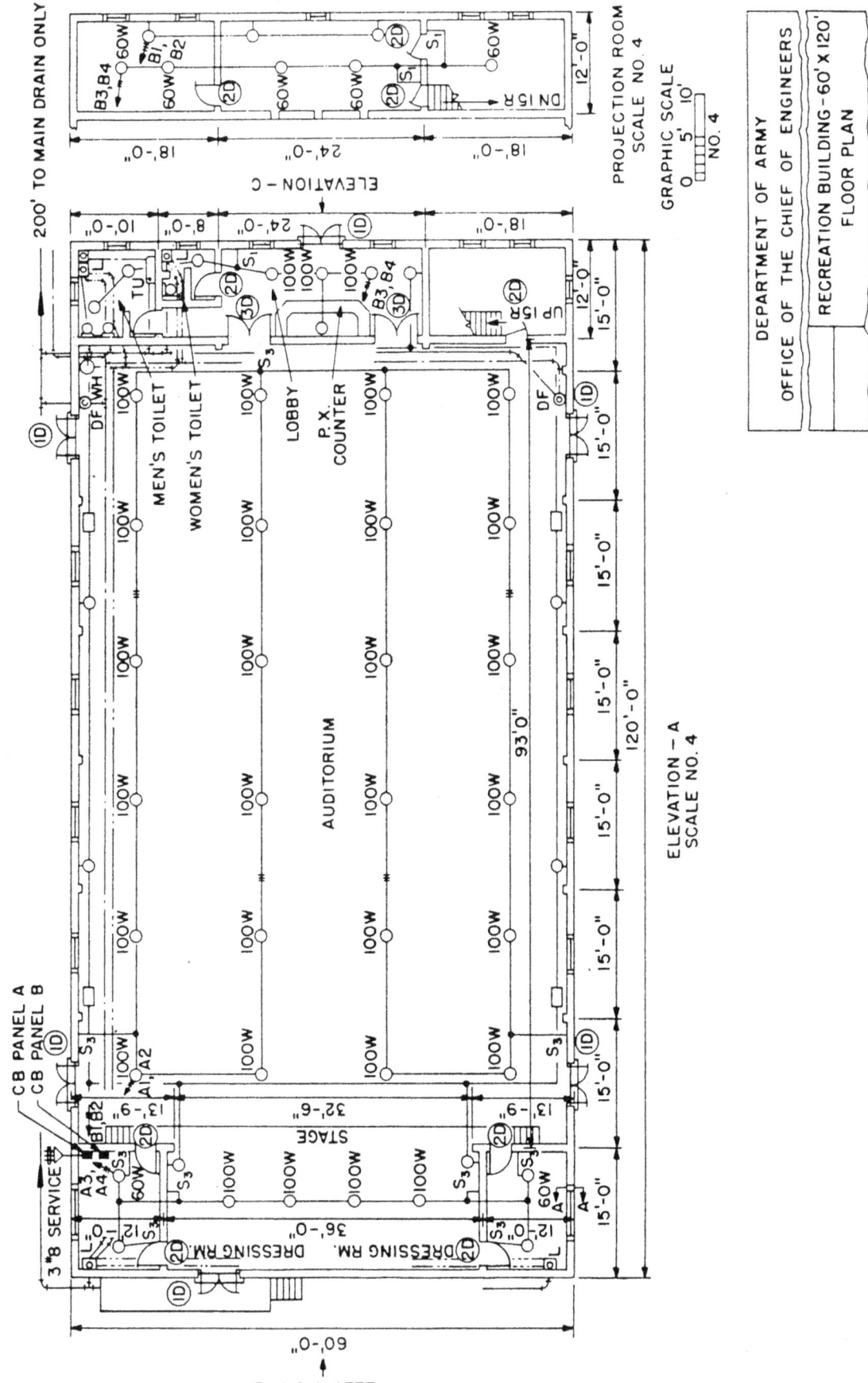

Figure 5. Typical floor plan.

windows are given on the drawing. Note that the recreation building shown in figure 3 has two double doors on each side and a double door at each end. The elevation also shows that at the end of the building with loading platform, the door is at the level of the stage floor and all the other doors are at grade level.

5. Floor Plans

a. A floor plan is a cross-sectional view of a building. The horizontal cut crosses all openings regardless of their height from the floor. The development of a floor plan is shown in figure 4. Note that a floor plan shows the outside shape of the building; the arrangement, size, and shape of the rooms; the type of materials; and the length, thickness, and character of the building walls at a particular floor. A floor plan also includes the type, width, and location of the doors and windows; the types and locations of utility installations; and the location of stairways. A typical floor plan is shown in figure 2

b. Read the floor plan shown in figure 5 and note the features of the recreation building. Basically, the lines with small circles show wiring for electrical outlets; appropriate symbols show the plumbing fixtures. These features are important to the carpenter from the standpoint of coordination. He may have to make special provisions, at various stages of construction, for the placement of electrical or plumbing fixtures. These provisions should be studied on the floor plan and coordinated with the electrician, plumber, and foreman.

c. Figure 6 shows how a stairway is drawn in a plan and how riser-tread information is given. The symbol shows the direction of the stairs from the floor shown in the plan and the amount of risers in the run. For example, 17 DN followed by an arrow means that there are 17 risers in the run of stairs going from the floor shown on the plan to the floor below in the direction indicated by the arrow. The riser-tread diagram provides height and width information. The standard for the riser, or height from step-to-step, is from 6 1/2 to 7 1/2 inches. The tread width is usually such that the sum of riser and tread is about 18 inches (a 7-inch riser and 11-

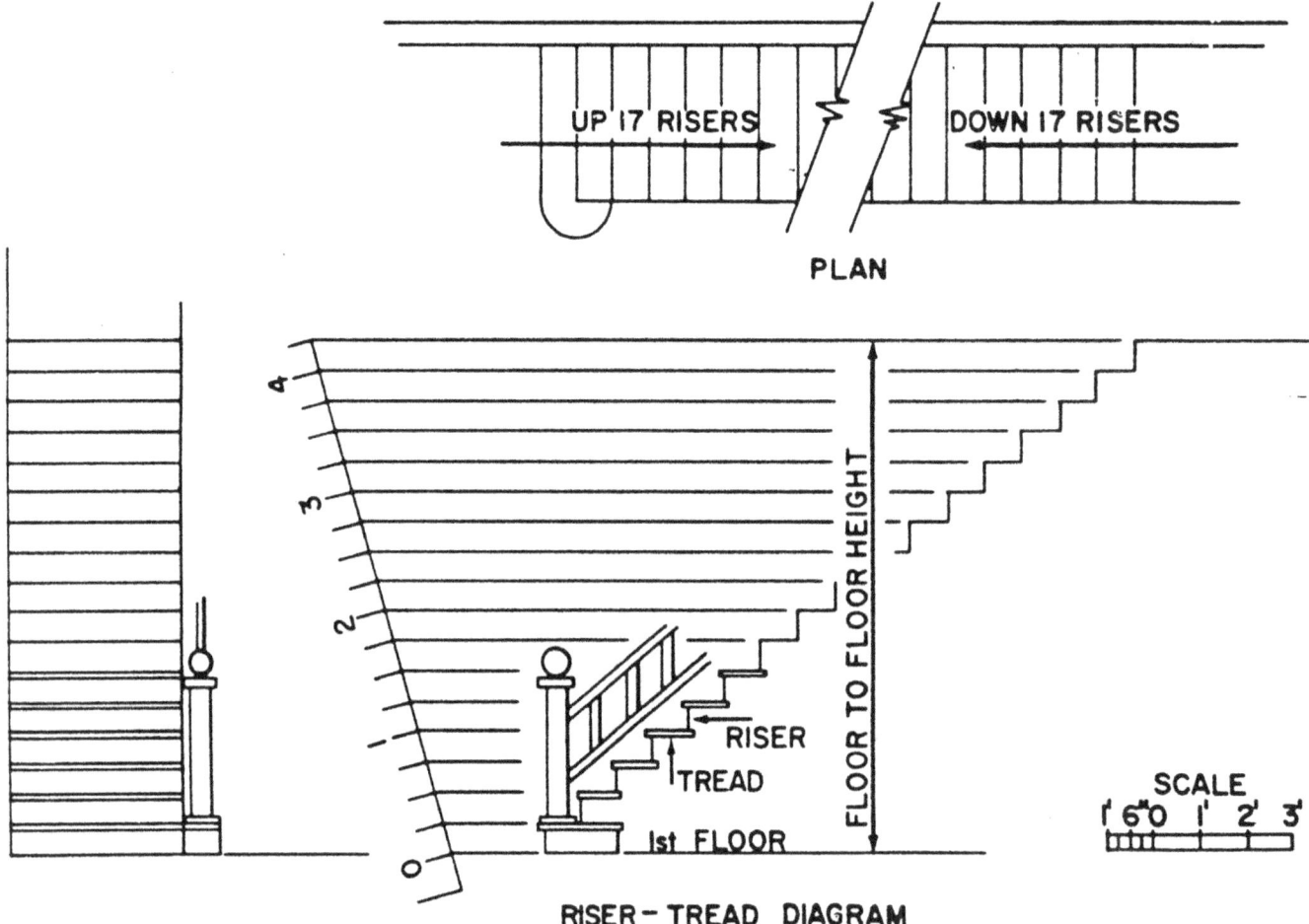

Figure 6. Stairway and steps.

inch tread is standard). On the plan, the distance between the riser lines is the width of the tread.

d. By examining the floor plan (fig. 5) it is seen that the interior of the building will consist of an auditorium, a lobby with a P.X. counter, a men's toilet, a women's toilet, a projection room on a second level above the lobby, two dressing rooms, and a stage. The stage may not be apparent but, by noting the steps adjacent to each dressing room, it can be seen that there is a change in elevation. The elevation view, as in figure 3, will show the stage and its elevation. The plan gives the dimensions of the areas specified. Note that all building entrances and/or exit doors are the same type (1D) and that all windows are the double-hung type. All interior single doors (2D) are the same and two double doors (3D) open into the lobby from the auditorium. The projection room will be reached via a 15-riser stairway located in a 12- by 18-foot room. Entrances to this room will be from the auditorium through a single door opening into the room. At the top of the stairway, a single door opens into the projection room. The wall of the projection room that faces the stage (inside wall) has three openings. Note that no windows are shown for the sides of the building where the projection room is located, but are shown at the main level.

e. The symbols shown in figure 7 are typical representations of exterior and interior walls. Note how the material conventions are used in the makeup of the symbols for masonry, brick, and concrete walls. The carpenter should become familiar with these symbols, which can be found in appendix B.

6. Sections

a. A section shows how a structure looks when

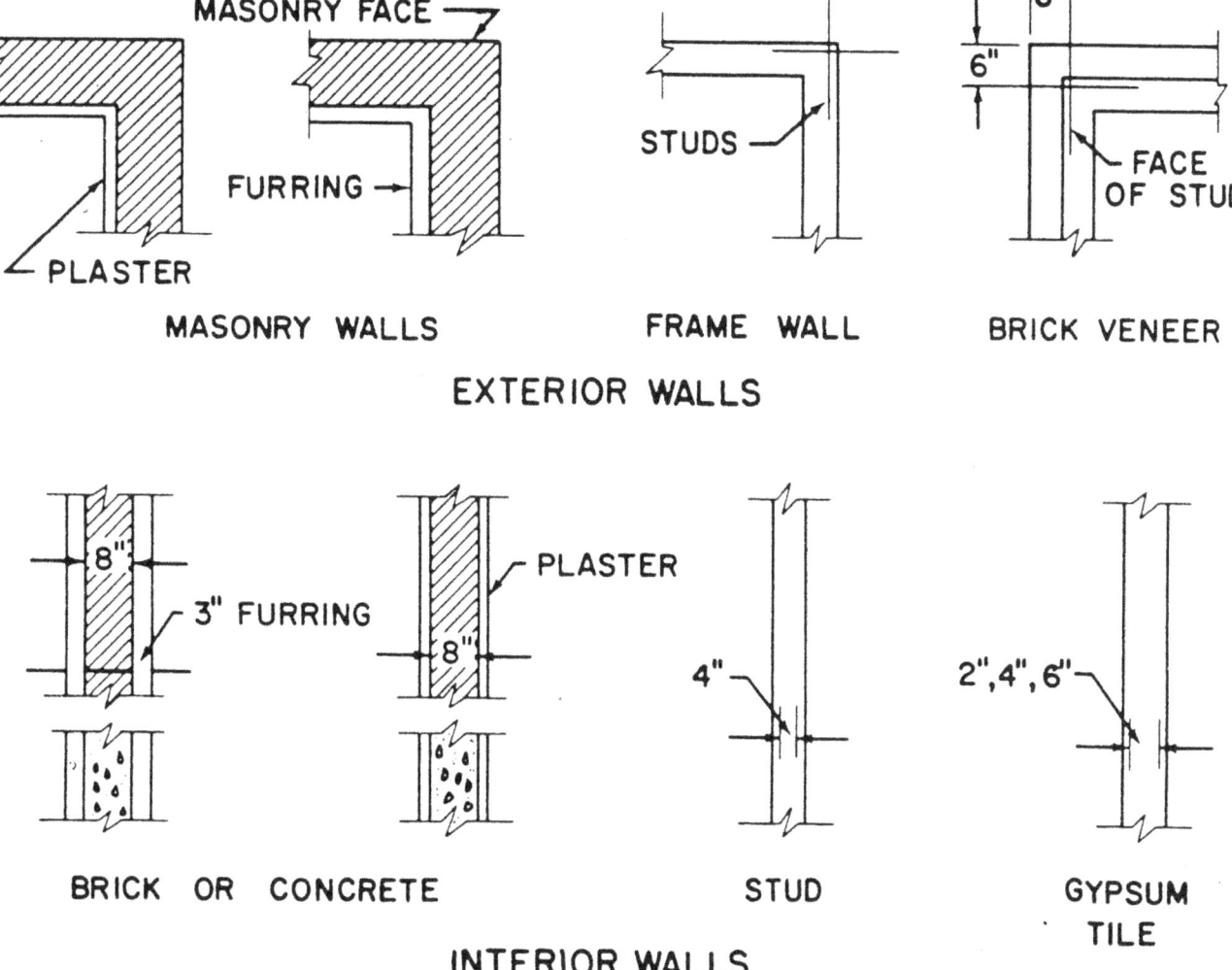

Figure 7. Typical wall symbols.

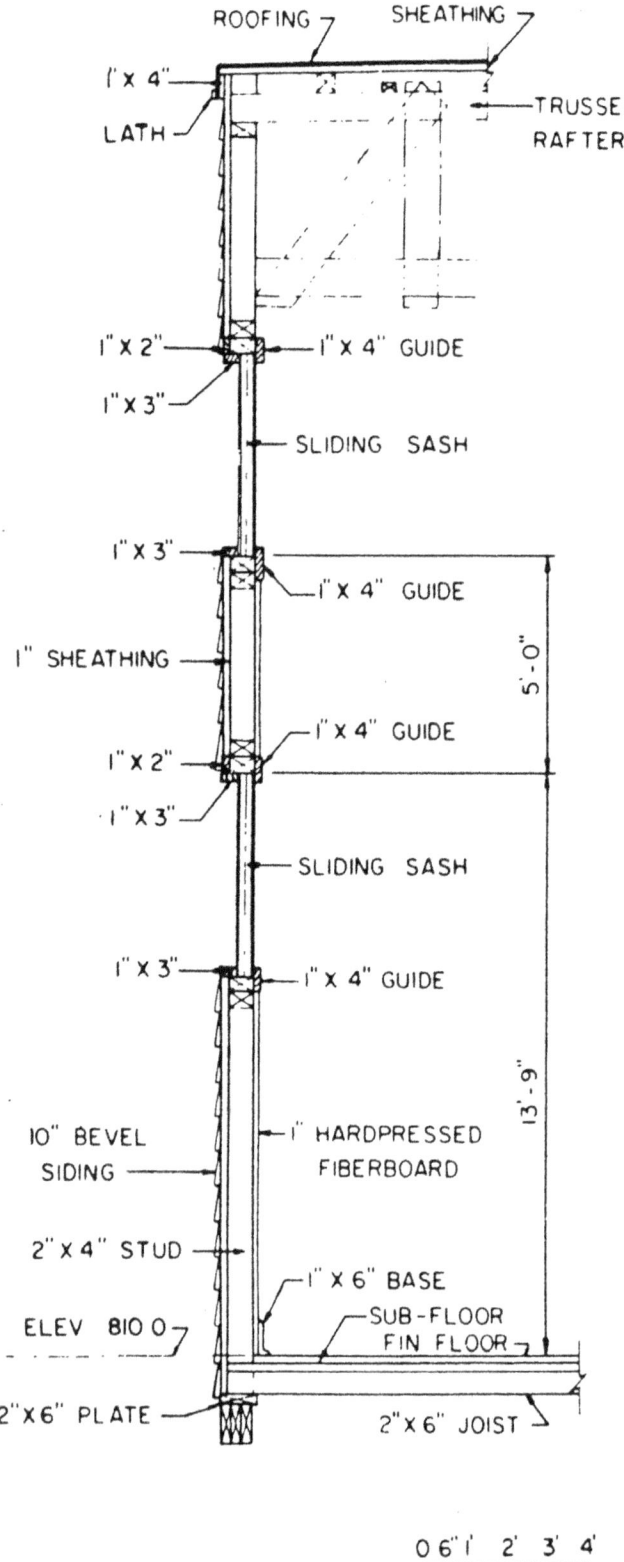

Figure 8. Typical wall section.

EXTERIOR DOOR DETAILS

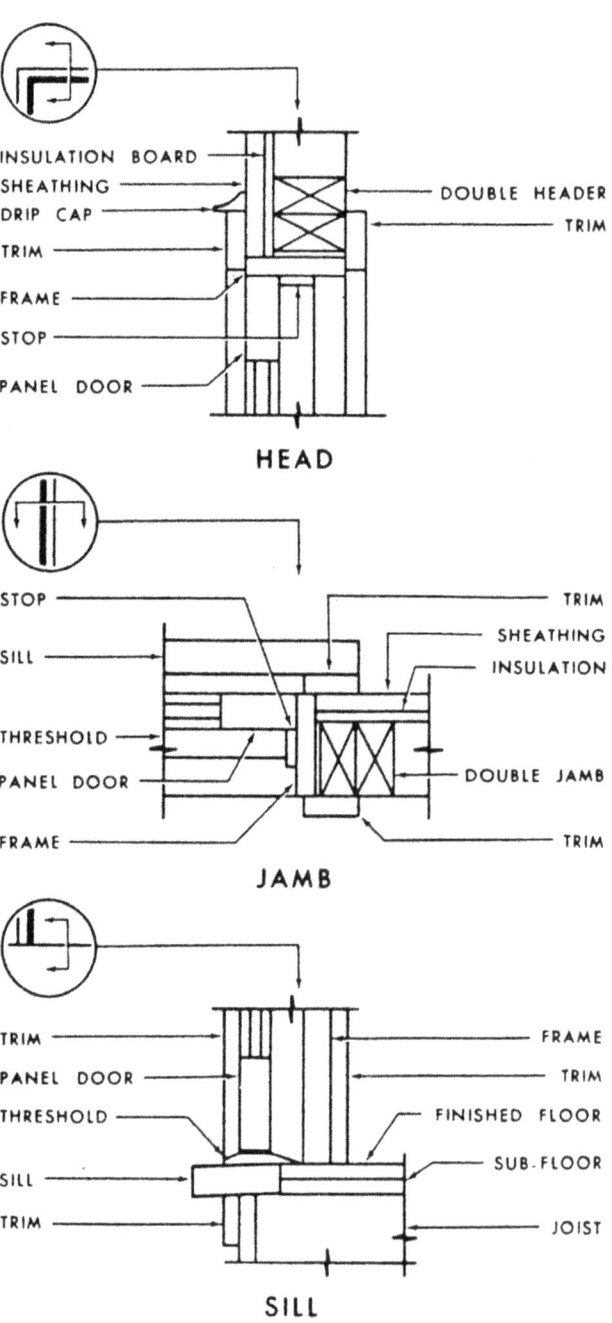

Figure 9. Typical door details.

general drawing. The section provides information on height, materials, fastening and support systems, and concealed features.

b. Of primary importance to construction supervisors and to the craftsmen who do the actual building are the wall sections. These show the construction of the wall as well as the way in which structural members and other features are joined to it. Wall sections extend vertically from the foundation bed to the roof. A typical wall cut vertically by a cutting plane. It is drawn to a large scale showing details of a particular construction feature that cannot be given in the

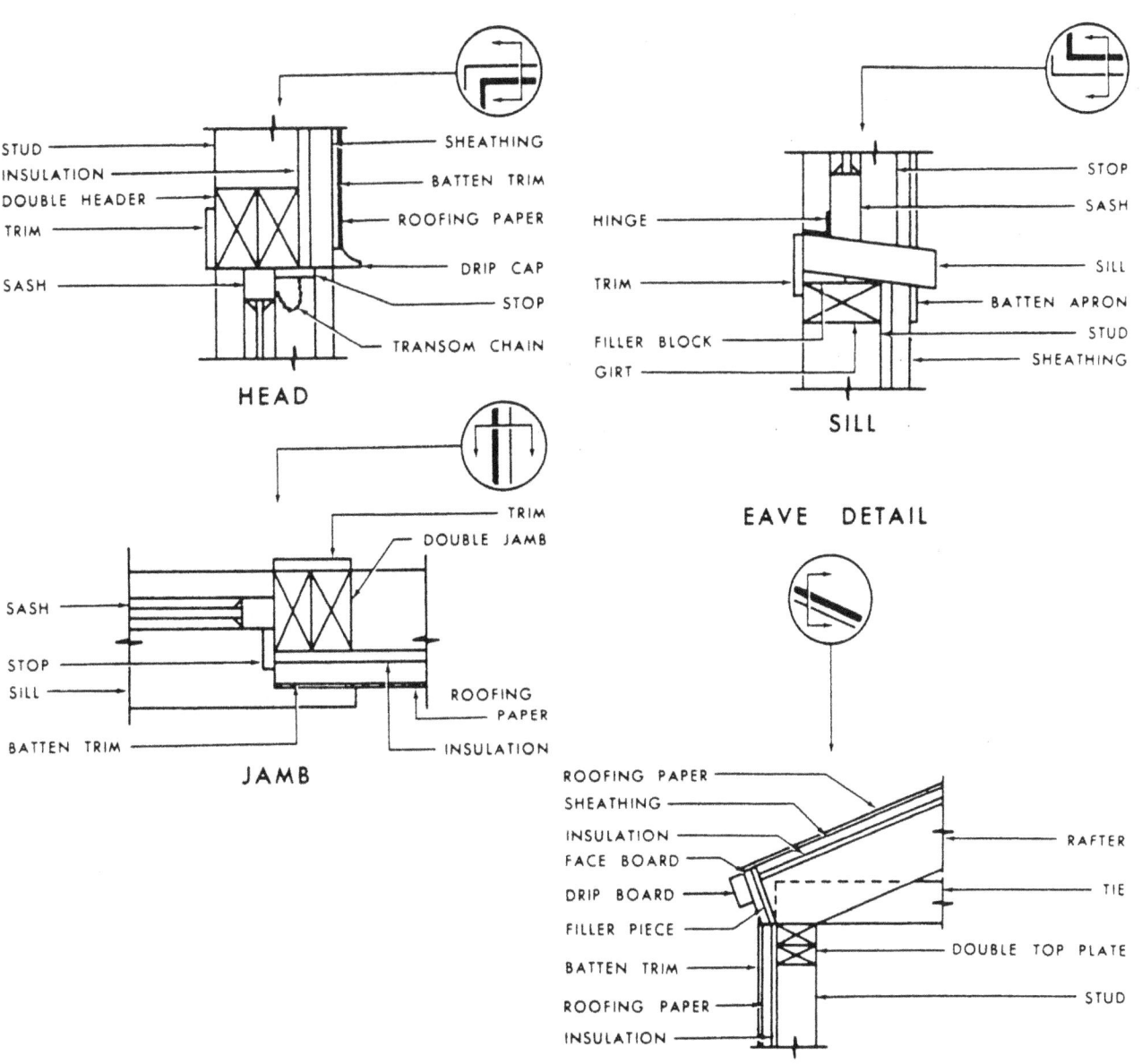

Figure 10. Typical window and eave details.

section with the parts identified by name and/or size is illustrated in figure 8.

7. Details

Details are large scale drawings which show features that do not appear (or appear on too small a scale) on the plans, elevations, and sections. Details do not have a cutting-plane indication, but are simply noted by a code. The construction of doors, windows, and eaves is usually shown in detail drawings. Figure 9 shows some typical door framing details and figure 10 shows that of window wood framing and an eave detail for a simple type of cornice. Other details which are customarily shown are sills, girder and joist connections, and stairways.

Section II. LIGHT AND HEAVY WOOD FRAMING

8. Light Wood Framing

Framing is the rough timberwork of a building. It includes exterior walls, flooring, roofing, beams, trusses, partitions, and ceilings. Working prints for theater of operations type buildings usually show details of all framing. Light framing is used in barracks, bathhouses, administration buildings, light shop buildings, hospital build-

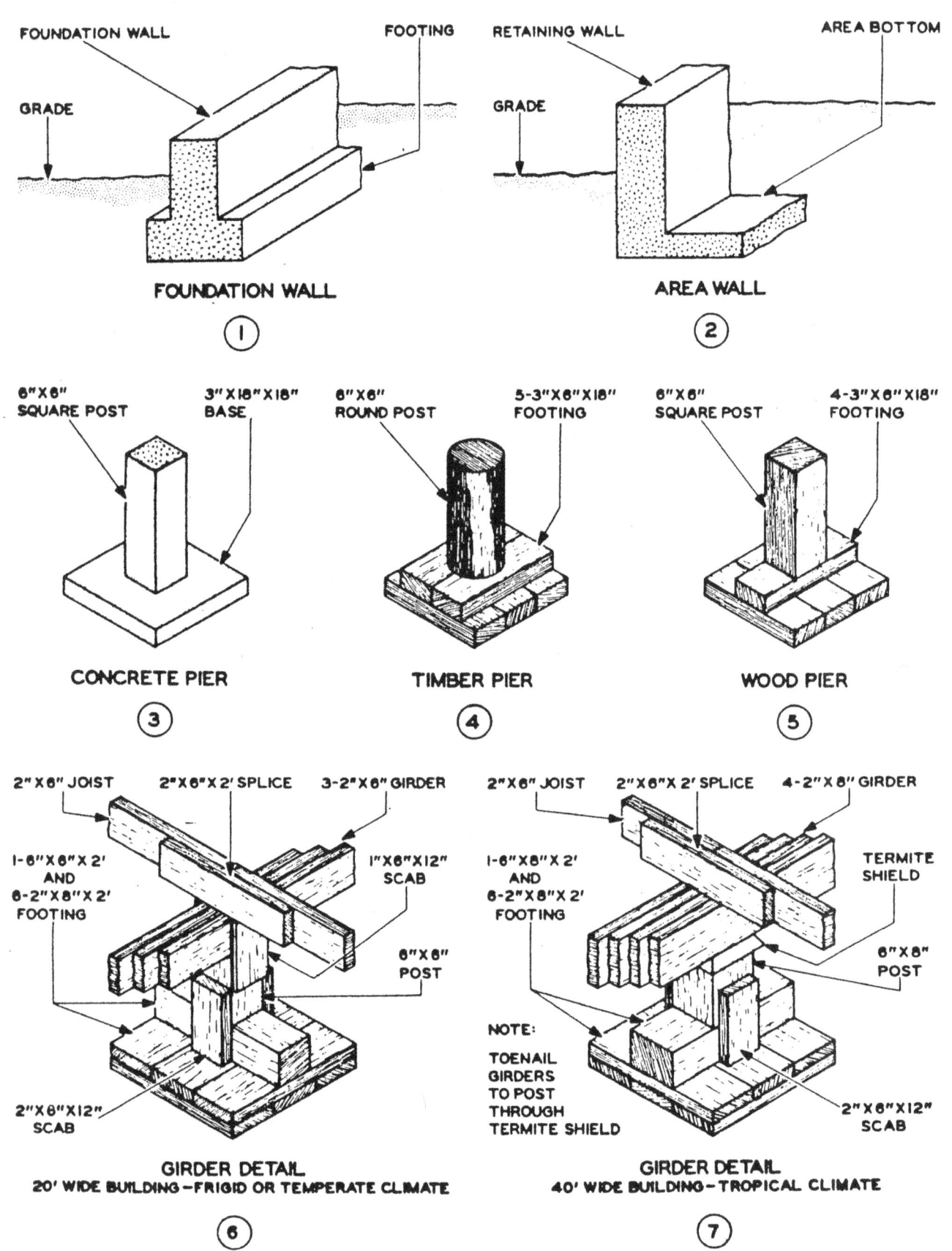

Figure 11. Typical foundation walls, piers, footings, and girder details.

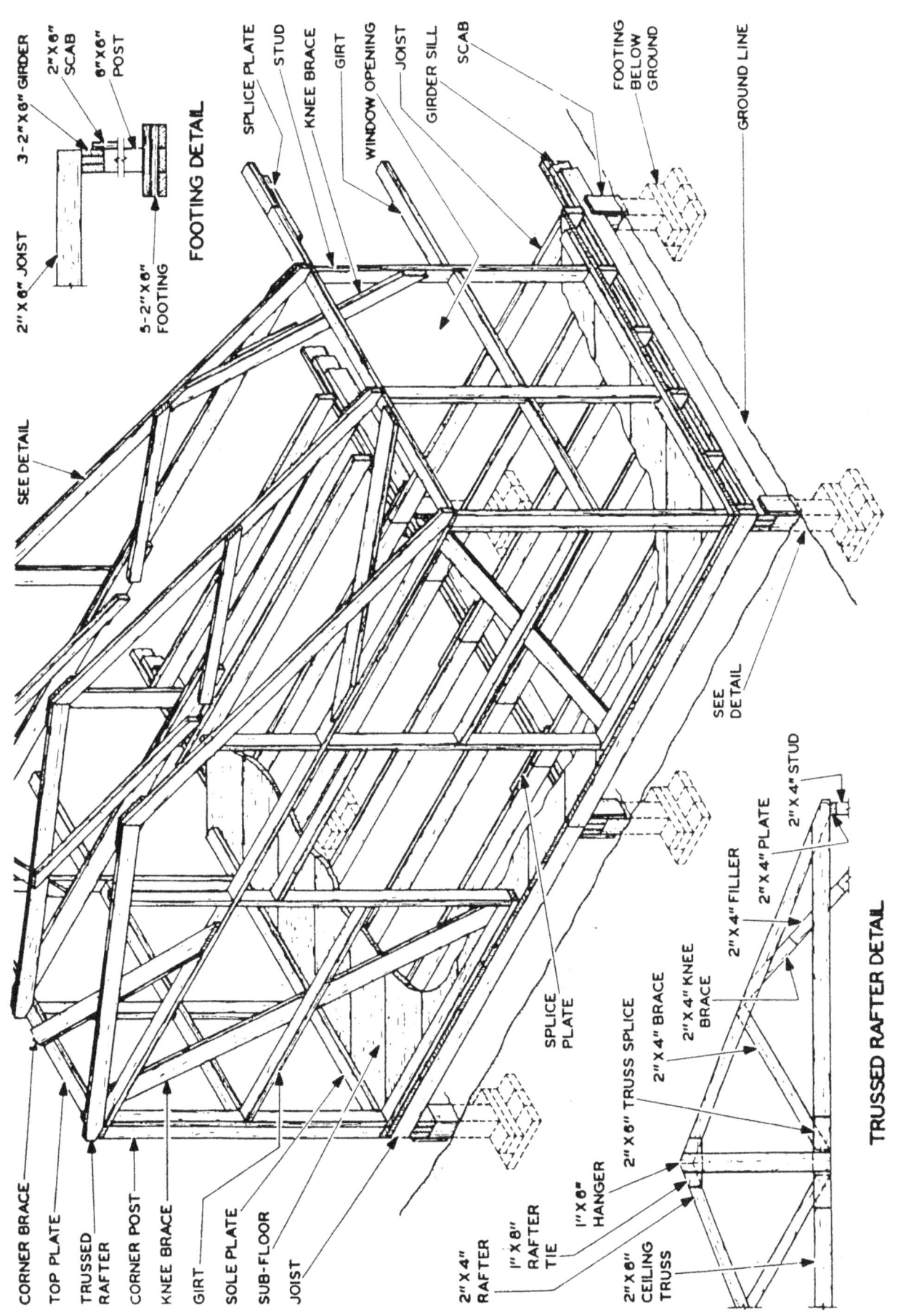

Figure 12. Light framing details (20-foot-wide building).

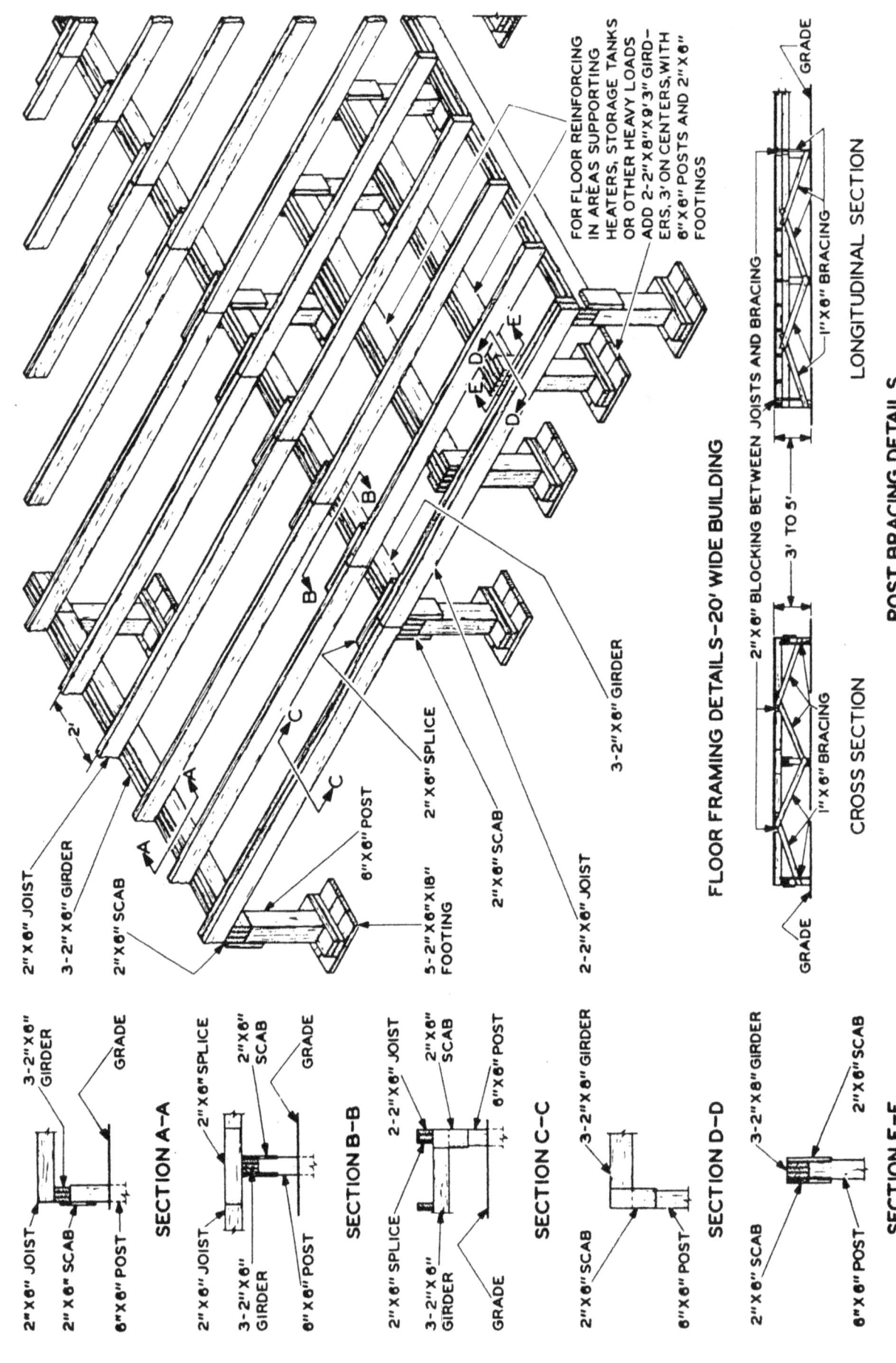

Figure 13. Floor framing details.

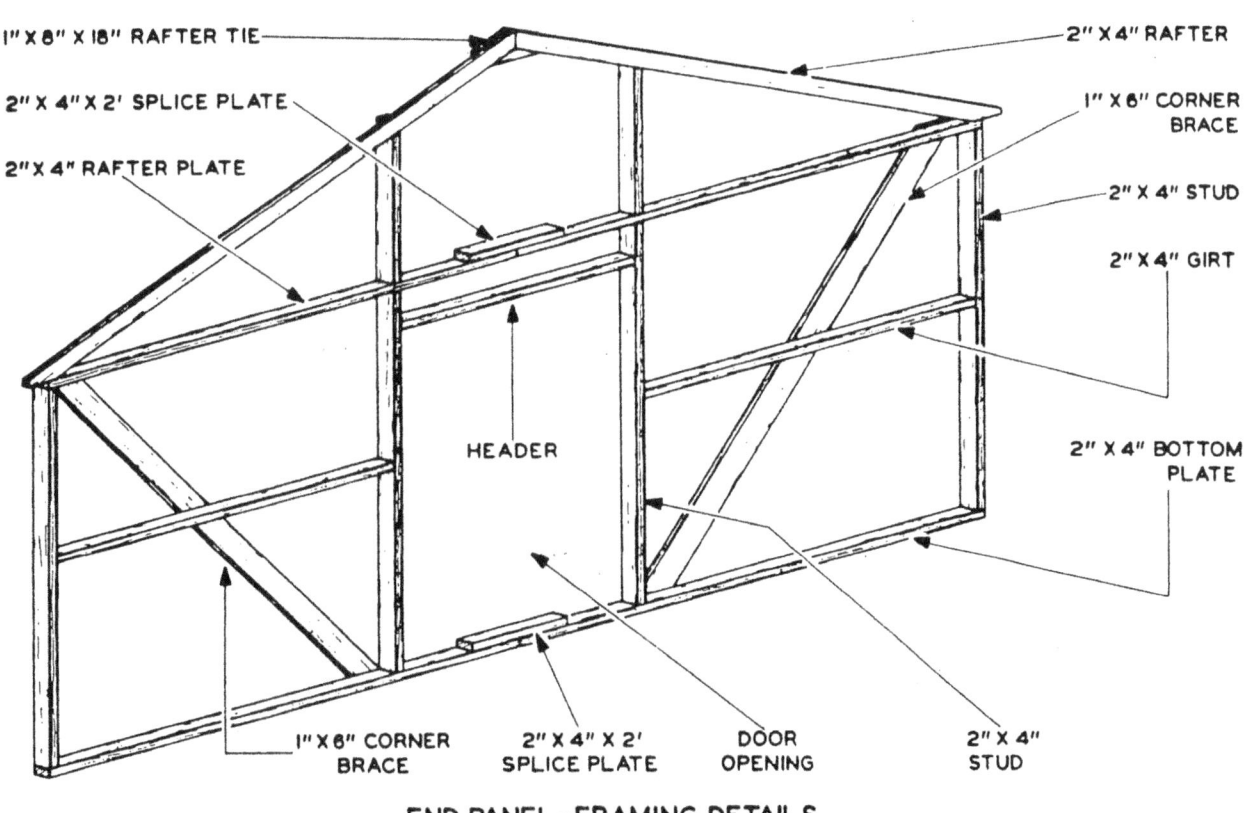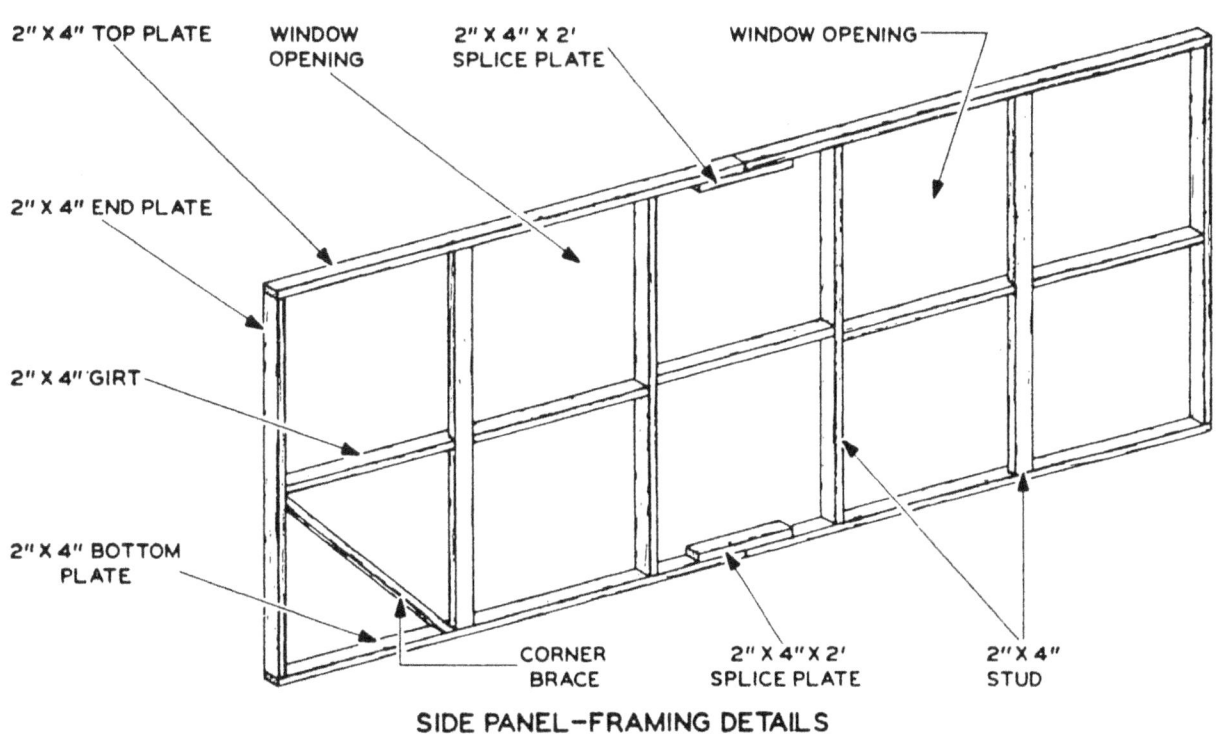

Figure 14. Typical wall panels—framing details.

ings, and similar structures.

a. The types of foundation walls, footings, and girder details normally used in standard theater of operations type construction are shown in figure 11. The various details for overall framing of a 20-foot-wide building showing ground level and including window openings, braces, splices, and nomenclature of framing are shown in figure 12.

b. Figure 13 illustrates floor framing details showing footings, posts, girders, joists, reinforced section of floor for heavy loads, section views covering makeup of certain sections, scabs for joining girders to posts, and post bracing details as placed for cross sections and longitudinal sections. On a construction print the type of footings and size of the various members are shown. In some cases the lengths are given while in others the bill of materials which accompanies the print specifies the required lengths of the various members.

c. Wall framing details for end panels are shown in ①, figure 14. The height of panels is usually shown and from this height the length of wall studs is determined by deducting the thickness of the top or rafter plate and the bottom plate. The space between studs is given in the drawing as well as height of girt from bottom plate, type of door opening, if any, and window opening. Details for side panels, ②, figure 14, cover the same type of information as listed for end panels. For window openings, the details specify whether the window is hinged to swing in or out or whether it is to be a sliding panel. Studs placed next to window openings may be placed either on edge or flat depending upon the type of window used.

d. The makeup of various trussed rafters is shown in figure 14. A 40-foot trussed rafter showing a partition bearing in the center is shown in ①, figure 15. This figure shows the splices required, bracing details, stud and top plate at one end of rafter, and size of members. The typical 20-foot truss rafter is shown in ②, figure 15. The use of filler blocks to keep the brace members in a vertical plane is needed since the rafter and bottom chord are nailed together rather than spliced. The rafter tie is placed on the opposite side from the vertical brace. Usually the splice plate for the bottom chord, if one is needed, is placed on the side on which it is planned to nail the rafters so that it can also serve as a filler block. A modified truss rafter is shown in ③, figure 15. This type of truss is used only when specified in plans for certain construction. It will not be used in areas subject to high wind velocities or moderate to heavy snowfall. In this type of trussed rafter, the bottom chord is placed on the rafters at a height above the top plate.

9. Heavy Wood Framing

Heavy wood framing consists of framing members at least 6 inches in dimension (timber construction). Examples of this type of framing can be found in heavy roof trusses, timber trestle bridges, and wharfs. The major differences between light and heavy framing are the size of timber used and the types of fasteners used. Fasteners for both light and heavy framing will be covered in a later chapter. Figure 16 shows the framing details for a heavy roof truss.

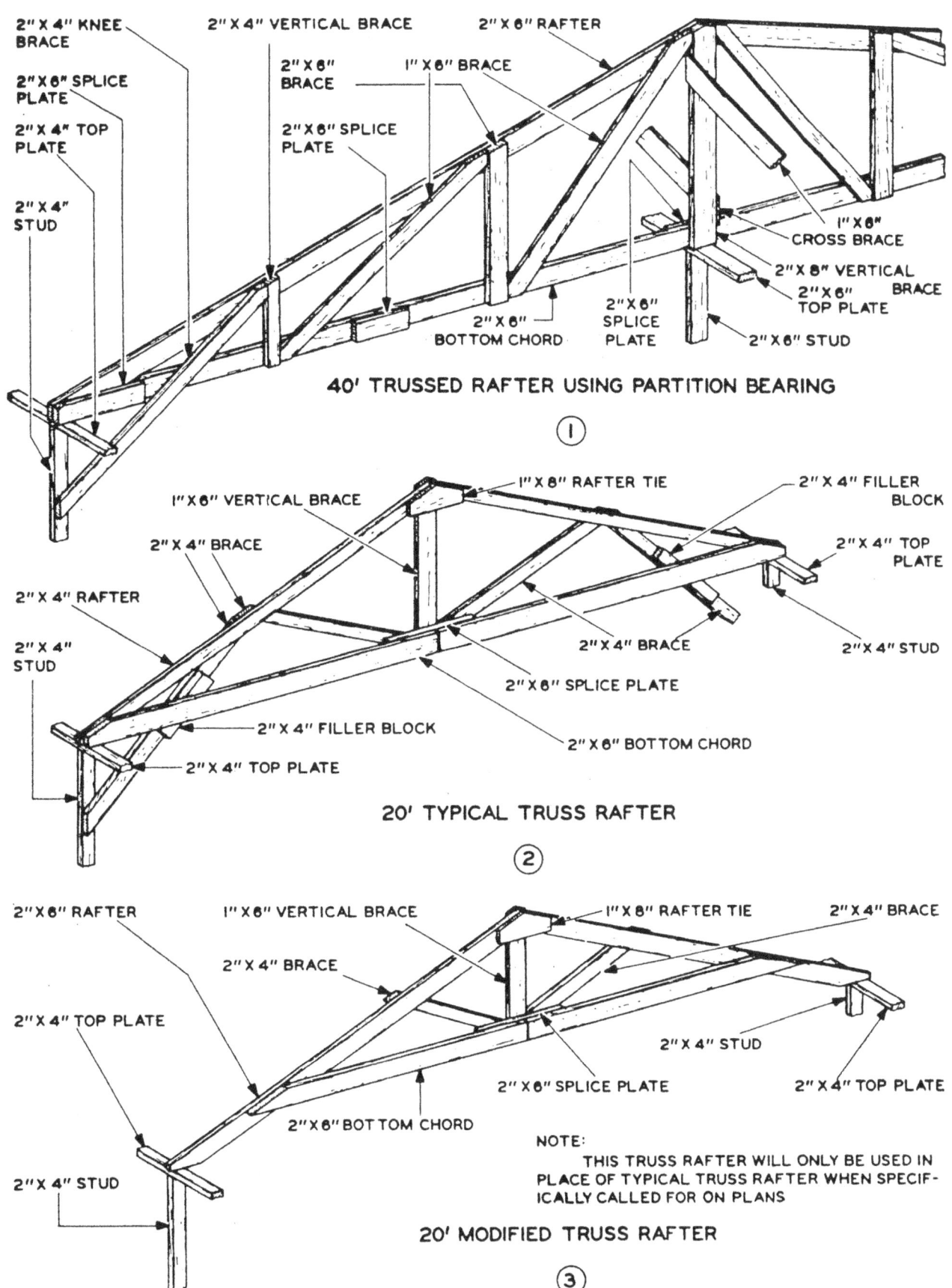

Figure 15. Trussed rafter details.

① TYPICAL LIGHT ROOF TRUSS

② TYPICAL HEAVY ROOF TRUSS

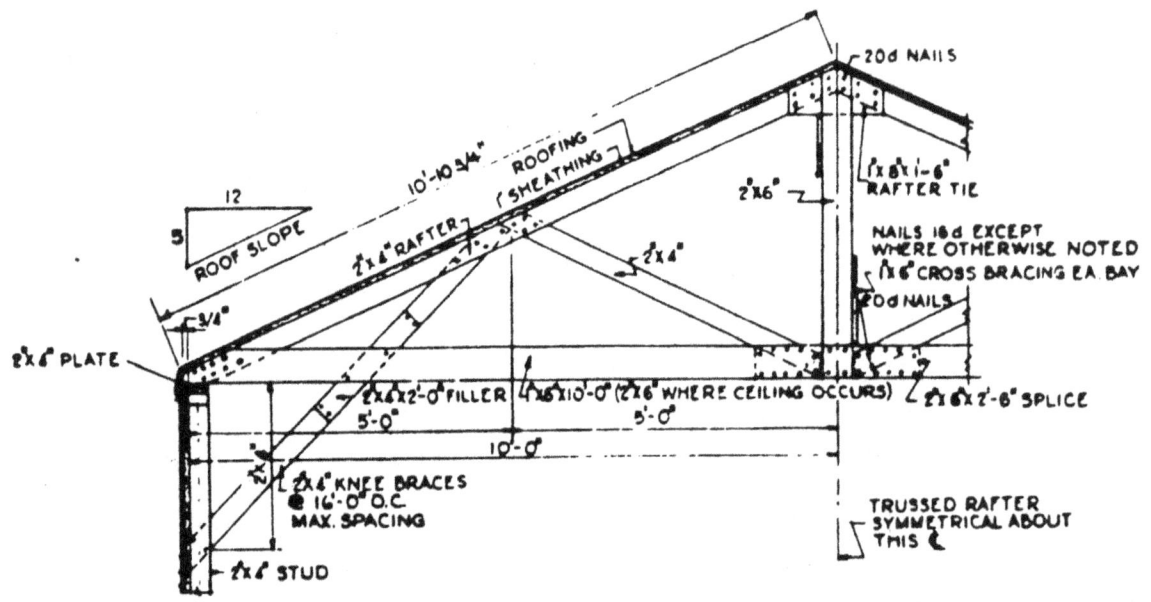

Figure 16. Typical heavy roof trusses.

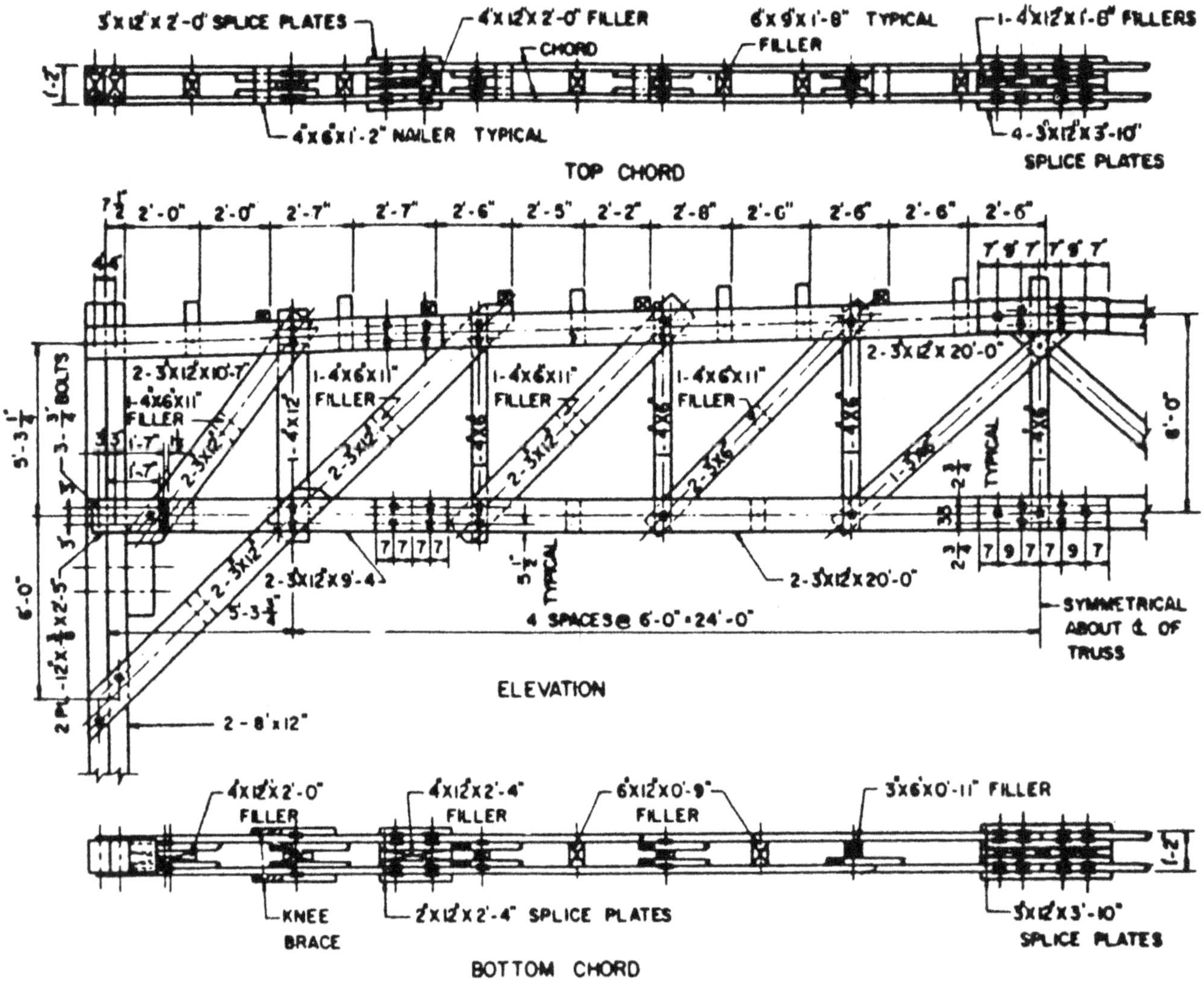

GLOSSARY OF HOUSING, BUILDING CONSTRUCTION, CARPENTRY, AND WOOD TERMS

CONTENTS

	Page
Air Dried Lumber...... Balusters	1
Balustrade ...... Blind Stop	2
Blinds ...... Built-up Timber	3
Butt Joint ...... Collar Beam	4
Column ...... Corner Braces	5
Cornerite ...... Density	6
Diffuse-Porous Wood ......Ducts	7
Early Wood...... Flat Paint	8
Flue ...... Full Frame	9
Fungi, Wood ...... Edge-Grained Lumber	10
Fine-Grained Wood ...... Gypsum Plaster	11
Hardwoods ...... Jamb	12
Joint ...... Ledger Strip	13
Ledgerboard......Lumber, Yard	14
Mantel ...... Mullion	15
Muntin ......Panel	16
Paper, Building ......Planing-Mill Products	17
Planks Or Lumber ......Primer	18
Pulley Stile ......Rays, Wood	19
Reflective Insulation......Run	20
Saddle Board ...... Semigloss Paint or Enamel	21
Shake ...... Soil Cover (Ground Cover)	22
Soil Stack ...... Stress	23
String, Stringer ...... Tin Shingle	24
To the Weather...... Sliced Veneer	25
Vent ...... Weatherstrip	26
Wind ......Workability	27

GLOSSARY OF HOUSING, BUILDING CONSTRUCTION, CARPENTRY, AND WOOD TERMS

A

AIR-DRIED LUMBER - Lumber that has been piled in yards or sheds for any length of time. For the United States as a whole the minimum moisture content of thoroughly air-dried lumber is 12 to 15 percent and the average is somewhat higher.

AIRWAY - A space between roof insulation and roof boards for movement of air.

ALLIGATORING - Coarse checking pattern characterized by a slipping of the new coating over the old coating to the extent that the old coating can be seen through the fissures.

ANCHOR - Irons of special form used to fasten together timbers or masonry.

ANCHOR BOLTS - (1) Bolts which fasten columns, girders, or other members to concrete or masonry.

(2) Bolts to secure a wooden sill to concrete or masonry floor or wall.

ANNUAL GROWTH RING - The growth layer put on in a single growth year, including springwood and summerwood.

APRON - The flat member of the inside trim of a window placed against the wall immediately beneath the stool.

AREAWAY - An open subsurface space adjacent to a building used to admit light or air or as a means of access to a basement or cellar.

ASPHALT - Most native asphalt is a residue from evaporated petroleum. It is insoluble in water but soluble in gasoline and melts when heated. Used widely in building for such items as waterproof roof coverings of many types, exterior wall coverings, and flooring tile.

ASTRAGAL - A molding, attached to one of a pair of swinging doors, against which the other door strikes.

ATTIC VENTILATORS - In houses, screened openings provided to ventilate an attic space. They are located in the soffit area as inlet ventilators and in the gable end or along the ridge as outlet ventilators. They can also consist of powerdriven fans used as an exhaust system. (See also LOUVER)

B

BACKBAND - Molding used on the side of a door or window casing for ornamentation or to increase the width of the trim.

BACKING - The bevel on the top edge of a hip rafter that allows the roofing board to fit the top of the rafter without leaving a triangular space between it and the lower side of the roof covering.

BACK-FILL - The replacement of excavated earth into a trench or pier excavation around and against a basement foundation.

BALLOON FRAME - The lightest and most economical form of construction, in which the studding and corner posts are set up in continuous lengths from first-floor line or sill to the roof plate.

BALUSTER - A small pillar or column used to support a rail.

BALUSTERS - Usually small vertical members in a railing used between a top rail and the stair treads or a bottom rail.

BALUSTRADE - A series of balusters connected by a rail, generally used for porches, balconies, and the like.

BAND - A low, flat molding.

BARK - Outer layer of a tree, comprising the inner bark, or thin, inner living part (phloem) and the outer bark, or corky layer, composed of dry, dead tissue.

BASE - The bottom of a column; the finish of a room at the junction of the walls and floor.

BASE OR BASEBOARD - A board placed around a room against the wall next to the floor to finish properly between floor and plaster or dry wall.

BASE MOLDING - Molding used to trim the upper edge of interior baseboard.

BASE SHOE - Molding used next to the floor on interior baseboard. Sometimes called a carpet strip.

BATTEN - Narrow strips of wood used to cover joints or as decorative vertical members over plywood or wide boards.

BATTEN (CLEAT) - A narrow strip of board used to fasten several pieces together.

BATTER BOARD - One of a pair of horizontal boards nailed to posts set at the corners of an excavation, used to indicate the desired level, also as a fastening for stretched strings to indicate outlines of foundation walls.

BAY WINDOW - Any window space projecting outward from the walls of a building, either square or polygonal in plan.

BEAM -   (1) An inclusive term for joists, girders, rafters, and purlins.
         (2) A large structural member transversely supporting a load.
One example is a beam under the floor of a house.

BEARING PARTITION - A partition that supports any vertical load in addition to its own weight.

BEARING WALL - A wall that supports any vertical load in addition to its own weight.

BED MOLDING - A molding in an angle, as between the overhanging cornice, or eaves, of a building and the sidewalls.

BEDDING - A filling of mortar, putty, or other substance in order to secure a firm bearing.

BELT COURSE - A horizontal board across or around a building, usually made of a flat member and a molding.

BENDING, STEAM - The process of forming curved wood members by steaming or boiling the wood and bending it to a form.

BEVEL - One side of a solid body is said to be on a bevel with respect to another when the angle between the two sides is greater or less than a right angle.

BEVEL BOARD (PITCH BOARD) - A board used in framing a roof or stairway to lay out bevels.

BEVEL SIDING (LAP SIDING) - Used as the finish siding on the exterior of a house or other structure. It is usually manufactured by "resaw-ing dry, square surfaced boards diagonally to produce two wedge-shaped pieces. These pieces commonly run from three-sixteenths inch thick on the thin edge to one-half to three-fourths inch thick on the other edge, depending on the width of the siding.

BIRD'S-EYE - Small localized areas in wood with the fibers indented and otherwise contorted to form few to many small circular or elliptical figures remotely resembling birds' eyes on the tangential surface. Common in sugar maple and used for decorative purposes; rare in other hardwood species.

BLIND-NAILING - Nailing in such a way that the nailheads are not visible on the face of the work. Usually at the tongue of matched boards.

BLIND STOP - A rectangular molding, usually 3/4 by 1 3/8 inches or more in width, used in the assembly of a window frame. Serves as a stop for storm and screen or combination windows and to resist air infiltration.

BLINDS (SHUTTERS) - Light wood sections in the form of doors to close over windows to shut out light, give protection, or add temporary insulation. Commonly used now for ornamental purposes, in which case they are fastened rigidly to the building.

BLUE STAIN - A bluish or grayish discoloration of the sapwood caused by the growth of certain moldlike fungi on the surface and in the interior of the piece, made possible by the same conditions that favor the growth of other fungi. BOARD - Lumber less than 2 inches thick.

BOARD FOOT - The equivalent of a board 1 foot square and 1 inch thick.

BOARDING IN - The process of nailing boards on the outside studding of a house.

BODIED LINSEED OIL - Linseed oil that has been thickened in viscosity by suitable processing with heat or chemicals. Bodied oils are obtainable in a great range of viscosity from a little greater than that of raw oil to just short of a jellied condition.

BOILED LINSEED OIL - Linseed oil in which enough lead, manganese, or cobalt salts have been incorporated to make the oil harden more rapidly when spread in thin coatings.

BOLSTER - A short horizontal timber resting on the top of a column for the support of beams or girders.

BOLTS, ANCHOR - Bolts to secure a wooden sill plate to concrete or masonry floor or wall or pier.

BOSTON RIDGE - A method of applying asphalt or wood shingles at the ridge or at the hips of a roof as a finish.

BOW - The distortion in a board that deviates from flatness lengthwise but not across its faces.

BRACE - An inclined piece of framing lumber used to complete a triangle and applied to wall or floor to stiffen the structure. Often used on walls as temporary bracing until framing has been completed.

BRACES - Pieces fitted and firmly fastened to two others at any angle in order to strengthen the angle thus threated.

BRACKET - A projecting support for a shelf or other structure.

BREAK JOINTS - To arrange joints so that they do not come directly under or over the joints of adjoining pieces, as in shingling, siding, etc.

BRICK VENEER - A facing of brick laid against frame or tile wall construction .

BRIDGING -   (1) Pieces fitted in pairs from the bottom of one floor joist to the top of adjacent joists, and crossed to distribute the floor load; sometimes pieces of width equal to the joists and fitted neatly between them.

(2) Small wood or metal members that are inserted in a diagonal position between the floor joists to act both as tension and compression members for the purpose of bracing the joists and spreading the action of loads.

BROAD-LEAVED TREES - (See HARDWOODS)

BUCK - Often used in reference to rough frame opening members. Door bucks used in reference to metal door frame.

BUILDING CODE - A collection of legal requirements the purpose of which is to protect the safety, health, morals, and general welfare of those in and about buildings.

BUILDING PAPER - Cheap, thick paper, used to insulate a building before the siding or roofing is put on; sometimes placed between double floors.

BUILT-UP ROOF - A roofing composed of three to five layers of asphalt felt laminated with coal tar, pitch, or asphalt. The top is finished with crushed slag or gravel. Generally used on flat or low-pitched roofs.

BUILT-UP TIMBER - A timber made of several pieces fastened together, and forming one of larger dimension.

BUTT JOINT - The junction where the ends of two timbers or other members meet in a square-cut joint.

C

CABINET - A shop-or-job-built unit for kitchens or other rooms. Often includes combinations of drawers, doors, and the like.

CAMBIUM - The one-cell-thick layer of tissue between the bark and wood that repeatedly subdivides to form new wood and bark cells.

CANT STRIP - A wedge or triangular-shaped piece of lumber used at gable ends under shingles or at the junction of the house and a flat deck under the roofing.

CAP - The upper member of a column, pilaster, door cornice, molding, and the like.

CARRIAGES - The supports or the steps and risers of a flight of stairs.

CASEMENT - A window in which the sash opens upon hinges.

CASEMENT FRAMES AND SASH - Frames of wood or metal enclosing part or all of the sash, which may be opened by means of hinges affixed to the vertical edges.

CASING - (1) Molding of various widths and thicknesses used to trim door and window openings at the jambs.

(2) The trimming around a door or window opening, either outside or inside, or the finished lumber around a post or beam, etc.

CEILING - Narrow, matched boards; sheathing of the surfaces that inclose the upper side of a room.

CELL - A general term for the minute units of wood structure, including wood fibers, vessels, members, and other elements of diverse structure and function.

CEMENT, KEENE'S - The whitest finish plaster obtainable that produces a wall of extreme durability. Because of its density it excels for a wainscoting plaster for bathrooms and kitchens and is also used extensively for the finish coat in auditoriums, public buildings, and other places where walls will be subjected to unusually hard wear or abuse.

CENTER-HUNG SASH - A sash hung on its centers so that it swings on a horizontal axis.

CHAMFER - A beveled surface cut upon the corner of a piece of wood.

CHECK - A lengthwise separation of the wood, usually extending across the rings of annual growth and commonly resulting from stresses set up in the wood during seasoning.

CHECKING - Fissures that appear with age in many exterior paint coatings, at first superficial, but which in time may penetrate entirely through the coating.

CHECKRAILS - Meeting rails sufficiently thicker than a window to fill the opening between the top and bottom sash made by the parting stop in the frame. They are usually beveled.

CHECKS - Splits or cracks in a board, ordinarily caused by seasoning.

CLAMP - A mechanical device used to hold two or more pieces together.

CLAPBOARDS - A special form of outside covering of a house; siding.

COLLAPSE - The flattening of groups of cells in heartwood during the drying or pressure treatment of wood, characterized by a caved-in or corrugated appearance.

COLLAR BEAM - (1) Nominal 1- or 2-inch-thick members connecting opposite roof rafters. They serve to stiffen the roof structure.

(2) A tie beam connecting the rafters considerably above the wall plate. It is also called a rafter tie.

(3) A beam connecting pairs of opposite roof rafters above the attic floor.

COLUMN - In architecture: A perpendicular supporting member, circular or rectangular in section, usually consisting of a base, shaft, and capital. In engineering: A structural compression member, usually vertical, supporting loads acting on or near and in the direction of its longitudinal axis.

COLUMNS - A support, square, rectangular, or cylindrical in section, for roofs, ceilings, etc., composed of base, shaft, and capital.

COMBINATION DOORS - Combination doors have an inside removable section so that the same frame serves for both summer and winter protective devices. A screen is inserted in warm weather to make a screen door, and a glazed or a glazed-and-wood paneled section in winter to make a storm door. The inconvenience of handling a different door in each season is eliminated.

COMBINATION DOORS OR WINDOWS - Combination doors or windows used over regular openings. They provide winter insulation and summer protection. They often have, self-storing or removable glass and screen inserts. This eliminates the need for handling a different unit each season.

COMBINATION FRAME - A combination of the principal features of the full and balloon frames.

CONCRETE - An artificial building material made by mixing cement and sand with gravel, broken stone, or other aggregate, and sufficient water to cause the cement to set and bind the entire mass.

CONCRETE, PLAIN - Concrete without reinforcement, or reinforced only for shrinkage or temperature changes.

CONDENSATION - Beads or drops of water, and frequently frost in extremely cold weather, that accumulate on the inside of the exterior covering of a building when warm, moisture-laden air from the interior reaches a point where the temperature no longer permits the air to sustain the moisture it holds. Use of louvers or attic ventilators will reduce moisture condensation in attics. A vapor barrier under the gypsum lath or dry wall on exposed walls will reduce condensation in walls.

CONDUCTORS - Pipes for conducting water from a roof to the ground or to a receptacle or drain; downspout.

CONDUIT, ELECTRICAL - A pipe, usually metal, in which wire is installed.

CONSTRUCTION, DRY-WALL - A type of construction in which the interior wall finish is applied in a dry condition, generally in the form of sheet materials or wood paneling, as contrasted to plaster.

CONSTRUCTION, FRAME - A type of construction in which the structural parts are of wood or depend upon a wood frame for support. In building codes, if masonry veneer is applied to the exterior walls, the classification of this type of construction is usually unchanged.

COPED JOINT - Fitting woodwork to an irregular surface. In moldings, cutting the end of one piece to fit the molded face of the other at an interior angle to replace a miter joint.

CORBEL OUT - To build out one or more courses of brick or stone from the face of a wall, to form a support for timbers.

CORNER BEAD - A strip of formed galvanized iron, sometimes combined with a strip of metal lath, placed on corners before plastering to reinforce them. Also, a strip of wood finish three-quarters-round or angular placed over a plastered corner for protection.

CORNER BOARDS - Used as trim for the external corners of a house or other frame structures against which the ends of the siding are finished.

CORNER BRACES - Diagonal braces at the corners of frame structure to stiffen and strengthen the wall.

CORNERITE - Metal-mesh lath cut into strips and bent to a right angle. Used in interior corners of walls and ceilings on lath to prevent cracks in plastering.

CORNICE - (1) Overhang of a pitched roof at the eave line, usually consisting of a facia board, a soffit for a closed cornice, and appropriate moldings.

(2) The molded projection which finishes the top of the wall of a building.

(3) A decorative element made up of molded members usually placed at or near the top of an exterior or interior wall.

CORNICE RETURN - That portion of the cornice that returns on the gable end of a house.

COUNTERFLASHING - A flashing usually used on chimneys at the roofline to cover shingle flashing and to prevent moisture entry.

COUNTERFLASHINGS - Strips of metal used to prevent water from entering the top edge of the vertical side of a roof flashing; they also allow expansion and contraction without danger of breaking the flashing.

COVE MOLDING - (1) A molding with a concave face used as trim or to finish interior corners.

(2) A three-sided molding with concave face used wherever small angles are to be covered.

CRAWL SPACE - A shallow space below the living quarters of a house. It is generally not excavated or paved and is often enclosed for appearance by a skirting or facing material.

CRICKET - A small drainage diverting roof structure of single or double slope placed at the junction of larger surfaces that meet at an angle.

CROOK - The distortion in a board that deviates edgewise from a straight line from end to end of the board.

CROWN MOLDING - A molding used on cornice or wherever a large angle is to be covered.

CUP - The distortion in a board that deviates flatwise from a straight line across the width of the board.

D

d - (See PENNY)

DADO - A rectangular groove across the width of a board or plank. In interior decoration, a special type of wall treatment.

DEADENING - Construction intended to prevent the passage of sound.

DECAY - The decomposition of wood substance by fungi.

DECAY, ADVANCED (OR TYPICAL) - The older stage of decay in which the destruction is readily recognized because the wood has become punky, soft and spongy, stringy, ringshaked, pitted, or crumbly. Decided discoloration or bleaching of the rotted wood is often apparent.

DECAY, INCIPIENT - The early stage of decay that has not proceeded far enough to soften or otherwise perceptibly impair the hardness of the wood. It is usually accompanied by a slight discoloration or bleaching of the wood.

DECK PAINT - An enamel with a high degree of resistance to mechanical wear, designed for use on such surfaces as porch floors.

DENSITY - (1) The mass of substance in a unit volume. When expressed in the metric system (in g. per cc), it is numerically equal to the specific gravity of the same substance.

(2) The weight of a body per unit volume. When expressed in the c. g. s. (centimeter-gram-second) system, it is numerically equal to the specific gravity of the same substance.

DIFFUSE-POROUS WOOD - Certain hardwoods in which the pores tend to be uniform in size and distribution throughout each annual ring or to decrease in size slightly and gradually toward the outer border of the ring.

DIMENSION - (See LUMBER)

DIMENSION STOCK - A term largely superseded by the term hardwood dimension lumber. It is hardwood stock processed to a point where the maximum waste is left at a dimension mill, and the maximum utility is delivered to the user. It is stock of specified thickness, width, and length, in multiples thereof. According to specification, it may be solid or glued; rough or surfaced; semifabricated or completely fabricated.

DIMENSIONAL STABILIZATION - Reduction through special treatment in swelling and shrinking of wood, caused by changes in its moisture content with changes in relative humidity.

DIRECT NAILING - To nail perpendicular to the initial surface, or to the junction of the pieces joined. Also termed face nailing.

DOORJAMB, INTERIOR - The surrounding case into which and out of which a door closes and opens. It consists of two upright pieces, called jambs, and a head, fitted together and rabbeted.

DORMER - (1) A projection in a sloping roof, the framing of which forms a vertical wall suitable for windows or other openings.

(2) An internal recess, the framing of which projects a sloping roof.

DOWNSPOUT - A pipe, usually of metal, for carrying rainwater from roof gutters.

DRESSED AND MATCHED (TONGUED AND GROOVED) - Boards or planks machined in such a manner that there is a groove on one edge and a corresponding tongue on the other.

DRIER, PAINT - Usually oil-soluble soaps of such metals as lead, manganese, or cobalt, which, in small proportions, hasten the oxidation and hardening (drying) of the drying oils in paints. DRIP - (1) The projection of a window sill or water table to allow the water to drain clear of the side of the house below it.

(2) A member of a cornice or other horizontal exterior-finish course that has a projection beyond the other parts for throwing off water.

(3) A groove in the underside of a sill to cause water to drop off on the outer edge, instead of drawing back and running down the face of the building.

DRIP CAP - A molding placed on the exterior top side of a door or window frame to cause water to drip beyond the outside of the frame.

DROP SIDING - Usually 3/4 inch thick and 6 inches wide, machined into various patterns. Drop siding has tongue and groove or shiplap joints, is heavier, and has more structural strength than bevel siding.

DRY KILN - (See KILN)

DRY ROT - A term loosely applied to any dry, crumbly rot but especially to that which, when in an advanced stage, permits the wood to be crushed easily to a dry powder. The term is actually a misnomer, since all wood-rotting fungi require considerable moisture for growth.

DRY-WALL - (See CONSTRUCTION, DRY WALL)

DUCTS - In a house, usually round or rectangular metal pipes for distributing warm air from the heating plant to rooms, or air from a conditioning device, or as cold air returns. Ducts are also made of asbestos and composition materials.

E

EARLY WOOD - (See SPRINGWOOD)
EAVES - (1) The overhang of a roof projecting over the walls.
(2) The margin or lower part of a roof projecting over the wall.
EDGE-GRAINED - (See GRAIN)
EXPANSION JOINT - A bituminous fiber strip used to separate blocks or units of concrete to prevent cracking due to expansion as a result of temperature changes.
EXTRACTIVES - Substances in wood, not an integral part of the cellular structure, that can be removed by solution in hot or cold water, ether, benzene, or other solvents that do not react chemically with wood components.

F

FACE NAILING - To nail perpendicular to the initial surface or to the junction of the pieces joined.
FACIA OR FASCIA - (1) A flat board, band, or face, used sometimes by itself but usually in combination with moldings, often located at the outer face of the cornice.
(2) A flat member of a cornice or other finish, generally the board of the cornice to which the gutter is fastened.
FIBER, WOOD - A comparatively long (one twenty-fifth or less to one-third inch), narrow, tapering wood cell closed at both ends.
FIGURE - The pattern produced in a wood surface by annual growth rings, rays, knots, deviations from regular grain such as interlocked and wavy grain, and irregular coloration.
FILLER (WOOD) - A heavily pigmented preparation used for filling and leveling off the pores in open-pored woods.
FINISH - Wood products to be used in the joiner work, such as doors and stairs, and other fine work required to complete a building, especially the interior.
FIRE-RESISTIVE - In the absence of a specific ruling by the authority having jurisdiction, applies to materials for construction not combustible in the temperatures of ordinary fires and that will withstand such fires without serious impairment of their usefulness for at least 1 hour.
FIRE-RETARDANT CHEMICAL - A chemical or preparation of chemicals used to reduce flammability or to retard spread of flame.
FIRE STOP - A solid, tight closure of a concealed space, placed to prevent the spread of fire and smoke through such a space.
FLAGSTONE (FLAGGING OR FLAGS) - Flat stones, from 1 to 4 inches thick, used for rustic walks, steps, floors, and the like. Usually sold by the ton.
FLAKES - (See RAYS, WOOD)
FLASHING - (1) The material used and the process of making watertight the roof intersections and other exposed places on the outside of the house.
(2) Sheet metal or other material used in roof and wall construction to protect a building from seepage of water.
FLAT-GRAINED - (See GRAIN)
FLAT PAINT - An interior paint that contains a high proportin of pigment, and dries to a flat or lusterless finish.

FLUE - The space or passage in a chimney through which smoke, gas, or fumes ascend. Each passage is called a flue, which, together with any others and the surrounding masonry, make up the chimney.

FLUE LINING - Fire clay or terracotta pipe, round or square, usually made in all of the ordinary flue sizes and in 2-foot lengths, used for the inner lining of chimneys with a brick or masonry work around the outside. Flue lining in chimneys runs from about a foot below the flue connection to the top of the chimney.

FLUSH - Adjacent surfaces even, or in some plane (with reference to two structural pieces).

FLY RAFTER - End rafters of the gable overhang supported by roof sheathing and lookouts.

FOOTING - (1) A masonry section, usually concrete, in a rectangular form, wider than the bottom of the foundation wall or pier it supports.

(2) The spreading course or courses at the base or bottom of a foundation wall, pier, or column.

(3) An enlargement at the lower end of a wall, pier or column, to distribute the load.

FOOTING FORM - A wooden or steel structure, placed around the footing that will hold the concrete to the deserved shape and size.

FOUNDATION - (1) The supporting portion of a structure below the first floor construction, or below grade, including the footings.

(2) That part of a building or wall which supports the super-structure.

FRAME - The surrounding or inclosing woodwork of windows, doors, etc., and the timber skeleton of a building.

FRAMING - (1) The rough timber structure of a building, including interior and exterior walls, floor, roof, and ceiling.

(2) Lumber used for the structural members of a building, such as studs and joists.

FRAMING SYSTEMS:

BALLOON FRAMING - A system of framing a building in which all vertical structural elements of the exterior walls, particularly the studs, consist of single pieces extending from the foundation sill to the roof plate, and support intermediate floor and ceiling joists.

BRACED FRAMING - A system of framing a building in which all vertical structural elements of the bearing walls and partitions except corner posts, extend for one story only, starting at the foundation sill for the first-story framing and at the top plate of the story below for all stories above the first. Corner posts extend from foundation sill to roof plate and are braced by diagonal members usually extending the full height of each story and crossing several of the studs in each outer wall.

PLATFORM FRAMING - A system of framing a building on which floor joists of each story rest on the top plates of the story below (or on the foundation sill for the first story) and the bearing walls and partitions rest on the subfloor of each story.

FRIEZE - (1) In house construction, a horizontal member connecting the top of the siding with the soffit of the cornice or roof sheathing.

(2) Any sculptured or ornamental band in a building. Also the horizontal member of a cornice set vertically against the wall.

FROSTLINE - The depth of frost penetration in soil. This depth varies in different parts of the country. Footings should be placed below this depth to prevent movement.

FULL FRAME - The old fashioned mortised-and-tenoned frame, in which every joint was mortised and tenoned. Rarely used at the present time.

FUNGI, WOOD - Microscopic plants that live in damp wood and cause mold, stain, and decay.

FUNGICIDE - A chemical that is poisonous to fungi.

FURRING - (1) Narrow strips of board nailed upon the walls and ceilings to form a straight surface upon which to lay the laths or other finish.

(2) Strips of wood or metal applied to a wall or other surface to even it and usually to serve as a fastening base for finish material.

G

GABLE - (1) The vertical triangular end of a building from the eaves to the apex of the roof.

(2) That portion of a wall contained between the slopes of a double-sloped roof, on a single-sloped roof, that portion contained between the slope of and a line projected horizontally through the lowest elevation of the roof construction.

GABLE END - An end wall having a gable.

GAGE - A tool used by carpenters; to strike a line parallel to the edge of a board.

GAMBREL - A symmetrical roof with two different pitches or slopes on each side.

GIRDER - (1) A timber used to support wall beams or joists.

(2) A large or principal beam of wood or steel used to support concentrated loads at isolated points along its length.

GIRT (RIBBAND) - The horizontal member of the walls of a full or combination frame house which supports the floor joists or is flush with the top of the joists.

GLOSS ENAMEL - A finishing material made of varnish and sufficient pigments to provide opacity and color, but little or no pigment of low opacity. Such an enamel forms a hard coating with maximum smoothness of surface and a high degree of gloss.

GLOSS (PAINT OR ENAMEL) - A paint or enamel that contains a relatively low proportion of pigment and dries to a sheen or luster.

GRADE - The designation of quality of a manufactured piece of wood or of logs.

GRAIN - The direction, size, arrangement, appearance, or quality of the elements in wood or lumber. To have a specific meaning the term must be qualified.

CLOSE-GRAINED WOOD - Wood with narrow, inconspicuous annual rings. The term is sometimes used to designate wood having small and closely spaced pores, but in this sense the term "fine textured" is more often used.

COARSE-GRAINED WOOD - Wood with wide conspicuous annual rings in which there is considerable difference between springwood and summer-wood. The term is sometimes used to designate wood with large pores, such as oak, ash, chestnut, and walnut, but in this sense the term "coarse textured" is more often used.

CROSS-GRAINED WOOD - Wood in which the fibers deviate from a line parallel to the sides of the piece. Cross grain may be either diagonal or spiral grain, or a combination of the two.

CURLY-GRAINED WOOD - Wood in which the fibers are distorted so that they have a curled appearance, as in "bird's-eye" wood. The areas showing curly grain may vary up to several inches in diameter.

DIAGONAL-GRAINED WOOD - Wood in which the annual rings are at an angle with the axis of a piece as a result of sawing at an angle with the bark of the tree or log. A form of cross grain.

EDGE-GRAINED LUMBER - Lumber that has been sawed so that the wide surfaces extend approximately at right angles to the annual growth rings. Lumber is considered edge grained when the rings form an angle of 45° to 90° with the wide surface of the piece.

FINE-GRAINED WOOD - (See GRAIN, CLOSE-GRAINED WOOD)

FLAT-GRAINED LUMBER - Lumber that has been sawed so the wide surfaces extend approximately parallel to the annual growth rings. Lumber is considered flat grained when the annual growth rings make an angle of less than 45° with the surface of the piece.

INTERLOCKED-GRAINED WOOD - Wood in which the fibers are inclined in one direction in a number of rings of annual growth, then gradually reverse and are inclined in an opposite direction in succeeding growth rings, then reverse again.

OPEN-GRAINED WOOD - Common classification by painters for woods with large pores, such as oak, ash, chestnut, and walnut. Also known as "coarse textured."

PLAINSAWED LUMBER - Another term for flat-grained lumber.

QUARTERSAWED LUMBER - Another term for edge-grained lumber.

SPIRAL-GRAINED WOOD - Wood in which the fibers take a spiral course around the trunk of a tree instead of the normal vertical course. The spiral may extend in a right-handed or left-handed direction around the tree trunk. Spiral grain is a form of cross grain.

STRAIGHT-GRAINED WOOD - Wood in which the fibers run parallel to the axis of a piece.

VERTICAL-GRAINED LUMBER - Another form for edge-grained lumber.

WAVY-GRAINED WOOD - Wood in which the fibers collectively take the form of waves or undulations.

GREEN - Freshly sawed lumber, or lumber that has received no intentional drying; unseasoned. The term does not apply to lumber that may have become completely wet through waterlogging.

GROOVE - A long hollow channel cut by a tool, into which a piece fits or in which it works. Two special types of grooves are the

DADO, a rectangular groove cut across the full width of a piece, and the

HOUSING, a groove cut at any angle with the grain and part way across a piece. Dados are used in sliding doors, window frames, etc.; housings are used for framing stair risers and threads in a string.

GROUND - A strip of wood assisting the plasterer in making a straight wall and in giving a place to which the finish of the room may be nailed.

GROUNDS - Strips of wood, of same thickness as lath and plaster, that are attached to walls before the plastering is done. Used around windows, doors, and other openings as a plaster stop and in other places for attaching baseboards or other trim.

GROUT - (1) Mortar made of such consistency by the addition of water that it will just flow into the joints and cavities of the masonry work and fill them solid.

(2) Mortar made so thin by the addition of water that it will all run into the joints and cavities of the masonwork and fill them up solid.

GUSSET - A flat wood, plywood, or similar type member used to provide a connection at the intersection of wood members. Most commonly used at joints of wood trusses. They are fastened by nails, screws, bolts, or adhesives.

GUTTER OR EAVE TROUGH - A shallow channel or conduit of metal or wood set below and along the eaves of a house to catch and carry off rainwater from the roof.

GYPSUM PLASTER - Gypsum formulated to be used with the addition of sand and water for base-coat plaster.

H

HARDWOODS - Generally, the botanical group of trees that have broad leaves, in contrast to the conifers or softwoods. The term has no reference to the actual hardness of the wood.

HEADER - (1) A beam placed perpendicular to joists and to which joists are nailed in framing for a chimney, stairway, or other opening. More generally, a piece or member that makes a T-joint with other members; often a short piece extending between other members and at right angles to them; frequently used instead of lintel.

(2) A short joist supporting tail beams and framed between trimmer joists; the piece of stud or finish over an opening; a lintel.

HEADROOM - The clear space between floor line and ceiling, as in a stairway.

HEARTH - The floor of a fireplace, usually made of brick, tile, or stone.

HEARTWOOD - The wood extending from the pith to the sapwood, the cells of which no longer participate in the life processes of the tree. Heartwood may be infiltrated with gums, resins, and other materials that usually make it darker and more decay resistant than sapwood.

HEEL OF A RAFTER - The end or foot that rests on the wall plate. HIP - The external angle formed by the meeting of two sloping sides of a roof.

HIP ROOF - (1) A roof that rises by inclined planes from all four sides of a building.

(2) A roof which slopes up toward the center from all sides, necessitating a hip rafter at each corner.

HONEYCOMBING - Checks, often not visible at the surface, that occur in the interior of a piece of wood, usually along the wood rays.

HUMIDIFIER - A device designed to discharge water vapor into a confined space for the purpose of increasing or maintaining the relative humidity in an enclosure.

I

I-BEAM - A steel beam with a cross"section resembling the letter "I." INSULATING BOARD OR FIBERBOARD - A low-density board made of wood, sugarcane, cornstalks, or similar materials, usually formed by a felting process, dried and usually pressed to thicknesses 1/2 and 25/32 inch.

INSULATION BOARD, RIGID - A structural building board made of wood or cane fiber in 1/2" and 25/32" thicknesses. It can be obtained in various size sheets, in various densities, and with several treatments.

INSULATION, BUILDING - Any material high in resistance to heat transmission that, when placed in the walls, ceilings, or floors of a structure, will reduce the rate of heat flow.

INSULATION, THERMAL - Any material high in resistance to heat transmission that, when placed in the walls, ceilings, or floors of a structure, will reduce the rate of heat flow.

J

JACK RAFTER - (1) A rafter that spans the distance from the wallplate to a hip, or from a valley to a ridge.

(2) A short rafter framing between the wall plate; a hip rafter.

JAMB - (1) The side piece or post of an opening; sometimes applied to the door frame.

(2) The side and head lining of a doorway, window, or other opening.

JOINT - (1) The space between the adjacent surfaces of two members or components joined and held together by nails, glue, cement, mortar, or other means.
(2) The junction of two pieces of wood or veneer.
JOINT-BUTT - Squared ends or ends and edges adjoining each other.
DOVETAIL - Joint made by cutting pins the shape of dovetails which fit between dovetails upon another piece.
DRAWBOARD - A mortise-and-tenon joint with holes so bored that when a pin is driven through, the joint becomes tighter.
FISHED - An end butt splice strengthened by pieces nailed on the sides.
HALVED - A joint made by cutting half the wood away from each piece so as to bring the sides flush.
HOUSED - A joint in which a piece is grooved to receive the piece which is to form the other part of the joint.
GLUE - A joint held together with glue.
LAP - A joint of two pieces lapping over each other.
MORTISED - A joint made by cutting a hole or mortise, in one piece, and a tenon, or piece to fit the hole, upon the other.
RUB - A flue joint made by carefully fitting the edges together, spreading glue between them, and rubbing the pieces back and forth until the pieces are well rubbed together.
SCARFED - A timber spliced by cutting various shapes of shoulders, or jogs, which fit each other.
JOINT CEMENT - A powder that is usually mixed with water and used for joint treatment in gypsum - wallboard finish. Often called "spackle."
JOIST - One of a series of parallel beams, usually 2 inches thick, used to support floor and ceiling loads, and supported in turn by larger beams, girders, or bearing walls.
JOISTS - Timbers supporting the floor boards.

K

KERF - The cut made by a saw.
KILN - A heated chamber for drying lumber, veneer, and other wood products.
KNEE BRACE - A corner brace, fastened at an angle from wall stud to rafter, stiffening a wood or steel frame to prevent angular movement.
KNOT - (1) That portion of a branch or limb which has been surrounded by subsequent growth of the wood of the trunk or other portion of the tree. As a knot appears on the sawed surface, it is merely a section of the entire knot, its shape depending upon the direction of the cut.
(2) In lumber, the portion of a branch or limb of a tree that appears on the edge or face of the piece.

L

LANDING - A platform between flights of stairs or at the termination of a flight of stairs.
LATH - A building material of wood, metal, gypsum, or insulating board that is fastened to the frame of a building to act as a plaster base.
LATHS - Narrow strips to support plastering.
LATTICE - (1) Crossed wood, iron plate, or bars.
(2) An assemblage of wood or metal strips, rods, or bars made by crossing them to form a network.
LEADER - (See DOWNSPOUT)
LEDGER STRIP - A strip of lumber nailed along the bottom of the side of a girder on which joists rest.

LEDGERBOARD - The support for the second-floor joists of a balloon-frame house, or for similar uses; ribband.

LEVEL - A term describing the position of a line or plane when parallel to the surface of still water; an instrument or tool used in testing for horizontal and vertical surfaces, and in determining differences of elevation.

LIGHT - Space in a window sash for a single pane of glass. Also, a pane of glass.

LINTEL - A horizontal structural member that supports the load over an opening such as a door or window.

LINTEL (HEADER) - The piece of construction or finish, stone, wood, or metal, which is over an opening; a header.

LONGITUDINAL - Generally, the direction along the length of the grain of wood.

LOOKOUT - (1) The end of a rafter, or the construction which projects beyond the sides of a house to support the eaves; also the projecting timbers at the gables which support the verge boards.

(2) A short wood bracket or cantilever to support an overhanging portion of a roof or the like, usually concealed from view.

LOUVER - (1) An opening with a series of horizontal slats so arranged as to permit ventilation but to exclude rain, sunlight, or vision. See also ATTIC VENTILATORS.

(2) A kind of window, generally in peaks of gables and the tops of towers, provided with horizontal slots which exclude rain and snow and allow ventilation.

LUMBER - (1) Lumber is the product of the sawmill and planing mill not further manufactured other than by sawing, resawing, and passing lengthwise through a standard planing machine, cross cutting to length, and matching.

(2) Sawed parts of a log such as boards, planks, scantling, and timber.

LUMBER, BOARDS - Yard lumber less than 2 inches thick and 2 or more inches wide.

LUMBER, DIMENSION - Yard lumber from 2 inches to, but not including, 5 inches thick, and 2 or more inches wide. Includes joists, rafters, studs, plank, and small timbers. The actual size dimension of such lumber after shrinking from green dimension and after machining to size or pattern is called the dress size.

LUMBER, DRESSED SIZE - The dimensions of lumber after shrinking from the green dimension and after planing, usually 3/8 inch less than the nominal or rough size. For example, a 2 by 4 stud actually measures 1 5/8 by 3 5/8 inches.

LUMBER, MATCHED - Lumber that is edge-dressed and shaped to make a close tongue-and-groove joint at the edges or ends when laid edge to edge or end to end.

LUMBER, NOMINAL SIZE - As applied to timber or lumber, the rough-sawed commercial size by which it is known and sold in the market.

LUMBER, SHIPLAP - Lumber that is edge-dressed to make a close rabbeted or lapped joint.

STRUCTURAL LUMBER - Lumber that is 2 or more inches thick and 4 or more inches wide, intended for use where working stresses are required. The grading of structural lumber is based on the strength of the piece and the use of the entire piece.

LUMBER, TIMBERS - Yard lumber 5 or more inches in least dimension. Includes beams, stringers, posts, caps, sills, girders, and purlins.

LUMBER, YARD - Lumber of those grades, sizes, and patterns which are generally intended for ordinary construction, such as framework and rough coverage of houses.

M

MANTEL - The shelf above a fireplace. Originally referred to the beam or lintel supporting the arch above the fireplace opening. Used also in referring to the entire finish around a fireplace, covering the chimney breast in front and sometimes on the sides.

MASONRY - Stone, brick, concrete, hollow-tile, concrete-block, gypsum-block, or other similar building units or materials or a combination of the same, bonded together with mortar to form a wall, pier, buttress, or similar mass.

MATCHING, OR TONGUING AND GROOVING - The method used in cutting the edges of a board to make a tongue on one edge and a groove on the other.

MEDULLARY RAYS - (See RAYS, WOOD)

MEETING RAIL - The bottom rail of the upper sash of a double-hung window. Sometimes called the check rail.

MEETING RAILS - Rails sufficiently thicker than a window to fill the opening between the top and bottom sash made by the parting stop in the frame of double-hung windows. They are usually beveled.

MEMBER - A single piece in structure, complete in itself.

METAL LATH - Sheets of metal that are slit and drawn out to form openings on which plaster is spread.

MILLWORK - Generally all building materials made of finished wood and manufactured in millwork plants and planing mills are included under the term "millwork." It includes such items as inside and outside doors, window and doorframes, blinds, porchwork, mantels, panel-work, stairways, moldings, and interior trim. It normally does not include flooring, ceiling, or siding.

MITER - (1) The joining of two pieces at an angle that bisects the angle of junction.

(2) The joint formed by two abutting pieces meeting at an angle.

MITER JOINT - The joint of two pieces at an angle that bisects the joining angle. For example, the miter joint at the side and head casing at a door opening is made at a 45° angle.

MOISTURE CONTENT OF WOOD - Weight of the water contained in the wood, usually expressed as a percentage of the weight of the oven-dry wood.

MOLDING - (1) A wood strip having a curved or projecting surface used for decorative purposes.

(2) Material, usually patterned strips, used to provide ornamental variation of outline or contour, whether projections or cavities, such as cornices, bases, window and doorjambs, and heads.

MOLDING BASE - The molding on the top of a base board.

BED - A molding used to cover the joint between the plancier and frieze; also used as a base molding upon heavy work, and sometimes as a member of a cornice.

LIP - A molding with a lip which overlaps the piece against which the back of the molding rests.

RAKE - The cornice upon the gable edge of a pitch roof, the members of which are made to fit those of the molding of the horizontal eaves.

PICTURE - A molding shaped to form a support for picture hooks, often placed at some distance from the ceiling upon the wall to form the lower edge of the frieze.

MORTISE - The hole which is to receive a tenon, or any hole cut into or through a piece by a chisel; generally of rectangular shape.

MULLION - The construction between the openings of a window frame to accommodate two or more windows.

MUNTIN - The vertical member between two panels of the same piece of panel work. The vertical sash-bars separating the different panels of glass.

N

NATURAL FINISH - (1) A transparent finish which does not seriously alter the original color or grain of the natural wood. Natural finishes are usually provided by sealers, oils, varnishes, water-repellent, preservatives, and other similar materials.

(2) A transparent finish, usually a drying oil, sealer, or varnish, applied on wood for the purpose of protection against soiling or weathering. Such a finish may not seriously alter the original color of the wood or obscure its grain pattern. NAVAL STORES - A term applied to the oils, resins, tars, and pitches derived from oleoresin contained in, exuded by, or extracted from trees chiefly of the pine species (genus *Pinus*) or from the wood of such trees.

NEWEL - (1) The principal post of the foot of a staircase; also the central support of a winding flight of stairs.

(2) A post to which the end of a stair railing or balustrade is fastened. Also, any post to which a railing or balustrade is fastened.

NONBEARING WALL - A wall supporting no load other than its own weight.

NONLOADBEARING WALL - A wall supporting no load other than its own weight.

NOSING - (1) The part of a stair tread which projects over the riser, or any similar projection; a term applied to the rounded edge of a board.

(2) The projecting edge of a molding or drip. Usually applied to the projecting molding on the edge of a stair tread.

NOTCH - A crosswise rabbet at the end of a board.

O

O.C. ON CENTER - The measurement of spacing for studs, rafters, joists, and the like in a building from center of one member to the center of the next.

O.G. OR OGEE - A molding with a profile in the form of a letter S; having the outline of a reversed curve.

OLD GROWTH - Timber growing in or harvested from a mature, naturally established forest. When the trees have grown most or all of their individual lives in active competition with their companions for sunlight and moisture, this timber is usually straight and relatively free of knots.

OVENDRY WOOD - Wood dried to constant weight in an oven at temperatures above that of boiling water (usually 101° to 105°C. or 214° to 221°F.).

P

PAINT — (1) A combination of pigments with suitable thinners or oils to provide decorative and protective coatings.

(2) L, pure white lead (basic-carbonate) paint; TLZ, titanium-lead-zinc paint; TZ, titanium-zinc paint.

PANEL - (1) A large, thin board or sheet of lumber, plywood, or other material. A thin board with all its edges inserted in a groove of a surrounding frame of thick material. A portion of a flat surface recessed or sunk below the surrounding area, distinctly set off by molding or some other decorative device. Also, a section of floor, wall, ceiling, or roof, usually prefabricated and of large size, handled as a single unit in the operations of assembly and erection.

(2) In house construction, a thin flat piece of wood, plywood, or similar material, framed by stiles and rails as in a door or fitted into grooves of thicker material with molded edges for decorative wall treatment.

PAPER, BUILDING - A general term for papers, felts, and similar sheet materials used in buildings without reference to their properties or uses.

PAPER, SHEATHING - A building material, generally paper or felt, used in wall and roof construction as a protection against the passage of air and sometimes moisture.

PARTING STOP OR STRIP - A small wood piece used in the side and head jambs of double-hung windows to separate upper and lower sash.

PARTITION A wall that subdivides spaces within any story of a building.

PARTITION TYPES:

BEARING PARTITION - A partition which supports any vertical load in addition to its own weight.

NONBEARING PARTITION - A partition extending from floor to ceiling but which supports no load other than its own weight.

PECK - Pockets or areas of disintegrated wood caused by advanced stages of localized decay in the living tree. It is usually associated with cypress and incense-cedar. There is no further development of peck once the lumber is seasoned.

PENNY - As applied to nails, it originally indicated the price per hundred. The term now serves as a measure of nail length and is abbreviated by the letter d.

PERM - A measure of water vapor movement through a material (grains per square foot per hour per inch of mercury difference in vapor pressure).

PIER - A column of masonry, usually rectangular in horizontal cross-section, used to support other structural members.

PIGMENT - A powdered solid in suitable degree of subdivision for use in paint or enamel.

PILASTER - A portion of a square column usually set within or against a wall.

PILES - Long posts driven into the soil in swampy locations or whenever it is difficult to secure a firm foundation, upon which the footing course of masonry or other timbers are laid.

PITCH - (1) The incline or rise of a roof. Pitch is expressed in inches or rise per foot of run, or by the ratio of the rise to the span.

(2) The incline slope of a roof, or the ratio of the total rise to the total width of a house; i.e., an 8-foot rise and a 24-foot width are a 1/3 pitch roof.

ROOF SLOPE is expressed in inches of rise per 12 inches of run.

(3) Inclination or slope, as for roofs or stairs, or the rise divided by the span.

PITCH BOARD - A board sawed to the exact shape formed by the stair tread, riser, and slope of the stairs and used to lay out the carriage and stringers.

PITCH POCKET - An opening that extends parallel to the annual growth rings and that contains, or has contained, either solid or liquid pitch.

PITCH STREAK - A well-defined accumulation of pitch in a more or less regular streak in the wood of certain softwoods.

PITH - The small, soft core occurring in the structural center of a tree trunk, branch, twig, or log.

PLAINSAWED - (See GRAIN)

PLAN - A horizontal geometrical section of a building, showing the walls, doors, windows, stairs, chimneys, columns, etc.

PLANING-MILL PRODUCTS - Products worked to pattern, such as flooring, ceiling, and siding.

PLANKS OR LUMBER - Material 2 or 3 inches thick and more than 4 inches wide, such as joists, flooring, etc.

PLASTER - A mixture of lime, hair, and sand, or of lime, cement, and sand, used to cover outside and inside wall surfaces.

PLATE - (1) The top horizontal piece of the walls of a frame building upon which the roof rests.

(2) A. A horizontal structural member placed on a wall or supported on posts, studs, or corbels to carry the trusses of a roof or to carry the rafters directly.

B. A shoe or base member, as of a partition or other frame.

C. A small, relatively thin member placed on or in a wall to support girders, rafters, etc.

(3) Sill plate - A horizontal member anchored to a masonry wall.

Sole plate - Bottom horizontal member of a frame wall.

Top plate - Top horizontal member of a frame wall supporting ceiling joists, rafters, or other members.

PLATE CUT - The cut in a rafter which rests upon the plate; sometimes called the seat cut.

PLOUGH - To cut a groove, as in a plank.

PLUMB - Exactly perpendicular; vertical.

PLUMB CUT - Any cut made in a vertical plane; the vertical cut at the top end of a rafter.

PLY - (1) A term used to denote a layer or thickness of building or roofing paper as two-ply, three-ply, etc.

(2) A term to denote the number of thicknesses or layers of roofing felt, veneer in plywood, or layers in built-up materials, in any finished piece of such material.

PLYWOOD - (1) A piece of wood made of three or more layers of veneer joined with glue and usually laid with the grain of adjoining plies at right angles. Almost always an odd number of plies are used to provide balanced construction.

(2) An assembly made of layers (plies) of veneer, or of veneer in combination with a lumber core, joined with an adhesive. The grain of adjoining plies is usually laid at right angles, and almost always an odd number of plies are used to obtain balanced construction.

PORCH - (1) An ornamental entrance way.

(2) A floor extending beyond the exterior walls of a building. It may be enclosed or unenclosed, roofed or uncovered.

(3) A roofed area extending beyond the main house. May be open or enclosed and with concrete or wood frame floor system.

PORE - (See VESSELS)

PORES - Wood cells of comparatively large diameter that have open ends and are set one above the other to form continuous tubes. The openings of the vessels on the surface of a piece of wood are referred to as pores.

POROUS WOODS - Another name for hardwoods, which frequently have vessels or pores large enough to be seen readily without magnification.

POST - A timber set on end to support a wall, girder, or other member of the structure.

PLOW - To cut a groove running in the same direction as the grain of the wood.

PRESERVATIVE - Any substance that, for a reasonable length of time, will prevent the action of wood-destroying fungi, borers of various kinds, and similar destructive life when the wood has been properly coated or impregnated with it.

PRIMER - The first coat of paint in a paint job that consists of two or more coats; also the paint used for such a first coat.

PULLEY STILE - The member of a window frame which contains the pulleys and between which the edges of the sash slide.

PURLIN - A timber supporting several rafters at one or more points, or the roof sheeting directly.

PUTTY - A type of cement usually made of whiting and boiled linseed oil, beaten or kneaded to the consistency of dough, and used in sealing glass in sash, filling small holes and crevices in wood, and for similar purposes.

Q

QUARTER ROUND - A small molding that has the cross-section of a quarter circle.

R

RABBET or REBATE - (1) A corner cut out of an edge of a piece of wood.
(2) A rectangular longitudinal groove cut in the corner of a board or other piece of material.

RADIAL - Coincident with a radius from the axis of the tree or log to the circumference. A radial section is a lengthwise section in a plane that extends from pith to bark.

RADIANT HEATING - A method of heating, usually consisting of coils or pipes placed in the floor, wall, or ceiling.

RAFTER - One of a series of structural members of a roof designed to support roof loads. The rafters of a flat roof are sometimes called roof joists.

RAFTERS, COMMON - Those which run square with the plate and extend to the ridge.

CRIPPLE - Those which cut between valley and hip rafters.

HIP - Those extending from the outside angle of the plates toward the apex of the roof.

JACKS - Those square with the plate and intersecting the hip rafter.

VALLEY - Those extending from an inside angle of the plates toward the ridge or center line of the house.

RAIL - (1) The horizontal members of a balustrade or panel work.
(2) Cross members of panel doors or of a sash. Also the upper and lower members of a balustrade or staircase extending from one vertical support, such as a post, to another.
(3) A horizontal bar or timber of wood or metal extending from one post or support to another as a guard or barrier in a fence, balustrade, staircase, etc. Also, the cross or horizontal members
of the framework of a sash, door, blind, or any paneled assembly.

RAKE - (1) The trim of a building extending in an oblique line, as rake dado or molding.
(2) The trim members that run parallel to the roof slope and from the finish between wall and roof.
(3) The inclined edge of a gable roof (the trim member is a rake molding).

RATE OF GROWTH - The rate at which a tree has laid on wood, measured radially in the trunk or in lumber cut from the trunk. The unit of measure in use is number of annual growth rings per inch.

RAW LINSEED OIL - The crude product expressed from flaxseed and usually without much subsequent treatment.

RAYS, WOOD - Strips of cells extending radially within a tree and varying in height from a few cells in some species to 4 or more inches in oak. The rays serve primarily to store food and transport it horizontally in the tree.

REFLECTIVE INSULATION - Sheet material with one or both surfaces of comparatively low heat emissivity that, when used in building construction so that the surfaces face air spaces, reduces the radiation across the air space.

REINFORCING - Steel rods or metal fabric placed in concrete slabs, beams, or columns to increase their strength.

RELATIVE HUMIDITY - The amount of water vapor expressed as a percentage of the maximum quantity that could be present in the atmosphere at a given temperature. (The actual amount of water vapor that can be held in space increases with the temperature.)

RESIN-EMULSION PAINT - Paint, the vehicle (liquid part) of which consists of resin or varnish dispersed in fine droplets in water, analogous to cream, which consists of butterfat dispersed in water.

RESIN PASSAGE (OR DUCT) - Intercellular passages that contain and transmit resinous materials. On a cut surface, they are usually inconspicuous. They may extend vertically parallel to the axis of the tree or at right angles to the axis and parallel to the rays.

RETURN - The continuation of a molding or finish of any kind in a different direction.

RIBBAND - (See LEDGERBOARD)

RIBBON - A narrow board let into the studding to add support to joists.

RIDGE - The horizontal line at the junction of the top edges of two sloping roof surfaces. The rafters of both slopes are nailed to the ridge board. (See PLUMB CUT)

RIDGE BOARD - The board placed on edge at the ridge of the roof into which the upper ends of the rafters are fastened.

RING-POROUS WOODS - A group of hardwoods in which the pores are comparatively large at the beginning of each annual ring and decrease in size more or less abruptly toward the outer portion of the ring, thus forming a distinct inner zone of pores, known as the springwood, and an outer zone with smaller pores, known as the summerwood.

RISE - (1) The height a roof rising in horizontal distance (run) from the outside face of a wall supporting the rafters or trusses to the ridge of the roof. In stairs, the perpendicular height of a step or flight of steps.

(2) The vertical distance through which anything rises, as the rise of a roof or stair.

RISER - Each of the vertical boards closing the spaces between the treads of stairways.

ROLL ROOFING - Roofing material, composed of fiber and saturated with asphalt, that is supplied in rolls containing 108 square feet in 36-inch widths. It is generally furnished in weights of 55 to 90 pounds per roll.

ROOF - The entire construction used to close in the top of a building.

ROOF SHEATHING - The boards or sheet material fastened to the roof rafters on which the shingle or other roof covering is laid.

ROOFING - The material put on a roof to make it wind and waterproof.

ROUTED - (See MORTISED)

RUBBER-EMULSION PAINT - Paint, the vehicle of which consists of rubber or synthetic rubber dispersed in fine droplets in water.

RUBBLE - Roughly broken quarry stone.

RUBBLE MASONRY - Uncut stone, used for rough work, foundations, backing, and the like.

RUN - (1) The length of the horizontal projection of a piece such as a rafter when in position.

(2) In reference to roofs, the horizontal distance from the face of a wall to the ridge of the roof. Referring to stairways, the net width of a step; also the horizontal distance covered by a flight of steps.

S

SADDLE BOARD - The finish of the ridge of a pitch-roof house. Sometimes called comb board.

SAP - All the fluids in a tree except special secretions and excretions, such as oleoresin.

SAPWOOD - (1) The living wood of pale color near the outside of the log. Under most conditions the sapwood is more susceptible to decay than heartwood.

(2) The outer zone of wood, next to the bark. In the living tree it contains some living cells (the heartwood contains none), as well as dead and dying cells. In most species, it is lighter colored than the heartwood. In all species, it is lacking in decay resistance. SASH-(1) A single light frame containing one or more lights of glass.

(2) The framework which holds the glass in a window.

SASH BALANCE - A device, usually operated with a spring, designed to counterbalance window sash. Use of sash balances eliminates the need for sash weights, pulleys, and sash cord.

SATURATED FELT - A felt which is impregnated with tar or asphalt.

SAWING, PLAIN - Lumber sawed regardless of the grain, the log simply squared and sawed to the desired thickness; sometimes called slash or bastard sawed.

SCAB - (1) A short piece of lumber used to splice, or to prevent movement of two other pieces.

(2) A short piece of wood or plywood fastened to two abutting timbers to splice them together.

SCAFFOLD or STAGING - A temporary structure or platform enabling workmen to reach high places.

SCALE - A short measurement used as a proportionate part of a larger dimension. The scale of a drawing is expressed as 1/4 inch = 1 ft.

SCANTLING - Lumber with a cross-section ranging from 2 by 4 inches to 4 by 4 inches.

SCARFING - A joint between two pieces of wood which allows them to be spliced lengthwise.

SCOTIA - A hollow molding used as a part of a cornice, and often under the nosing of a stair tread.

SCRATCH COAT - The first coat of plaster, which is scratched to form a bond for the second coat.

SCRIBING - (1) The marking of a piece of work to provide for the fitting of one of its surfaces to the irregular surface of another.

(2) Fitting woodwork to an irregular surface.

SEALER - A finishing material, either clear or pigmented, that is usually applied directly over uncoated wood for the purpose of sealing the surface.

SEASONING - Removing moisture from green wood in order to improve its serviceability.

AIR-DRIED - Dried by exposure to air, usually in a yard, without artificial heat.

KILN-DRIED - Dried in a kiln with the use of artificial heat.

SEAT CUT or PLATE CUT - The cut at the bottom end of a rafter to allow it to fit upon the plate.

SEAT OF A RAFTER - The horizontal cut upon the bottom end of a rafter which rests upon the top of the plate.

SECOND GROWTH - Timber that has grown after removal by cutting, fire, wind, or other agency, of all or a large part of the previous stand.

SECTION - A drawing showing the kind, arrangement, and proportions of the various parts of a structure. It is assumed that the structure is cut by a plane, and the section is the view gained by looking in one direction.

SEMIGLOSS PAINT OR ENAMEL - A paint or enamel made with a slight insufficiency of nonvolatile vehicle so that its coating when dry, has some luster but is not very glossy.

SHAKE - A thick handsplit shingle, resawed to form two shakes, usually edge grained.
SHAKES - Imperfections in timber caused during the growth of the tree by high winds or imperfect conditions of growth.
SHEATHING - (1) The structural covering, usually wood boards or plywood, used over studs or rafters of a structure. Structural building board is normally used only as wall sheathing.

(2) Wall boards, roofing boards; generally applied to narrow boards laid with a space between them, according to the length of a shingle exposed to weather.
SHEATHING PAPER - (1) The paper used under siding or shingles to in-sulate in the house; building papers.

(2) A building material used in wall, floor, and roof construction to resist the passage of air.
SHELLAC - A transparent coating made by dissolving lac, a resinous secretion of the lac bug (a scale insect that thrives in tropical countries, especially India), in alcohol.
SHINGLES - Roof covering of asphalt, asbestos, wood, tile, slate, or other material cut to stock lengths, widths, and thicknesses.
SHINGLES, SIDING - Various kinds of shingles, such as wood shingles or shakes and non-wood shingles, that are used over sheathing for exterior sidewall covering of a structure.
SHIPLAP - (See LUMBER, SHIPLAP)
SIDING - The finish covering of the outside wall of a frame building, whether made of horizontal weatherboards, vertical boards with battens, shingles, or other material.
SIDING, BEVEL (LAP SIDING) - Used as the finish siding on the exterior of a house or other structure. It is usually manufactured by resawing dry square-surfaced boards diagonally to produce two wedge-shaped pieces. These pieces commonly run from 3/16 inch thick on the thin edge to 1/2 to 3/4 inch thick on the other edge, depending on the width of the siding.
SIDING, DROP - Usually 3/4 inch thick and 6 inches wide, machined into various patterns. Drop siding has tongue-and-groove joints, is heavier, has more structural strength, and is frequently used on buildings that require no sheathing, such as garages and barns.
SIDING, PANEL - Large sheets of plywood or hardboard which serve as both sheathing and siding.
SILL - The lowest member of the frame of a structure, resting on the foundation and supporting the floor joists or the uprights of the wall. The member forming the lower side of an opening, as a door sill, window sill, etc.
SILLS - The horizontal timbers of a house which either rest upon the masonry foundations or, in the absence of such, form the foundations.
SIZING - Working material to the desired size; a coating of glue, shellac, or other substance applied to a surface to prepare it for painting or other method of finish.
SLEEPER - A timber laid on the ground to support a floor joist.
SOFFIT - The underside of the members of a building, such as staircases, cornices, beams, and arches, relatively minor in area as compared with ceilings.
SOFTWOODS - Generally, the botanical group of trees that bear cones and in most cases have needlelike or scalelike leaves; also the wood produced by such trees. The term has no reference to the actual hardness of the wood.
SOIL COVER (GROUND COVER) - A light covering of plastic film, rool roofing, or similar material used over the soil in crawl spaces of buildings to minimize moisture permeation of the area.

SOIL STACK - A general term for the vertical main of a system of soil, waste, or vent piping.

SOLE OR SOLEPLATE - A member, usually a 2 by 4, on which wall and partition studs rest.

SPAN - The distance between structural supports such as walls, columns, piers, beams, girders, and trusses.

SPECIFIC GRAVITY - The ratio of the weight of a body to the weight of an equal volume of water at 4°C. or other specified temperature.

SPECIFICATIONS - The written or printed directions regarding the details of a building or other construction.

SPLASH BLOCK - A small masonry block laid with the top close to the ground surface to receive roof drainage and to carry it away from the building.

SPLICE - Joining of two similar members in a straight line.

SPRINGWOOD - The portion of the annual growth ring that is formed during the early part of the season's growth. In most softwoods and in ring-porous hardwoods, it is less dense and weaker mechanically than summerwood.

SQUARE - (1) A tool used by mechanics to obtain accuracy; a term applied to a surface including 100 square feet.

(2) A unit of measure - 100 square feet - usually applied to roofing material. Sidewall coverings are sometimes packed to cover 100 square feet and are sold on that basis.

STAIN - A discoloration in wood that may be caused by such diverse agencies as micro-organisms, metal, or chemicals. The term also applies to materials used to color wood.

STAIN, SHINGLE - A form of oil paint, very thin in consistency, intended for coloring wood with rough surfaces, like shingles, without forming a coating of significant thickness or gloss.

STAIR CARRIAGE - (1) Supporting member for stair treads. Usually a 2-inch plank notched to receive the treads; sometimes termed a "rough horse."

(2) A stringer for steps on stairs.

STAIR LANDING - A platform between flights of stairs or at the termination of a flight of stairs.

STAIR RISE - The vertical distance from the top of one stair tread to the top of the cne next above.

STAIRS, BOX - Those built between walls, and usually with no support except the wall strings.

STANDING FINISH - Term applied to the finish of the openings and the base, and all other finish work necessary for the inside.

STOOL - (1) The flat, narrow shelf forming the top member of the interior trim at the bottom of a window.

(2) A flat molding fitted over the window sill between jambs and contacting the bottom rail of the lower sash.

STORM SASH OR STORM WINDOW - An extra window usually placed on the outside of an existing window as additional protection against cold weather.

STORY - That part of a building between any floor and the floor or roof next above.

STRENGTH - The term in its broader sense includes all the properties of wood that enable it to resist different forces or loads. In its more restricted sense, strength may apply to any one of the mechanical properties, in which event the name of the property under consideration should be stated, thus: strength in compression parallel to grain, strength in bending, hardness, and so on.

STRESS - Force per unit of area.

STRING, STRINGER - A timber or other support for cross members in floors or ceilings. In stairs, the support on which the stair treads rest; also stringboard.

STRINGER - A long horizontal timber in a structure supporting a floor.

STUCCO - (1) Most commonly refers to an outside plaster made with Portland cement as its base.

(2) A fine plaster used for interior decoration and fine work; also for rough outside wall coverings.

STUD - (1) An upright beam in the framework of a building.

(2) One of a series of slender wood or metal vertical structural members placed as supporting elements in walls and partitions. (Plural: studs or studding.)

STUDDING - The framework of a partition or the wall of a house; usually referred to as 2 by 4's.

SUBFLOOR - (1) A wood floor which is laid over the floor joists and on which the finished floor is laid.

(2) Boards or plywood laid on joists over which a finish floor is to be laid.

SUMMERWOOD - The portion of the annual growth ring that is formed after the springwood formation has ceased. In most softwoods and in ring-porous hardwoods, it is denser and stronger mechanically than springwood.

T

TAIL BEAM - A relatively short beam or joist supported in a wall on one end and by a header at the other.

TANGENTIAL - Strictly, coincident with a tangent at the circumference of a tree or log, or parallel to such a tangent. In practice, however, it often means roughly coincident with a growth ring. A tangential section is a longitudinal section through a tree or limb and is perpendicular to a radius. Flat-grained and plainsawed lumber is sawed tangentially.

TERMITE SHIELD - A shield, usually of noncorrodible metal, placed in or on a foundation wall or other mass of masonry or around pipes to prevent passage of termites.

TERMITES - Insects that superficially resemble ants in size, general appearance, and habit of living in colonies; hence, frequently called "white ants." Subterranean termites do not establish themselves in buildings by being carried in with lumber, but by entering from ground nests after the building has been constructed. If unmolested they eat out the woodwork, leaving a shell of sound wood to conceal their activities, and damage may proceed so far so to cause collapse of parts of a structure before discovery. There are about 56 species of termites known in the United States; but the two main species, classified from the manner in which they attack wood, subterranean (ground-inhabiting) termites, the most common, and drywood termites, found almost exclusively along the extreme southern border and the Gulf of Mexico in the United States.

TEXTURE - A term often used interchangeably with grain. Sometimes used to combine the concepts of density and degree of contrast between springwood and summerwood. In this publication, texture refers to the finer structure of the wood (see GRAIN) rather than the annual rings.

THRESHOLD - (1) A strip of wood or metal with beveled edges used over the finished floor and the sill of exterior doors.

(2) The beveled piece over which the door swings; sometimes called a carpet strip.

TIE BEAM (COLLAR BEAM)- A beam so situated that it ties the principal rafters of a roof together and prevents them from thrusting the plate out of line.

TIMBER - Lumber with cross-section over 4 by 6 inches; such as posts, sills, and girders.

TIN SHINGLE - A small piece of tin used in flashing and repairing a shingle roof.

TO THE WEATHER - A term applied to the projecting of shingles or siding beyond the course above.
TOENAILING - To drive a nail at a slant with the initial surface in order to permit it to penetrate into a second member.
TREAD - The horizontal board in a stairway on which the foot is placed.
TRIM - (1) The finish materials in a building, such as moldings, applied around openings (window trims, door trim) or at the floor and ceiling of rooms (baseboard, cornice, picture molding).
(2) A term sometimes applied to outside or interior finished woodwork and the finish around openings.
TRIMMER - A beam or joist to which a header is nailed in framing for a chimney, stairway, or other opening.
TRIMMING - Putting the inside and outside finish and hardware upon a building.
TRUSS - (1) Structural framework of triangular units for supporting loads over long spans.
(2) A frame or jointed structure designed to act as a beam of long span, while each member is usually subjected to longitudinal stress only, either tension or compression.
TURPENTINE - A volatile oil used as a thinner in paints, and as a solvent in varnishes. Chemically, it is a mixture of terpenes.
TWIST - A distortion caused by the turning or winding of the edges of a board so that the four corners of any face are no longer in the same plane.
TYLOSES - Masses of cells appearing somewhat like froth in the pores of some hardwoods, notably white oak and black locust. In hardwoods, tyloses are formed when walls of living cells surrounding vessels extend into the vessels. They are sometimes formed in softwoods in a similar manner by the extension of cell walls into resin-passage cavities.

U

UNDERCOAT - A coating applied prioT to the finishing or top coats of a paint job. It may be the first of two or the second of three coats. In some usage of the word it may become synonymous with priming coat.

V

VALLEY - The internal angle formed by the junction of two sloping sides of a roof.
VAPOR BARRIER - Material used to retard the flow of vapor or moisture into walls and thus to prevent condensation within them. There are two types of vapor barriers, the membrane that comes in rolls and is applied as a unit in the wall or ceiling construction, and the paint type, which is applied with a brush. The vapor barrier must be a part of the warm side of the wall.
VARNISH - A thickened preparation of drying oil or drying oil and resin suitable for spreading on surfaces to form continuous, transparent coatings, or for mixing with pigments to make enamels.
VEHICLE - The liquid portion of a finishing material; it consists of the binder (nonvolatile) and volatile thinners.
VENEER - A thin layer or sheet of wood cut on a veneer machine.
ROTARY-CUT VENEER - Veneer cut in a lathe which rotates a log or bolt, chucked in the center, against a knife.
SAWED VENEER - Veneer produced by sawing.
SLICED VENEER - Veneer that is sliced off a log, bolt, or flitch with a knife.

VENT - A pipe installed to provide a flow of air to or from a drainage system or to provide a circulation of air within such system to protect trap seals from siphonage and back pressure.

VERGE BOARDS - The boards which serve as the eaves finish on the gable end of a building.

VERMICULITE - A mineral closely related to mica, with the faculty of expanding on heating to form lightweight material with insulation quality. Used as bulk insulation and also as aggregate in insulating and acoustical plaster and in insulating concrete floors.

VERTICAL GRAIN - (See GRAIN)

VESSELS - Wood cells of comparatively large diameter that have open ends and are set one above the other so as to form continuous tubes. The openings of the vessels on the surface of a piece of wood are usually referred to as *pores.*

VESTIBULE - An entrance to a house; usually inclosed.

VIRGIN GROWTH - The original growth of mature trees.

VOLATILE THINNER - A liquid that evporates readily and is used to thin or reduce the consistency of finishes without altering the relative volumes of pigments and nonvolatile vehicle.

W

WAINSOOTING - Matched boarding or panel work covering the lower portion of a wall.

WALE - A horizontal beam.

WALL, BEARING - A wall which supports any vertical load in addition to its own weight.

WALLBOARD - Wood pulp, gypsum, or similar materials made into large, rigid sheets that may be fastened to the frame of a building to provide a surface finish.

WANE - Bark or lack of wood from any cause on the edge or corner of a piece of lumber.

WARP - Any variation from a true or plane surface. Warp includes bow, crook, cup, and twist, or any combination thereof.

WASH - (1) The upper surface of a member or material when given a slope to shed water.

(2) The slant upon a sill, capping, etc., to allow the water to run off easily.

WATER REPELLENT - A liquid designed to penetrate into wood and to impart water repellency to the wood.

WATER-REPELLENT PRESERVATIVE - A liquid designed to penetrate into wood and impart water repellency and a moderate preservative protection. It is used for millwork, such as sash and frames, and is usually applied by dipping.

WATER TABLE - (1) A ledge or offset on or above a foundation wall, for the purpose of shedding water.

(2) The finish at the bottom of a house which carries the water away from the foundation.

WEATHERING - The mechanical or chemical disintegration and discoloration of the surface of wood that is caused by exposure to light, the action of dust and sand carried by winds, and the alternate shrinking and swelling of the surface fibers with the continual variation in moisture content brought by changes in the weather. Weathering does not include decay.

WEATHERSTRIP - (1) Narrow strips made of metal, or other material, so designed that when installed at doors or windows they will retard the passage of air, water, moisture, or dust around the door or window sash.

(2) Narrow or jamb-width sections of thin metal or other material to prevent infiltration of air and moisture around windows and doors.

WIND ("i" pronounced as in kind) - A term used to describe the surface of a board when twisted (winding) or when resting upon two diagonally opposite corners, if laid upon a perfectly flat surface.

WOODEN BRICK - Piece of seasoned wood, made the size of a brick, and laid where it is necessary to provide a nailing space in masonry walls.

WOOD RAYS - Strips of cells extending radially within a tree and varying in height from a few cells in some species to 4 inches or more in oak. The rays serve primarily to store food and to transport it horizontally in the tree.

WOOD SUBSTANCE - The solid material of which wood is composed. It usually refers to the extractive-free solid substance of which the cell walls are composed, but this is not always true. There is no wide variation in chemical composition or specific gravity between the wood substance of various species; the characteristic differences of species are largely due to differences in infiltrated materials and variations in relative amounts of cell walls and cell cavities.

WORKABILITY - The degree of ease and smoothness of cut obtainable with hand or machine tools.

www.ingramcontent.com/pod-product-compliance
Lightning Source LLC
Chambersburg PA
CBHW081810300426
44116CB00014B/2304